ARAB NATIONALISM, OIL, AND THE POLITICAL ECONOMY OF DEPENDENCY

Recent Titles in
Contributions in Economics and Economic History

ARAB NATIONALISM, OIL, AND THE POLITICAL ECONOMY OF DEPENDENCY

Abbas Alnasrawi

CONTRIBUTIONS IN ECONOMICS AND ECONOMIC HISTORY,
NUMBER 120
Dominick Salvatore, *Series Adviser*

Greenwood Press
NEW YORK • WESTPORT, CONNECTICUT • LONDON

Library of Congress Cataloging-in-Publication Data

Alnasrawi, Abbas.
    Arab nationalism, oil, and the political economy of dependency /
Abbas Alnasrawi.
        p. cm.—(Contributions in economics and economic history,
ISSN 0084–9235 ; no. 120)
    Includes bibliographical references and index.
    ISBN 0–313–27610–2 (alk. paper)
        1. Arab countries—Economic conditions.   2. Arab countries—
Economic integration.   3. Petroleum industry and trade—Political
aspects—Arab countries.   4. Panarabism.   5. Arab countries—
Dependency on foreign countries.   I. Title.   II. Series.
HC498.A667   1991
337′.0917′4927—dc20   90–25225

British Library Cataloguing in Publication Data is available.

Library of Congress Catalog Card Number: 90–25225
ISBN: 0–313–27610–2
ISSN: 0084–9235

First published in 1991

Greenwood Press, 88 Post Road West, Westport, CT 06881
An imprint of Greenwood Publishing Group, Inc.

Printed in the United States of America

∞™

The paper used in this book complies with the
Permanent Paper Standard issued by the National
Information Standards Organization (Z39.48–1984).

10 9 8 7 6 5 4 3 2 1

to Susan, Leyla, and Kara with love

CONTENTS

ACKNOWLEDGMENTS

It gives me great pleasure to acknowledge with a deep sense of gratitude the assistance and support I received in the long process of researching and writing this manuscript. The publication of this book at this time was facilitated considerably by a sabbatical leave from the University of Vermont.

An enormous intellectual debt to the Beirut-based Centre for Arab Unity Studies under the energetic leadership of Dr. Khair El Din Hasseb for the books, the seminars, and the monthly *Al Mustaqbal Al Arabi* is cheerfully acknowledged. The Centre's publications provided an indispensable source of research materials for the entire book.

Professor Anthony S. Campagna's support and friendship contributed to this project in more than one way and gave a special meaning to collegiality. I would like to express my appreciation to my longtime friend Professor Ibrahim al-Mansour of the University of Baghdad for his reading of the first three chapters and for his comments and criticisms. I greatly benefited from Professor Dominick Salvatore who read the entire manuscript and made important suggestions.

I am greatly indebted to Professor Cheryl A. Rubenberg of Florida International University for her comprehensive and insightful critique of the work and for the numerous suggestions she made.

I owe Sandra A. Mable a special debt of gratitude for her patience and understanding as she prepared several drafts of the manuscript. Thanks are due to Elizabeth L. Hovinen for the excellent copy editing and for the numerous and insightful suggestions she made.

At Greenwood Press I am grateful to my editor, Sally M. Scott, for her understanding and support and for her meticulous guidance of the book at the various stages of production. I am particularly indebted to Cynthia Harris, Executive Editor, for her support of the project and for her wise counsel.

The help, the patience, the constant encouragement, and the tolerance shown by Susan, Leyla, and Kara are deeply appreciated.

I alone am responsible for any error that may remain.

1

EMERGENCE OF MODERN ARAB
ECONOMIC DEPENDENCE

Economic dependence, according to Theotonio Dos Santos, refers to a situation in which one economy is conditioned by the development and expansion of another economy. The economies of Arab oil-exporting countries, for example, can be said to be influenced directly by changing demand for their oil. Given the fact that most of the exported oil is destined for the industrial countries, it follows that changes in economic conditions in the latter group of countries would inevitably affect their demand for oil and consequently the export earnings of and economic conditions in oil-exporting countries.

In other words, economic interdependence under the above assumption becomes dependence when some countries (the dominant ones) can expand and be self-sustaining, while other countries (the dependent ones) can do this only as a reflection of the expansion in the dominant countries.[1] From this perspective change and development in the weaker or dependent economies will be determined to a considerable extent by change and development in the dominant economies.

It should be stressed at the outset that dependence entails more than the mere transmission of change in demand or other economic conditions from one region to another. Indeed, such transmission could occur only in the context of certain historical development and changes—social, cultural, colonial, political, military, economic, institutional, and so forth—that result in a whole array of linkages that in turn make possible the emergence of dependency relations. The evolution of the economies of the geographical area known as the Arab region or the Arab world illustrates how the structures of these economies changed in response to external stimuli, which in time led to the breakdown of their relative isolation and eventual integration into the world capitalist system.

The process that led to the inclusion of Arab economies in the world economic system was complicated by the fact that these economies were colonies of the Ottoman Empire. This meant that the entry of European influence into the Arab region took place through the Ottoman Empire, which exhibited the dual status of being an imperial power vis-à-vis the Arabs on the one hand and a dependent state vis-à-vis Europe on the other. This dual status was not unique to the Ottoman Empire. Portugal played a similar role in the eighteenth century when, although it had political control over Brazil, it nevertheless allowed Britain to penetrate the economy to the point of virtual control.

Rising Arab dependence status in the European-dominated world economy was facilitated by the outright military and political control that Britain and France exerted over the Arab region in the aftermath of the defeat of the Ottoman Empire during World War I. This control enabled these European powers to create economic, political, and government institutions that accelerated the process of integrating Arab economies in the world economic system, a process that had already been launched when the Arab world was part of the ailing Ottoman Empire. While the collapse of the Ottoman system of control and its replacement by the European system of domination were important forces in shaping Arab economic and social development, it was the entry of foreign investment, especially multinational oil capital, in the early part of this century that completed and deepened the dependency status of both oil-producing and non-oil-producing Arab economies, as will be seen in the following pages and chapters.

In this chapter the process of evolving Arab dependency will be divided into four phases. The first phase extends from the early sixteenth century to the early nineteenth century. During these three centuries the Ottoman Empire controlled the Arab region either directly through its appointed governors, generals, and other officials, or indirectly through local rulers. During the latter part of this phase the economies of the Arab region were gradually introduced into the world economy by European powers as part of their penetration and eventual control of the economies of the empire and its provinces, colonies, or periphery.

The second phase extends from the early part of the nineteenth century to the period of World War I, when Britain and France completed their control over the Arab world. This control culminated a process that had started in the nineteenth century. European economic penetration and political influence were underscored by the 1838 Anglo-Turkish Commercial Convention, which gave European merchants a privileged position and European imports a competitive advantage in the Ottoman economy.

The third phase extended from the end of World War I to the late 1940s and early 1950s when the modern state system in most of the Arab countries was established. This period was also characterized by the emergence of the Arab region as the most important oil-producing and oil-exporting region in the world. In this phase also Arab economies, due to the conditions of the Great Depression and World War II, embarked on various programs of import-substitution industrialization.

The fourth and present phase began in the early 1970s when Arab oil-producing countries, in cooperation with other members of the Organization of Petroleum Exporting Countries (OPEC), succeeded in raising oil prices sharply and assuming control over the operation of their national oil sectors.

FIRST PHASE OF ARAB DEPENDENCY: THE OTTOMAN PERIOD, 1500–1800

The evolution of Arab dependency during this period was closely associated with the effects of the annexation of the Arab region by the Ottoman Empire and with the changing nature of Ottoman rule under the impact of the emerging European economic and political power on the world scene. The Ottoman annexation of the Arab region provided certain stimuli to the agriculture-based Arab economies throughout the sixteenth century. Repairs to the irrigation systems, institution of a more regular and a more efficient system of tax collection, and general improvement in rural security stimulated increased agricultural production. The annexation of Arab provinces into the larger Ottoman market and the removal of trade barriers to intraregional trade created economic integration of some sort, which in turn increased efficiency and expanded output. Arab agriculture also benefited from population growth in major Ottoman urban centers as well as from continuous increases in European cereal grain prices. Although sixteenth-century agricultural growth could not be maintained in the next two centuries, there was no evidence to suggest that agriculture suffered from any major setbacks.[2] Foreign trade was another major economic activity in addition to agriculture.

In addition to the region's own exports and imports, the area of the Middle East—comprising the territories located at the juncture of Europe, Asia, and Africa—served as a major route for the trade between Asia and Europe during the sixteenth century. The area benefited from this locational advantage by providing both overland routes across central Asia and overseas routes through the Mediterranean, the Red Sea, the Arabian/Persian Gulf (the Gulf), and the Indian Ocean. This locational advantage yielded revenues in the form of customs duties to the Ottoman government and provided employment opportunities for thousands of merchants, shipbuilders, clerks, sailors, camel drivers, and all the rest who were directly or indirectly connected with the trade.[3]

Increased Ottoman and Arab dependence on the international economy of the day, however, exposed the Ottoman Empire to changing economic conditions over which it had no control. One such change was the discovery of the route around the Cape of Good Hope in 1498 by Vasco da Gama, which set the stage for the declining importance of the Middle East as the major transit trade route between Asia and Europe. As the cape route proved to be cheaper, more trade was routed away from the traditional routes in the Middle East. Although Sultan Suleiman, supported by Venetian merchants, attempted to restore trade through the old channels by sending several expeditions to the Indian Ocean to drive the Portuguese out, these failed attempts proved that the changes were irreversible.

Even more important, the new trade routes were symptomatic of more serious changes in the balance of economic power in Europe as the preeminence of Venice and the Mediterranean was successfully challenged first by the Portuguese, and later by the Dutch, the British, and the French. This rerouting of trade had the effect of relegating the Middle East to economic obscurity until the second half of the nineteenth century when the Suez Canal was opened. The rerouting of trade and the emergence of new economic powers in Europe resulted in the establishment of a new pattern of international trade: European manufactured products such as woolen cloth were exchanged for Middle Eastern primary commodities.[4] This new pattern of trade inaugurated the era of modern Arab economic dependency on the West in the manner outlined by Dos Santos.

Of course, as expected, the effects of the new pattern of trade on Middle Eastern economies were uneven. According to Roger Owen, while the production of cash crops was stimulated by European demand, the local textile industry began to suffer from European competition as early as mid-eighteenth century. Thus while Egypt's textile industry suffered from European imports, that of Iraq was subjected to competition from cloth imports from British India. Moreover, a sudden increase in French or British demand for cotton or silk meant that all existing stocks were exported, leaving local industry with little or nothing to work with. Another fact that affected indigenous industries was the growth of a European pattern of consumption among the ruling elites during the Ottoman period even prior to the high tide of nineteenth-century European economic penetration of the Middle East.[5]

It is worth noting that one of the vehicles that helped seventeenth-century European economic penetration of the Ottoman Empire and its Arab provinces was European access to and use of new sources of gold and silver of the New World. Such access gave European commerce the unfair competitive advantage of substantially greater purchasing power than the Ottomans, who had no similar access to sources of gold and silver, enjoyed.[6]

The flow of gold and silver from America to the Mediterranean countries of Europe led to a rise in prices that dislocated the finances of the Ottoman state and brought hardship to the productive classes. In turn, this led to an increase in taxation, decline in the agriculture and crafts, and depopulation of the countryside.[7]

This imbalance in the power and the resources between the declining Ottoman economy and the rising European economies was aggravated in the case of the Arab provinces of the empire. The interests of the Ottoman government in the Arab provinces were centered on military preparedness, urban and rural security, and raising money.[8] These tasks were undertaken by appointed officials or by local chieftains in areas where Ottoman authority was weak.

Although there were nonagricultural activities such as craft and commerce, land remained the most important source of revenue for the empire. All landownership was vested in the Ottoman government. Peasants were allowed to work the land in exchange for payment of taxes. The empire's rising revenue needs to finance its armies led to the evolution of a system of tax-farms where the right to collect taxes was auctioned in advance. Under this system many tax-farmers found themselves in a position where they could increase their own income and wealth at the expense of both the state and the peasants, depending on the ability of the state to assert its power and authority in the provinces. This lack of control on the part of the state led to the emergence of what may be described as landed aristocracies in many parts of the Arab region.

While the Arab region was producing revenue or economic surplus to finance the needs of a wide but weakened empire, the economic system of the entire Ottoman Empire and its peripheries continued to be challenged by the vastly more powerful European or Atlantic economy, which was being shaped by Europe's Industrial Revolution. But even before the impact of Europe's factory-based economies was felt, another change with serious consequences for the economies of the Ottoman Empire was taking place: the discovery of an alternate route to India via the Cape of Good Hope, which reduced the cost of foreign trade drastically and led trade routes to shift away from the Ottoman Empire and its provinces. Associated with the shift in trade routes was the rise of the European-owned Levant trading companies. With their financial resources and special privileges they were able to establish a near monopoly over foreign trade. These companies also benefited from the technological superiority of their home industry, even before the use of steam as a source of energy. They played a crucial role in undermining the Ottoman economy and in helping the process of European economic penetration into all parts of the Ottoman Empire. Although the imperial decline cannot be attributed to external factors alone, the importance of these global considerations should not be underestimated either. The decline of the economic system of the empire was hastened by the establishment in Western Europe of an Atlantic economy of tremendous vitality and force. According to O. L. Barkan, these immense historical changes destroyed the equilibrium of the imperial economy and arrested its natural economic evolution. These changes were clearly evident long before the Industrial Revolution during the second half of the sixteenth century. In that period European commerce, sustained by strong organization and encouraged by powerful nation-states, began to be a threat to local Ottoman industry as the new European national commerce, driven by mercantilism, intended to sell the greatest possible quantity of goods abroad while restricting imports of any finished products. By denying entry of Ottoman products to European markets, they changed the pattern of trade relations and thus the nature of trade to one of "colonial commerce," turning Turkey, and by extension its Arab provinces, into clients for European industry. The empire was to buy finished products from Europe and sell only primary materials to it.[9]

An important factor that helped this process was the series of special treaties, known as the Capitulations Treaties, which the Ottoman government concluded with some of the European powers. The significance of these treaties was to give the nationals of European countries certain extraterritorial privileges such as exemption from business and personal taxes and immunity from trial by

Ottoman courts. The treaties also extended special privileges to certain ethnic minority groups who had become middlemen between European exporters, importers, and bankers on the one hand and local merchants and producers on the other.[10] It is obvious that these treaties had the effect of giving clear competitive advantage to European economies, segmenting the managerial markets in favor of certain minorities, creating enclave economies, and distorting the process of economic development.

The impact of European penetration—the privileged position given to European nationals and their dependent ethnic minorities within the empire and the rising dependency of the empire on Europe—led the French ambassador in Constantinople in 1788 to describe the Ottoman Empire as "one of the richest colonies of France."[11] The particular conditions that resulted in this special form of dependency had serious implications for the evolution of the economies of the Arab provinces. These provinces found themselves coping in what might be described as conditions of derivative or secondary dependency. This came about as a result of the change in the relative importance of Ottoman economy in the world economy.

Prior to the rise of the Atlantic economy the Ottoman economy was an important force in the world. Turkey was the center through which Arab economies were related to the larger world economic system. The transformation of the status of the Ottoman central economy from an independent force in the world economy to a dependent of the European economy did not change its dominant status vis-à-vis the Arab economies. Yet the privileges that the Ottoman center extended to Europe affected the Arab economies as well. This meant that the Arab economies were placed in the untenable position of having to serve the needs of the imperial economy on the one hand while at the same time remaining responsive to the demands of the European economies on the other. In other words the new dependency status of the Turkish economy and institutions served to diffuse the new linkages of dependency to the economies of the Arab provinces. In summary the process of integrating Arab economies into the European-dominated international economic system during the period that ended in the early part of the last century was accelerated by two interrelated factors. First, the rise of European economies, which brought about an expansion in foreign trade, found the Arab economies increasing their interaction with Europe through the export of their raw materials and the import of finished products. Second, the Ottoman economy's change to dependent status added another layer of dependency to Arab economies. These forces of integration and dependency were strengthened in the course of the nineteenth century.

ARAB DEPENDENCY IN THE CONTEXT OF WORLD CAPITALISM

The nineteenth century witnessed important changes in the status of the Arab region vis-à-vis Europe and the Ottoman Empire as well. Those same years also witnessed important changes in the position of the Ottoman Empire vis-à-vis

Europe, which in turn had their impact on patterns of economic development in the Arab region. The principal force behind the changes was the emergence of Britain as the leading capitalist power in the world economy.

The forces of the Industrial Revolution, which was initially a British phenomenon, gave the British economy a wide and strong competitive edge over its main European rival, France. The successful application of new technologies, which resulted in the reduction of the cost of producing manufactured products and which increased the competitiveness of the British economy in the world market, was also helped by concomitant reduction in shipping costs and in the cost of imported raw materials.[12] Britain's free trade policy received a major boost in 1846 when the Corn Laws were repealed. The repeal allowed for the relatively free entry of agricultural products, allowing a restructuring of the distribution of national income in favor of the capitalists and at the expense of agricultural interests. This redistribution of national income was accomplished as a result of a decline in food prices, which in turn lowered the cost of living and real wages and allowed the capitalist class to increase profits and expand productive and export capacity.

These developments in the British economy, which had already been involved in the logic of specialization and international division of labor, were also linked to colonial expansion and maritime trade. The rising importance of foreign trade to the British economy is reflected in the rise in the share of exports to total production from one-fifth in the 1830s to two-fifths by 1870.[13] But the reliance of economic growth on exports meant that all barriers to trade, both exports and imports, should be removed. Thus, the British economy had to encourage cheaper imports of food and raw materials in order to be able to keep its competitive advantage. This dependence on foreign suppliers added support to those who advocated free trade, acquisition of more colonies, and control over more foreign markets. This phenomenal economic expansion of Britain led C. F. Bastiat to note that "England . . . has broken down all the barriers which separated it from other nations; England had 50 colonies, and now has only one, the universe."[14]

Like all other parts of the Third World the Arab region was subjected to European political, military, and economic domination. Thus as early as 1798 Napoleon invaded Egypt, which remained under French occupation until 1801. But no sooner had the French left than a whole new chapter of invasion and domination began in the Arab region, which was still under formal Ottoman control. Thus in rapid succession through the last century Egypt, Morocco, Tunisia, Algeria, Sudan, Aden, and the sheikdoms of the Gulf had fallen under either British or French control. The process was completed in the aftermath of World War I when Britain and France divided up Iraq, Syria, Lebanon, Palestine, and Jordan and strengthened their control over the areas that they had occupied earlier. The Ottoman Empire ceased to exist.

Parallel with this political/military control, the worldwide impact of the economic expansion of Britain and other European countries in the last century was transmitted to the Ottoman economy and those of the Arab region through other mechanisms. The most important was, naturally, foreign trade. European economic impact on the Arab region was also felt in capital inflow, a decline in indigenous industry, and large-scale settlement of Europeans especially in Egypt, North Africa, and Palestine. It also manifested itself in the expansion in export agriculture and change in the land-tenure system in favor of private over communal or tribal ownership. A new class of landless peasantry emerged, trade supports such as transportation and communication networks were built, and banking and financial systems were introduced. In short, these mechanisms were developed to accelerate the process of integrating these economies in the network of world trade and finance.[15]

It is perhaps correct to say that none of these mechanisms and linkages of integration would have been developed had there been no expansion in trade between the Arab region and Europe, since all these activities are designed to facilitate the flow of imports and exports between countries and regions. The role of trade in accelerating the process of Arab dependency will be dealt with in some detail in the following paragraphs.

The successful application in nineteenth-century Europe of modern technology; inventions; low-cost, large-scale production; and availability of finance stimulated large-scale movement of goods, capital, and people from Europe to other parts of the world. These changes found their economic rationalization in David Ricardo's theory of international trade, which provided the theoretical underpinning for those European phenomena. It is relevant to note that one of the most important effects of Britain's preoccupation with the Napoleonic Wars was the forced reductions in its exports to continental Europe. This in turn forced Britain to find markets in other parts of the world including the Middle East. The wars, in other words, had the unintended consequence of hastening the integration of Arab economies into the European-dominated international economic system. By the middle of the century France joined Britain in expanding its presence in the Middle Eastern market. Several methods, instruments, and policies were used to facilitate trade. European merchants through trading houses or local firms paid cash for exportable crops and provided imports on credit with funds borrowed from Europe. European merchants were active in copying designs, so that their factories could compete with local industry in meeting the domestic demand for textile. British and French merchants were also helped by their governments, which supported their commercial interests.

The Anglo-Turkish Commercial Convention of 1838, as noted earlier, provided for special tax privileges for European merchants at the expense of their local counterparts. The British and French governments also exerted pressure on the Ottoman authorities to conduct business according to British or French practices. This led to the enactment of the Ottoman Commercial Code of 1850, based on French practice, and its widespread introduction throughout the provinces. In addition the Ottoman government was persuaded to have disputes involving European merchants settled by European-dominated special commercial tribunals. The 1838 treaty also helped European merchants by stipulating that the Ottoman government would abolish domestic commodity monopolies as well as internal duties on movements of goods within the empire. The monopolies had been designed for the purchase, sale, and even export of a number of agricultural products in order to stabilize domestic prices and stimulate local industry. But the monopolies and the internal duties constricted the freedom of foreign merchants who wanted to increase exports of agricultural products and imports of manufactured goods. Thus, the British government had an interest in seeing both types of constraints removed.[16] Beyond the immediate stimulus that the removal of these constraints gave to foreign trade, the broader effect of this forced trade liberalization was to bring the Arab economies within the scope of the world economic system and subject them to its cyclical fluctuations. This was reflected, as Roger Owen observed, in the fact that an increasing number of Ottoman districts had become directly affected by fluctuations in the European business cycle, and their level of agricultural and commercial activity was immediately influenced by movements in international commodity prices or changes in the availability of bank credit.[17]

Another important element in the integration and dependency process was the series of reforms that the Ottoman government attempted in the last century. In order to cope with the impact of the French and the Industrial Revolutions, the government attempted a series of military, administrative, fiscal, and educational reforms designed to help withstand the threat of political and military intervention by Britain and other European powers on the one hand and the externally induced rise in trade on the other. Yet the major effect of the reforms turned out to be entirely the opposite of what was originally intended: instead of making the empire and its provinces less dependent on Europe, they made them more dependent. Instead of allowing them to control the process of European economic penetration, they made the whole process of penetration a great deal easier.[18]

The economic penetration found its most important and lasting effects through the change in the composition of national output and foreign trade, which was facilitated and influenced by a series of economic, political, and juridical privileges extended to European as well as certain local minorities who performed intermediary functions between the Europeans and the local economy. The position of foreign minorities in Egypt illustrates the critical role that they played in integrating its economy in the world market.

In the second half of the nineteenth century there was a large inflow of foreigners and foreign capital in Egypt. Banks were established to finance Egypt's expanding trade with Europe and to provide loans to Egypt's rulers.

The cotton boom of 1861–1866 attracted more foreigners and expanded their role in finance, banking, and trade. By the 1870s these foreigners had almost complete domination over these activities. They also acted as agents of European capitalist expansion, which introduced market relations into the Egyptian countryside. This expansion into the countryside accelerated the creation of a class of landowners whose economic fortunes became intimately dependent on the world market.[19]

One of the most important effects of trade on Arab economies was the change in the agricultural sector from a subsistence activity producing to meet the needs of the local market to an export sector that had to be responsive to the international economy. The international demand that provided stimulus for cash crops such as cotton, silk, wool, and cereals had other economic and social effects that went far beyond mere responsiveness to changing demand conditions. One was the change in the relative importance of the agricultural sector and by extension the institution of landownership in the national economies. Another important effect was a change in the nature of the land-tenure system whereby communal ownership was transformed to private ownership.

According to Charles Issawi, the rise in the value of agricultural produce greatly strengthened the desire to own land outright. This desire was helped by governments anxious to increase their revenues from taxes. This led to the development of land tenure characterized by large estates tilled by sharecroppers, a huge number of a very small peasant proprietors, short and precarious leases, high rents absorbing one- to two-thirds of gross output, large debts, rising land values, and a growing landless proletariat earning very low wages.[20]

The gradual integration of the Arab region into the world economic order led not only to the restructuring of the agricultural sector and landownership but also to what had been described as a process of de-industrialization. Again prior to European penetration and the advent of the era of foreign privileges cities contained large numbers of craftsmen who supplied the bulk of the region's requirements of manufactured goods. But in the first half of the nineteenth century the full impact of European factory-produced, low-cost manufactured goods and the low tariffs frozen by the commercial treaties crippled local industries. Thus in 1845 a French consul reported that the number of looms in Damascus and Aleppo had fallen to 2,500 from a total of 12,000 and that Aleppo's output of textiles in the ten-year period ending in 1862 had fallen from 4 million pieces to 1.5 million.[21]

It is very clear from these observations that indigenous industry had to surrender to foreign competition and that income from agricultural exports could not keep pace with the cost of manufactured imports. According to Oya Koymen the free market forces acting upon the underdeveloped economy of the Ottoman Empire created a situation of compulsory bilateralism with Britain in particular that was little removed from colonial tutelage.[22] But Egyptian industry felt most the combined impact of the effects of free trade and the provisions of the 1838 convention. Egypt had a thriving industry that was built by Muhammad Ali around the needs of an army of 130,000. By forcing Muhammad Ali to accept the restrictions of the convention and by reducing the size of his army to only 18,000, Britain succeeded in eliminating the need for most of the factories and with them Egypt's drive for industrialization and political and economic independence.[23]

The virtual halt to Egypt's drive for industrialization illustrates an important dimension of Arab dependency under Ottoman rule. Arab economies, especially their agricultural sectors, were considered the primary sources of revenue for the Ottoman government and its agents. This meant that from the perspective of the Ottomans economic development was not necessary. The paramount concern under these conditions was the appropriation of the largest possible share of the economic surplus that the provinces could generate. This transfer of resources from the Arab region reached its peak as the Ottoman government was trying to cope with its external debt problem, which toward the end of the last century was absorbing about four-fifths of the budget. This in turn pushed the Ottomans to draw an increasing share of the Arab region's revenues. Thus it was estimated that by the end of the nineteenth century more than 80 percent of the fiscal revenue generated in Syria and Iraq was handed to the Ottoman government as a tribute, leaving less than one-fifth of the revenue for local administrative expenditure.[24] In addition to the direct Ottoman domination, the exposure of Arab economies to European forms of economic domination constituted another layer of dependency over these economies. Arab economies found that they had to respond to the dictates of Ottoman rulers as well to economic stimuli generated in the course of carrying out international transactions with the Europeans.

Moreover, the effects of integrating Arab economies into the world economic system went beyond restructuring the economies and blunting internally induced agricultural and industrial development. An important force in shaping economic development and change in the Middle East was the impact of the consumption demonstration effect as Middle Eastern upper and middle classes rushed to adopt European ways of dress and to build European-style houses. This effect had several important consequences. In the first place it affected the market for old-style handicrafts. The fashion for things European also meant that foreign factory goods would be preferred over domestic products.[25] More important, the consumption demonstration effect creates the illusion of development or modernization where none exists. Not only might the demonstration effect confuse imported consumption with development, but it may also look as though the way to development is through consumption. The danger with this line of reasoning is that by its very nature consumption tends to divert domestic savings away from investment, the critical ingredient for economic growth, and therefore it acts as a brake on development. Furthermore, imported patterns of consumption have the unavoidable effect of orienting the use of domestic savings to payments to European producers and inducing investment in sectors that are not basic to the economy.[26]

These changes in the structures of Arab economies and the continued expansion in foreign trade brought about a number of other changes in the pattern of relations between the Arab region and Europe. These include the development of transport networks to serve the needs of foreign trade, the influx of finance capital and banking, rising balance-of-trade deficits, and rising external debt, which led to Britain's invasion and occupation of Egypt in 1882. These linkages between the Arab region and Europe, which gave rise to dependency without formal colonization (except in parts of Arab Africa) considerably facilitated further European and later American economic expansion in this century. This economic domination was supported by a political power structure that rested in the hands of either foreign invading powers or their local agents. In either case the economies were directed to serve the needs of the European-dominated world capitalist system. Given the fact that most of the population was tied to the land and that local industry was either destroyed or not allowed to grow, Arab economies were left to the mercy of international market fluctuations, which in time had become more dependent than ever on changing economic conditions and policies in Europe. In short:

By 1914, Europeans held all the commanding heights of the economy except for landownership in the Middle East, and the minority groups occupied the middle and some of the lower slopes. But already forces were gathering to retake these positions. . . . The reaction was against Western penetration and control, which not only subjected the peoples of the region to rulers alien in race, religion, and culture but disrupted some of their most fundamental and cherished social and economic values and institutions.[27]

OIL AND ARAB DEPENDENCY IN THE TWENTIETH CENTURY

In this phase, which began at the end of World War I, there were two seemingly contradictory trends at work. In the first place a clear economic trend worked toward expanding, strengthening, and consolidating Western economic domination. Concurrently there were other forces at work that shaped events and outcomes and attempted to loosen Western control.

The defeat of the Ottoman Empire removed whatever administrative and bureaucratic obstacles the Ottomans may have presented to European economic domination of the Arab region. Britain's control over Egypt, which had begun in 1882, was extended now, with the blessing of the League of Nations, to Iraq, Palestine, and Transjordan. France's control of Arab North Africa was extended to Syria and Lebanon, again with the blessing of the League of Nations. In the meantime Britain had already converted the Gulf sheikdoms into British protectorates. Thus by the early 1920s the entire Arab region from the Gulf to the Atlantic Ocean, with the exception of Saudi Arabia and Yemen, had fallen under the military and/or political control of Britain and France, with Italy retaining control over Libya. The removal of Ottoman impediments enabled Britain and France to shape political institutions and economic relations and to recast dependency relations to serve the needs of twentieth-century Europe. In cases where a local or indigenous regime was viewed to be more efficient and less costly, such regime was installed. Thus in the case of Iraq, where Britain installed Faisal as king, it made certain that his regime would be no more than a puppet. A British official statement described the goals of the political arrangements in Iraq in these terms: "What we want . . . is some administration with Arab institutions which we can safely leave while pulling the strings ourselves; something that won't cost very much . . . but under which our economic and political interests will be secure."[28] While the trend of foreign domination was succeeding in imposing regimes like the one in Iraq, there was a nationalist trend at work that attempted to free the Arab region from such domination. The economic dimensions of this trend will be explored in more detail in the next chapter.

The most important economic development in the Arab region during this phase was the influx of foreign capital—European and American—to develop the region's oil resources. This influx came to the Middle East during the first half of the twentieth century and to Arab Africa in the second half of this century. In all the countries where oil concession agreements were signed these agreements exhibited more or less the same general features whether the concessions were signed by Iraq, Kuwait, Saudi Arabia, Qatar, Bahrain, or Abu-Dhabi (now part of the United Arab Emirates). The most outstanding feature is that they were signed by a government of an oil-producing country on the one hand and a number of multinational oil corporations on the other. In the case of Iraq the concession was with Iraq Petroleum Company (IPC), which was owned by British Petroleum (BP), Exxon, Mobil, Shell, and Compagnie Française des Pétroles (CFP). The same group of companies obtained oil concessions with similar provisions in Qatar and the United Arab Emirates. In Kuwait the concession was obtained by Gulf and BP. In Saudi Arabia the concession was granted to Standard Oil of California (Chevron), which took Texaco as a partner, and the two became four when they agreed to accept Exxon and Mobil as partners. Once an oil concession had been obtained, a host government had no control over how resources were developed or over how much oil was produced or the price at which it was sold. Instead the multinational oil companies created jointly owned operating companies such as the Arabian-American Oil Company (Aramco) or IPC that were entrusted with the task of producing oil and delivering it to their owners, the parent companies. Other major features of the concession system were: (1) the life of the concession extended over several decades. IPC's concession was slated to last for seventy-five years (1925–2000), Aramco's sixty years (1933–1993), and Kuwait's seventy-five years (1933–2008); (2) the governments were to receive a fixed sum of money per unit of output (amounting to about twenty-four cents per barrel of crude oil for the decades prior to the early 1950s); and (3) the concessions covered either the entire country as in Iraq and Kuwait or almost all of it as in Saudi Arabia. George W. Stocking captured the exploitive essence of this system when he said, "Never in modern times have governments granted so much to so few for so long."[29]

This long-term exclusive monopoly over the development of natural resources and national economies gave concession holders the freedom to develop, accelerate, or decelerate the development of the oil sector in Arab oil-producing countries. Far more significant than the preemption of entry by competitors was the rise of a new and different form of dependency. Instead of relying on agricultural exports for their foreign exchange earnings economies, oil-producing countries have become dependent on the export of one raw material, the production and the price of which were determined by a half dozen oil companies.

The glaring asymmetry in the power of the companies and the governments may be explained by at least two historical conditions. When the concessions were being negotiated, oil-producing countries were under the military or the political control of the home countries of the oil companies. Iraq, for instance, was under virtual British control, and Kuwait was a British protectorate. Another contributing factor to the asymmetry was the ignorance of Arab governments of the nature of the oil wealth when they had signed over its exploitation to oil companies. Nor did the governments have much knowledge of the international economy or the oil industry. Governments, furthermore, did not have the technocrats or bureaucrats who could negotiate with or challenge oil companies.[30] But the development of Arab oil resources did not take place in earnest until the end of World War II. In the meantime agriculture continued to be the most important source of employment and output in Arab economies.

During the first half of this century agriculture was the predominant form of economic activity employing the majority of the labor force and supporting the majority of population. The land-tenure system inherited from the Ottoman Empire continued a pattern of lack of interest in agricultural investment and innovation. Export of agricultural raw materials and cereals constituted the main source of foreign exchange.

Industrial activity accelerated during this period under the impact of the Great Depression and World War II, which disrupted normal supplies and cut the availability of commercial ocean transport. Like most other regions in the Third World industrialization in the Arab region was import substitution. And as was to be expected, most of the industries catered to domestic demand for building materials, textiles, food processing, and furniture. Other consumer and durable goods, industrial inputs and capital goods, and transportation and communication equipment continued to be imported, since there was no local industry that could supply them.

The 1950s witnessed certain important economic and political developments in the entire Arab region. The most serious development was the creation of the state of Israel in Palestine in 1948, which continues to influence developments in the Arab region to this day. Development of Arab oil resources, which had been held back during the interwar period, was accelerated to accommodate the rise in demand for oil as Europe and Japan embarked on the tasks of reconstructing and developing their war-shattered economies.

In the early 1950s the fiscal terms of concession agreements were amended, so that governments were to receive 50 percent of the difference between the cost of production and the posted price of crude oil. Included in government revenue was a royalty payment, an issue that was to be contested by governments in future years, since the new formula had the effect of reducing government share by the 16.5 percent royalty rate. The change in the method of payment from a fixed amount to what amounted to a corporate income tax rate of 50 percent received a major boost from the Iranian government when in 1951 it nationalized the oil concession in a dispute with BP, the sole holder of the Iranian concession, over government revenue. The nationalization of the Iranian concession was the first major challenge to Western economic interests in the Third World in the postwar period. The restructuring of the Iranian concession that followed the 1953 overthrow of the government of Dr. Muhammed Mossadegh paved the way for United States multinational oil companies to acquire a major share of the Iranian concession.

In 1956 the Egyptian government under the leadership of Jamal Abdel Nasser nationalized another major Western-controlled resource, the Suez Canal. A few months later France, Britain, and Israel invaded Egypt. In 1958 the Iraqi monarchy, which had been installed by the British in 1921, was overthrown and replaced by a government that was bent upon changing the terms of the concession system.

We can make several generalizations regarding Arab dependency during the early stages of this phase. First and foremost, oil over time had become the most important export, the primary source of foreign exchange earnings and the primary source of government revenue. This meant that prospects for economic development, imports, and ordinary government spending had all become dependent on the demand conditions and prices of oil, both of which were beyond the influence of Arab governments. The oil sector also had no appreciable impact on employment, since the oil industry is a capital-intensive industry. Moreover, oil companies tended to rely on foreigners rather than nationals for most of their managerial, technical, skilled, and clerical jobs.

Not unlike those in other parts of the Third World, governments in the Arab region were, in this period, preoccupied with the task of building the institutions necessary for the functioning of a modern state. These institutions included schools, hospitals, roads, harbors, and other forms of infrastructure, armed forces, bureaucracies, and the like. Governments also had to develop banking, financial, trade, and fiscal systems. Like other Third World countries, governments in the Arab region had to develop public sectors in those areas of the economy where the private sector was unwilling or unable to take risk and invest capital. Political independence and the evolving national bureaucratic structures and policies induced the formulation of economic policies that had the effect, whenever possible, of encouraging local industry to emerge under the shield of protection. As was to be expected, these industries were light industries, which relied heavily but not exclusively on local raw materials and inputs.

Before dealing with the evolving new forms of dependency, it is useful to recapitulate some of the more important aspects of Arab economic development during the last century and the early part of this century. In the nineteenth century the Arab population, as was mentioned earlier, was subjected to double or two-tier dependency. In the first place most of the Arab area was subject to the rule of the Ottoman Empire, either directly or indirectly. The paramount interest of the Ottomans was to extract as much as they could of the economic surplus that the Arab provinces were capable of generating, with agriculture being the primary source of revenue and surplus. The Ottomans adopted various methods and mechanisms for extracting the surplus, including the auctioning of revenue to the highest bidders who inserted themselves between the central authorities and the peasants. The emergence of the Atlantic economy following the commercial and Industrial revolutions and the rise of the modern factory system led to a decline in the relative economic position of the Ottoman Empire vis-à-vis European powers and turned it eventually into a debtor country and a peripheral state. European economic penetration and domination were helped by the extraterritorial privileges extended to European nationals doing business in the empire and its provinces. The process of underdevelopment of the Arab region and its integration into the European-dominated world economic system was accelerated in the second half of the nineteenth century, greatly facilitated by the signing of the 1838 convention. Arab economies found themselves being exploited by a bankrupt and weak empire on the one hand and by modern, powerful, factory-based industrialized European economies on the other. Not only did Britain and France succeed in orienting Arab economies to meet the demand of their economies and that of the larger world economy, but they also succeeded in invading, occupying, colonizing, or controlling most of the Arab region and its population.

The defeat of the Ottoman Empire in World War I allowed France, Britain, and the United States to exercise their control over the Arab region and its resources without any external challenge. The hallmark of the interwar period was the introduction of multinational capital in the Arab region to exploit oil resources. The influx of foreign investment into this sector resulted in the deepening and strengthening of the dependency of Arab economies on changing economic conditions and policies in the industrialized West. It should be stressed that although the oil concessions were obtained in the 1920s and the 1930s, the big push for developing the region's oil resources was not undertaken in earnest until the 1950s when the growing needs of Western Europe and Japan could not be met from the oil-producing regions in the Western Hemisphere, Venezuela and the United States.

Irrespective of the evolution of their political and economic systems and the nature of their resource endowments or the evolution of the patterns of their external economic linkages, the countries of the Arab region have in common many features of the Third World. These features include heavy reliance on one economic sector as a major source of income (such as oil or agriculture), reliance on one or a few raw material exports to generate foreign exchange earnings, lack of an industrial sector, high rates of underemployment and unemployment, and heavy dependence on foreign markets for finished products, inputs, and food items.

It is also striking to note that in the early 1960s differences in per capita incomes among Arab countries were much narrower than they became a decade later. Thus in 1962 the combined Arab population was 100 million with a combined gross national product of $19 billion and per capita income of $190 per year. Oil-producing states accounted for 26 percent of the population and 36 percent of the GNP with per capita GNP of $270. Per capita GNP in nonoil states was $164, with these states accounting for 74 percent of the combined Arab population and 64 percent of its GNP. The gap in per capita GNP was significant, but it was nothing compared to the gap that developed a few years later. Indeed, except for Kuwait, Lebanon had the highest per capita GNP in the Arab region, $400. Per capita GNP in Syria, Jordan, Tunisia, and Iraq was comparable. Egypt, on the other hand, was the richest country in the Arab region in terms of the level of its GNP, which was twice that of Saudi Arabia in that year.[31]

Moreover, a number of non-oil-producing countries had larger and more diversified economies than those of oil-producing countries, because countries like Egypt, Syria, Lebanon, Morocco, and Tunisia had a much earlier start in the process of economic growth in agriculture, industry, and the service sectors than in the oil-producing states. These differences in the structures of Arab economies and the level of income reflect the nature and the timing of the process of integrating these economies into the world economy. The countries with agriculture-based economies, which could meet world demand for their products, started the integrative process before oil-producing states. The latter group had to wait for the world demand for their oil to materialize before their resources could be developed and their dependency enhanced. In addition to the role of foreign trade and foreign capital serving as catalysts in shaping the structures of Arab economies there were two other important forces in this period. First, due to Western political control either through open colonialism or semicolonial arrangements such as the mandate system, Arab monetary and financial systems became part of the currency blocs of imperial powers. Egypt, Iraq, and the Gulf emirates, for instance, were part of the sterling area, while Syria and Lebanon were part of the French franc zone. These arrangements meant that exchange rates were based on the British pound or the French franc and that foreign exchange reserves were managed by banking systems in England and France. They also meant that borrowing had to be done also through the financial systems of these two countries. Second, the adoption by Arab countries of Western technology, educational systems, and culture tended to strengthen the linkages between these countries and the industrialized countries. Schools, universities, and curricula were organized along European models with little attention to national cultural heritage, needs, and resources. Large numbers of students were sent to European and later to American universities to acquire knowledge and skills. This in turn enabled Western-influenced local elites to determine the orientation and the structure of Arab economies. Although some Arab economies and societies were beginning to feel the impact of the rising importance of the oil sector in the interwar period, its full impact had to await the emergence of the oil era in the 1950s.

One of the hallmarks of current Arab economic history was the entry of

European and American multinational oil capital in the Arab region. The collapse of the Ottoman Empire allowed the monopolization of the development of oil resources by a small number of interconnected multinational oil firms. European capital in partnership with the Ottoman government was about to exploit Iraq's oil resources when the empire collapsed and the spoils went to the victors. Britain's mandatory power over Iraq made it possible for it to organize an oil concession that excluded Turkish but included French, American, Dutch, and of course British interests. Following the conclusion of the Iraqi concessions, other concessions, as was indicated earlier, were concluded in the Arab region.

Yet, Arab oil resources were not fully developed until the decade of the 1950s. Thus in the period 1940 to 1944 Arab oil exports averaged only 14,000 barrels per day (TAD) compared with a daily average of 176 TAD for the period 1945–1949. The picture changed drastically in the 1950s when exports averaged 1.7 million barrels per day (MBD) during the period 1950–1954 and 2.8 MBD for the period 1955–1959. By 1973 Arab oil exports reached 16.7 MBD.[32]

Several factors account for the steady rise in Arab oil exports. In the first place the number of Arab oil-exporting countries increased from five in 1950 to twelve in 1973. The nationalization of the Iranian oil concession by the government of Dr. Muhammad Mossadegh forced the oil companies to expand Arab oil exports to offset Iranian oil exports, which the oil companies had boycotted in retaliation for Iranian nationalization. The rise in oil exports and consequently government revenue increased the reliance of many states on this particular source of revenue. As the needs of the state increased over time, so did the pressure on the oil companies to raise output and exports. The increase in output was made possible by the rise in the world demand for oil. The process of economic reconstruction after World War II, which was followed by a long period of sustained economic growth in the 1950s and the 1960s in the industrialized economies of Europe and Japan, entailed a steady growth in the demand for Arab oil. Yet, during this period Arab oil-exporting countries received about 80 cents per barrel of crude oil exported. This low-cost Arab oil played a crucial role in helping industrialized countries to sustain economic growth. It is relevant in this context that purchasing power of oil revenue declined steadily as the terms of trade deteriorated for Arab oil-exporting countries as a result of the continued rise in prices of imports. It would be no exaggeration, therefore, to say that the decline in real cost of oil meant in effect that Arab oil was close to being a free input that made a major contribution to the sustained economic growth of Western Europe, the United States, and Japan.

The increased importance of oil as a source of national income, government revenue, and foreign exchange meant a rise in the importance of the oil sector relative to other sectors of the economy. This rise in the relative importance of oil was also the unavoidable outcome of the failure of the industrial and agricultural sectors to grow at the same rate as the oil sector. This in turn explains the ability of governments to increase public consumption and public sector investment and allow private consumption to rise without having to raise taxes.

But these imbalances only increased dependence on the oil sector. The contribution of oil was determined by forces outside the sphere of influence of Arab government economic policymakers. The most important of these forces were the policies of multinational oil corporations and economic and energy policies of major oil-importing countries.

The ability of the oil companies to regulate output, exports, and prices and consequently the size of the oil sector placed them in a position to influence the entire economy. The power of the companies was demonstrated to all oil-producing countries when they decided not to buy Iran's oil after the nationalization of 1951. The boycott deprived Iran of foreign exchange earnings, which forced it to reduce imports and government spending, and which resulted in economic disruptions that set the stage for the eventual military overthrow in 1953 of the Iranian government. Similarly when Iraq decided in 1961 after long and fruitless negotiations with the oil companies to expropriate the nonutilized areas covered by the concession agreement, the companies retaliated by freezing Iraq's output and export of crude oil.

The other determining force that falls outside the influence of Arab oil-exporting countries is the very nature of the pattern of economic relations between Third World raw material–exporting countries and the industrialized countries. Export earnings are determined by demand conditions, policies, and prices, all of which are decided in industrialized countries. Even when Arab oil-producing countries succeeded as they did in 1973 in raising prices, one of the major consequences of the price increase was to deepen the dependency of both oil- and non-oil-producing countries. These consequences will be explored more fully in subsequent chapters. Suffice it to say at this juncture, the oil price increases of the 1970s led to a major expansion in the role of the oil sector in the economy. The availability of oil revenues made it easier for governments to expand imports of consumer, capital, and military goods without having to pay attention to balance-of-payments implications. Again the availability of revenues led to the neglect of goods-producing sectors and ever heavier reliance on imports.

Moreover, the accelerated pace of public and private spending in labor-short oil-producing countries prompted these countries to import workers from other Arab countries. Worker remittance transfers and other forms of financial flows such as economic assistance and loans led to an increase in public and private spending on domestic and imported goods—an increase that was not accompanied by expansion in domestic output or exports.

The rising dependence of Arab economies manifested itself also in the sharp rise in the relative importance of oil-based Arab economies in the Arab region. In 1962 non-oil-producing states received 62 percent of the combined Arab GNP with the oil states getting the remaining 38 percent. By 1974 the share of the oil states increased to 70 percent and to 75 percent by 1981. Within the oil states the share of the oil sector in the GNP in 1962 ranged from 18 percent in Iraq to 25 percent in Kuwait and to 38 percent in Saudi Arabia. In 1974 the contribution of the oil sector had increased to 56 percent in Iraq, 61 percent in Kuwait, and 91 percent in Saudi Arabia. The magnitude of the change may be appreciated by realizing that the combined national income of Arab oil states tripled from $26 billion in 1972 to $79 billion in 1974. By contrast the national income of nonoil states increased from $25 billion to $34 billion. Saudi Arabia's GNP in 1972 was $5.8 billion or 74 percent of that of Egypt. By 1974 Saudi Arabia's GNP had increased to $23.2 billion, or 234 percent of Egypt's.[33]

The importance of Arab oil went far beyond mere commercial considerations. Oil has always been considered a strategic commodity, and its control could not be left to oil companies or to the governments of oil-producing countries alone. Oil companies and oil agreements were viewed by the United States government as important components in the process of United States foreign policymaking. In addition to approving oil agreements, the State Department looked at the oil companies as instruments of United States foreign policy. The objectives of the policy were: (1) that the United States provide a steady supply of oil to Europe and Japan at a reasonable price for post–World War II recovery and sustained economic growth; (2) that stable governments be maintained in pro-Western oil-producing countries; and (3) that American-based firms be the dominant force in world oil trade. In this context the State Department viewed the interests of the companies to be basically identical with United States national interests.[34]

The system of concessions, however, was inherently unstable in view of the pattern of asymmetrical power relations between the governments and the companies. The Iranian government which was driven by the instability of the system to nationalize the oil concession in 1951 discovered to its detriment that it could not sell its oil, since the companies that also controlled transportation refused to buy oil produced by the Iranian government. The failure of the Iranian attempt to nationalize its oil industry persuaded other governments in the region to seek other ways to lessen the inequitable distribution of benefits derived from oil.

Although the creation of the Organization of Petroleum Exporting Countries (OPEC) in 1960 helped governments to exert some influence, albeit a passive one, on prices, it was not until 1973 that the October 1973 Arab-Israeli war provided the historical context for the sharp increase in the price of oil and for the eventual transfer of ownership of the concession agreements to the governments of the oil-producing countries.

The quadrupling of oil prices introduced certain important structural changes in the pattern of relations among the Arab states themselves on the one hand and between the Arab states and the international capitalist system on the other. Within the Arab state system there occurred a shift in the center of economic and political power from the core states of Egypt, Iraq, and Syria to Saudi Arabia and the other Arab Gulf states. The war between Iraq and Iran that broke out in 1980 had the effect of strengthening the position of the oil states in the region.

The oil price revolution of the 1970s changed inter-Arab relations in other ways. The desire on the part of the oil states to develop their economies prompted them to rely on imported Arab labor, since they lacked appropriate indigenous manpower. The transfer of remittances by these workers together with official development assistance provided by the oil states as well as private capital flow became an important source of foreign exchange surpassing in many instances export earnings. Transfer of funds from oil states also made it possible for the nonoil states to engage in levels of public and private consumption that could not be supported by local resources and had to be met by imports. Consumption demonstration effect was at work again, thanks to the oil bonanza.

The sharp rise in national income in the oil states prompted them to increase private and public spending (especially defense spending) and channel the balance-of-payments surplus to the money and capital markets of the major industrialized economies. The sharp increase in spending on development projects, the military, and imports, and the recycling of balance-of-payments surpluses to the financial and capital markets in industrialized countries gave rise to new linkages and new forms of dependency. Although both oil and nonoil states proclaimed that economic independence and development were their main national objectives, the rise in the importance of the oil sector in the former and the increased dependence of the latter on financial flows from the oil states precluded both groups from realizing their national objectives. On the contrary, the increased dependence of both groups of states on oil meant that the realization of national objectives had become increasingly dependent on economic conditions and policy considerations in industrialized countries, which in turn determined how much oil was to be imported from oil-exporting countries. The collapse of the OPEC oil price structure in 1986, which resulted in dramatic decline in oil export earnings, is a powerful reminder, to all producers, of this simple fact.

Paradoxically the rise in the importance of the oil sector and in the revenue from oil had the effect of widening and deepening economic dependency as the Arab countries found themselves relying more heavily on imports of food, consumer goods, capital goods, arms, technology, and a wide range of services. Another aspect of this phenomenon was the emergence of classes and interest groups such as contractors, importers, exporters, agents, bankers, lawyers, military and civilian bureaucrats, and technocrats whose economic, political, and social prosperity had become closely dependent on the foreign sector of the economy, which in turn has become increasingly dependent on oil export earnings.

In short, the oil states, like all other raw material exporters, are not in a position to determine the level of their oil export earnings or their contribution to their national economies. Yet the rising relative importance of the oil sector means that the economies of the oil as well as the nonoil Arab states have become increasingly dependent in their growth and stability on the economic and noneconomic policies of the United States, Western Europe, and Japan.

NOTES

1. For further articulation of this concept see Theotonio Dos Santos, "The Structure of Dependence," *American Economic Review*, Vol. 60 (May 1970): 231–236.

2. For a more detailed analysis of developments in this period see Roger Owen, *The Middle East in the World Economy, 1800–1914* (London: Methuen, 1981), 3–5.

3. See L. S. Stavrianos, *Global Rift: The Third World Comes of Age* (New York: Morrow, 1981), 131–132.

4. Owen, *The Middle East*, 8–10.

5. Ibid, 9.

6. See André Gunder Frank, *World Accumulation, 1492–1789* (New York: Monthly Review Press, 1978), 69–70.

7. See Albert Hourani, *Arabic Thought in the Liberal Age, 1798–1939* (London: Oxford University Press, 1962), 35.

8. Owen, *The Middle East*, 10–23.

9. For a fuller analysis of this point, see Omer Lutfi Barkan, "The Price Revolution of the Sixteenth Century: A Turning Point in the History of the Near East," *International Journal of Middle East Studies*, Vol. 6, No. 1 (1975): 3–28.

10. For a good analysis of the forces at work at this period see Stavrianos, *Global Rift*, 131–137.

11. Ibid, 139.

12. For a good statement of the issues see Celso Furtado, "Economic Development of Latin America," in Peter F. Klaren and Thomas J. Bossert (eds.), *Promise of Development: Theories of Change in Latin America* (Boulder, Colo.: Westview Press, 1986), 125–129.

13. See Michel Beaud, *A History of Capitalism, 1500–1980* (New York: Monthly Review Press, 1983), 96–101.

14. Ibid, 96. It is relevant to note that it was in this period of Britain's economic rise in the world economy that David Ricardo's theory of comparative advantage with its strong advocacy of free trade gained intellectual and political acceptance.

15. For a good outline of these mechanisms see Charles Issawi, *An Economic History of the Middle East and North Africa* (New York: Columbia University Press, 1982), 1–9.

16. Owen, *The Middle East*, 90–92.

17. Ibid, 92.

18. Ibid, 57–58. It is relevant to note that reforms were inspired by waves of liberal ideological enlightenment from Europe. The phenomenon was not confined to the Middle East but also took place in Latin America at the same time. According to Frank such reforms occurred at times when demand for agricultural products was accelerating and new administrative and institutional frameworks were needed, such as the introduction of private property over communal ownership. Thus, land became concentrated in the hands of few speculators. See André Gunder Frank, "The Development of Underdevelopment," in James D. Cockcroft, André Gunder Frank, and Dale I. Johnson, *Dependence and Underdevelopment: Latin America's Political Economy* (Garden City, N.Y.: Anchor Books, 1972), 32–35.

19. A good analysis of the role of local foreign minorities in the Egyptian economy may be found in Marius Deeb, "The Socioeconomic Role of the Local Foreign Minorities in Modern Egypt, 1805–1961," *International Journal of Middle East Studies* 9, no. 1 (1978): 11–22.

20. Issawi, *An Economic History*, 138.

21. Ibid, 151.

22. Quoted in Stavrianos, *Global Rift*, 205.

23. Ibid, 208–209. See also Nadya Ramsis, "Western Theory and Arab Development" (in Arabic), *Al Mustaqbal Al Arabi*, No. 64 (June 1984), 31–50.

24. Samir Amin, *The Arab Nation: Nationalism and Class Struggles* (London: Zed Press, 1978), 39.

25. Issawi, *An Economic History*, 156–157.

26. For an elaboration on these points see Fernando Henrique Cardoso and Enzo Falleto, *Dependency and Development in Latin America* (Berkeley: University of California Press, 1979), 10–14.

27. Ibid, 9–10.

28. Quoted in Stavrianos, *Global Rift*, 535. For a more comprehensive analysis of the forces that shaped events and relations in that part of the Arab region and the role that the United States government played see William Stivers, *Supremacy and Oil: Iraq, Turkey, and the Anglo-American World Order, 1918–1930* (Ithaca, N.Y.: Cornell University Press, 1982).

29. See George W. Stocking, *Middle East Oil: A Study in Political and Economic Controversy* (Nashville, Tenn.: Vanderbilt University Press, 1970), 130.

30. In Iraq, for instance, the oil department in 1935 was composed of a director who did not have a high school diploma and a junior clerk. And as late as 1951 Iraqi oil officials had not heard of posted prices, much less technical and economic studies. See N. Pachachi, "The Development of Concession Arrangements in the Middle East," *Middle East Economic Survey (MEES)*, March 29, 1968.

31. National income data were derived from, Arab Monetary Fund, *National Income Accounts for the Arab States, 1972–1983* (in Arabic), Abu Dhabi, 1983; International Monetary Fund, *International Financial Statistics Yearbook*; The World Bank, *World Development Report* (Annual); OPEC, *Annual Bulletin of Statistics*.

32. For oil production data see OPEC, *Annual Bulletin of Statistics*.

33. See note 31 for sources.

34. For a comprehensive analysis of the interrelationship between United States foreign policy objectives and United States–based multinational corporations see U.S. Senate, Committee on Foreign Relations, Subcommittee on Multinational Corporations, *Multinational Oil Corporations and U.S. Foreign Policy* (Washington, D.C.: U.S. Government Printing Office, 1975).

2

ARAB NATIONALISM, DEPENDENCY, AND WORLD CAPITALISM

The evolution of Arab nationalism in the modern era cannot be said to be unrelated to the modern form of nationalism that has slowly evolved in Europe since the end of the Middle Ages. In this context Arab nationalism acquires content and clarity that distinguishes it from the vague awareness of belonging to or membership in the Arab group and also differentiates it from ethno-national ideology. Instead it relates to the historical growth of nationalism as an indispensable ideology for the market-based growth of modern European economies. This growth, which required national markets, called for the different parts of a given ethno-national group to be brought together. This in turn called for the creation and the evolution of a powerful national state and its various institutions. The national state under the leadership of the bourgeoisie with its advocacy of freedom of individual, freedom of contracts, free enterprise, and property rights gained its legitimacy initially in Europe and America. It was subsequently adopted and adapted to local conditions by elites in colonized countries and regions.[1]

EMERGENCE OF MODERN ARAB NATIONALISM

Although it is difficult to determine the particular historical period that marked the rise of Arab nationalism, it can be said that it was during the eighteenth century that awareness on the part of some of the Ottoman-dominated Arab groups of their particularism began to emerge. The Ottoman authorities who had ruled the Arab region for centuries used Islam as the ideological force and rationalization for their colonial rule. The empire was a Muslim state in which theoretically all Muslims of free status were equals as first-class subjects. By the eighteenth century there were at least three important trends that worked to undermine Ottoman rule and eventually give rise to Arab nationalist sentiments.

First, there was the realization on the part of non-Turkish communities that whether they were Muslims or not, they were not equals as far as the Ottoman rulers were concerned. The concept of the equality applied in other words primarily to the Turks. The Arabs must have resented this Turkish domination, since the Turks succeeded not only in displacing them as the guardians of Islam but also in dominating them. This explains in part why the Arabs described as decadent (*inhitat*) the entire period during which supremacy in the Islamic world passed into the hands of states ruled by Turks particularly when these states dominated the Arab region.[2]

The second force of change was the European economic and political penetration of the empire and its provinces. The rise of European influence throughout the empire and later the outright invasion and occupation of Arab lands was a clear demonstration of the failure of the Ottoman system of government to protect the "nation" of Islam against foreign invaders. Yet, Arab exposure to European culture and ideas prompted the Arabs to reexamine their cultural heritage and use it to challenge the hegemonic control exerted by the Ottomans.[3]

The third trend that was at work in the eighteenth century was the decline of control by the Ottoman central authorities over the periphery, including the Arab provinces. This in turn helped local elites to assert a measure of autonomous control in the provinces. These elites in the Arab region were drawn from three groups: (1) the *ulama*, or men of religion, who usually held most of the positions in the religious hierarchy. Given the fact that Islam was the official ideology of the state, the upper ranks of the *ulama* tended to become an exclusive and privileged clique. They were the guardians and beneficiaries of *awqaf* (property earmarked for religious purposes), they had political and social influence, and as a religious group they were relatively free from the danger of confiscation; (2) the *a'yan* or local notables who acquired power through tax-farming or in other ways and gradually obtained official recognition from the government as local representatives; (3) the *ashraf*, or those who claimed to be descendants of the prophet Muhammad, who were recognized as a separate body, with fiscal and legal privileges.[4]

Several important factors tended to provide a degree of cohesion among these groups. In the first place they relied on the agricultural sector as the main source of income and economic privilege and power. It is important to note that the Ottoman Empire was a feudal state and was the sole proprietor of all the land.[5] The state derived the major portion of its revenue from leasing land according to a tax-farming system. It was this system of farming that also provided the political power base for these groups in that they played the role of intermediary between the people and the Ottoman central authorities. Another important force that gave these groups a special commonality of interest was their Arab origin and the fact that Arabic was their native language. The centrality of Arabic in the long history of the Arabs and the development of Arab nationalism was captured by Albert Hourani in his *Arabic Thought in the Liberal Age*. Although Hourani is fully aware of the fact that the belief that those who speak Arabic form a nation became articulated and acquired political strength during this century, the Arabs, as far back in history as one can see, have always been conscious of their language and have always been proud of it. Furthermore, the Arabs had a special part in the history of Islam as well as in its essential structure. The Quran is in Arabic, the Prophet was an Arab, and it was through the Arabs that the religion and its authority spread and that Arabic became and has remained the language of devotion, theology, and law.[6] Hourani goes on to assert that even when power finally passed to the Turks and Ottoman became the language of government, Arabic kept its privileged position as the language of religious culture and law.[7]

The decline of authority of the central government was another factor that afforded these elite groups in the Arab region a historic opportunity to enjoy a degree of autonomy that they had not enjoyed for centuries. And when the assertion of autonomy came into conflict with the central authorities, revolts and local movements took on an anti-Turkish character. By the nineteenth century and especially after the success of the revolt of the Greeks for independence from the Ottoman Empire (1821–1829), the idea of an Arab nation based on ethno-linquistic association achieved new strength and clarity and increasingly eroded the idea of a religiously based allegiance.[8]

A contributing influence toward the emergence of *Arab* nationalist sentiment was what might be called the linquistic-literary-cultural renaissance, which was helped considerably by the work of European and American Christian mission-aries. The missions, especially the American ones, were concerned with Arabic, since Protestantism places Christianity firmly within the local language. This in turn found the missions encouraging their members to learn Arabic. The missions also employed Arab scholars to translate the Bible into Arabic, helped other scholars who were attempting to revitalize the Arabic language, and encouraged the writing of religious texts in Arabic for use in missionary schools. It should be noted that the extent of the contribution of the American missions to the revitalization of Arabic is a matter of debate. It has been asserted, for instance, that there were textbooks written in Arabic and that there was an Arabic trans-lation of the Bible. What the Americans did was to produce a different kind of religious literature and a different translation of the Bible. But the revitalization and the modernization of Arabic had the unintended but important consequence of revitalizing a national culture, which helped in the process of creating a national identity.

The revival of the national language that inaugurated a literary renaissance contributed to the emergence of a new national identity among the Arabs and had the effect of eroding their religion-based loyalty to the Ottoman Empire. Although Arab nationalism was apolitical, the cultural renaissance that charac-terized most of the last century meant by definition the struggle against the alien (the hegemonic) control of the Ottomans and the discovery by the Arabs of their own heritage.[9]

To the extent that this cultural awakening eroded the power of control of the

Ottomans, it served at the same time the objectives of the Europeans who were seeking the same goals. European penetration of the Ottoman Empire and its provinces pulled the nascent Arab nationalist movements in different directions. On the one hand, European ideals of political freedom and the rise of nationalism made deep impressions and provided further impetus for Arab nationalist sentiments. At the same time, the economic domination of the imperialist European powers over the empire and its provinces led to disillusionment and doubt and to a reexamination of European professed goals. This was particularly the case after the French invaded and occupied Arab North Africa and Britain occupied Egypt in 1882. Nineteenth-century developments and pressures, however, were not sufficient to change the nature of Arab nationalism as a movement that was interested in political independence from the Ottoman Empire. Instead, the political interest and activities of Ottoman Arabs were channeled in the general movement that sought to change the despotic regime of government into a constitutional monarchy with equal rights for Muslims and non-Muslims, Turks and non-Turks.[10] The failure to reform the political system of the empire from within and to achieve equality with the Turks persuaded many Arab political activists that they should push for local autonomy and decentralization within the overall Ottoman structure. Although certain writers asserted at the turn of the century that there was an Arab nation in the Middle East region of the Ottoman Empire and that such a nation should be independent of the Turks, such independence was not to be attained until after World War I.[11] Advocacy for political independence lost its appeal for a period of time when the Young Turks came to power in 1908 and pushed for constitutional government. The Arabs' hope for decentralization in government and more autonomy for the provinces was soon dashed when they found out that the Young Turks were moving in the opposite direction. This was demonstrated by their push for a strong central government dominated by the Turkish elements of the empire and their decision to turn these elements into Turks by enforcing the exclusive use of Turkish in schools and government offices.[12] The failure of the constitutional experiment of the Young Turks from the perspective of the Arabs pushed Arab nationalism in different directions. One tendency sought the regeneration of Islam under the auspices of an Arab caliphate while another proposed the establishment of an independent Arab empire.[13] It should be noted that early pioneers of Arabism were interested in the preservation of the Ottoman-Muslim rule so long as it offered the provinces a degree of autonomy within the Ottoman Empire. But the rise of nationalism in Turkey itself, which downgraded religion as the unifying force and advocated the superiority of the Turks over other nationalities, persuaded Arab notables, intellectuals, and civilian and military bureaucrats to rethink and reexamine the relationship between the Arab provinces and the Ottoman government. France, Britain, and Russia encouraged this tendency as they were plotting to divide up the Ottoman Empire. With France's encouragement, the First Arab Congress was convened in Paris in 1913 to discuss the future of the Arabs in the Ottoman Empire.

Significantly even at this late date congress participants looked at themselves not as enemies or even opponents of Ottoman rule. On the contrary they considered themselves to be citizens of an empire that they hoped to reform. Thus according to congress president Abdel Hameed al-Zahrawi, the idea to hold the meeting in Paris originated with young Arabs living in Paris who came from "respectable" and "well-known" families in Syria. Interestingly enough, al-Zahrawi referred to the participants as Ottoman Arabs or Turkish Arabs who were interested in asserting their autonomy within the Ottoman Empire. To attain this objective, congress participants thought that Islam as the basis for the then-existing political arrangements should be abandoned in favor of a political solution based on the principle of decentralization for the provinces. As one Lebanese delegate put it, "we are Ottomans and we want to remain Ottomans . . . but the obligation of the government at the center is to take some reform initiatives based on the principles of participation and decentralization."[14]

It must be rather curious that even as late as the early part of this century Arab nationalists would still consider themselves as Turkish Arabs who in spite of almost a century of European influence were still committed to the Ottoman Empire as long as the central government offered them administrative autonomy. The explanation for this phenomenon may be found in Maxime Rodinson's observation that the principal contradiction was with Europe and that solidarity with the Turks as Muslims and as victims of European domination remained a factor, even during the struggle against the Turks.[15]

To recapitulate, the evolution of Arab nationalism in the last century exhibited two distinct but related dimensions. There was in the first place a literary-cultural renaissance, which was helped by the modernization and the revitalization of Arabic, which had at any rate remained throughout the Ottoman centuries the language of devotion, theology, and law. This renaissance, which was helped considerably by European and American missionaries, had the important consequence of recreating an Arab national identity for the people who lived in the Arab provinces in the Middle East.

The other dimension, which could not be separated from the first one, was the advocacy by the Arab nationalists of local administrative autonomy rather than political independence. This should not be surprising, since the Arab national movement was not a political movement for independence. On the contrary, it repeatedly reiterated its commitment to the preservation of the empire. This was logical given the nature of the leadership of the movement, which came almost exclusively from the elites who believed that their own economic and social interests would be best served by retaining a less rigid structural affiliation with the imperial authorities. This was made clear by the delegates to the First Arab Congress, which was held in Paris in 1913. The outbreak of World War I in the following year and the entry of the Ottoman Empire on the side of Germany and against Britain, France, and Russia changed all that and heralded a new era in the evolution of Arab nationalism.

ARAB NATIONALISM IN THE TWENTIETH CENTURY

The entry of the Ottoman Empire into the war created a whole new situation, for the Arab nationalists had to consider their options seriously. For some the preservation and independence of the empire as a Muslim state was essential. Although they were opposed to the policies of the central government, they feared that its collapse would pave the way for European rule. Others felt that the war provided an opportunity to obtain independence for the Arabs with the help of the enemies of the empire.[16] The debate was settled in June 1916 when the Arabs decided to revolt against Ottoman rule and enter the war on the side of Britain and France.

The Arab revolt was declared and led by the Hashimite leader Sharif Hussain of Mecca, who had been promised by the British that they would guarantee the liberation of the Arabs and the throne of an Arab kingdom consisting of the Arab parts of Asia.[17] These promises strengthened the hands of the sharif and his sons in persuading reluctant nationalists to join the revolt. They succeeded also in persuading a large number of Arab army officers who had been part of the Ottoman officer corps to leave the Ottoman army and join the Arab revolt and its army.[18] Although the Arab nationalists were able to form a government in Syria in 1920 and declare Faisal, son of Sharif Hussain, as king, the government lasted only four months. French forces overthrew it in July. As Hourani has observed, neither the administration of the new government nor the nationalist movement as a whole had any military or diplomatic strength of its own and had to rely on the strength of Britain. The unavoidable consequence was being caught in the inescapable dilemma of a weak group looking to a great power to achieve its ends but unable to influence those actions.[19]

But the dilemma of the Arab nationalists proved to be far more serious and devastating than their inability to influence the direction of British policies, because when Britain had promised Sharif Hussain that it would support the formation of an Arab kingdom, it had no intention of doing so. Britain had already agreed with France to carve up the Arab East between them with France assuming control over Syria and Lebanon and Britain assuming control over Iraq, Jordan, and Palestine. The League of Nations sanctioned this colonial control by calling it a mandate system under which Britain and France were expected to prepare the mandated areas for political independence. By 1921 Britain had succeeded in installing Faisal as king of Iraq, and his brother Abdullah was given the crown of Transjordan, again under British mandate. Syria and Lebanon were ruled directly by France, as was Palestine by Britain.

Another important historical event that had serious impact on the Arab nationalist movement was the British government's declaration in November 1917 of support for the creation of a Jewish National Home in Palestine. These commitments on Britain's part were obviously irreconcilable with those made to the Arabs. "If it came to the point, Britain would always prefer her need for good relations with France to her desire to establish an Arab State in Syria; and the Zionists could bring greater pressure to bear in London than could the Arabs."[20]

The Arab revolt of 1916, its beneficiaries, and its impact on subsequent developments of Arab nationalism were summed up by Anis al-Sayigh as follows: "This national movement was largely a political movement in the narrow sense; it had no social or humanitarian perspectives. It fought merely for formal independence and was unable to achieve real independence. . . . Second, it was a right-wing conservative movement . . . which had been adjusted to the needs of a particular leadership and was monopolized by traditional politicians who were usually either rich feudalists or their agents. They saw their own interests as being the interests of the homeland and excluded workers, peasants and the middle classes from the power which they were able to gain for themselves for a third of a century [until the 1950s]. . . . Third, the movement had no confidence in itself or in the nation; hence it was based more on foreign capital than on the people, and tended to dance to the tunes played in foreign capitals."[21]

The first generation of Arab nationalists who led the Arab revolt and fought for the independence of the Arab region from Ottoman rule ended up in power but with the approval and under the patronage of a new colonial regime that was imposed on their countries by France and Britain. This was made easier by the very nature of the mandate system, which tended to rule indirectly through indigenous elites. For the elites it was an act of replacing one dominant foreign power by another. Once their economic interests were preserved, they found no reason to challenge the ruling foreign power.

From the elites' perspective the mandatory system provided new advantages that were lacking under the Ottomans. In the first place the elites had become the *de facto* as well as the *de jure* rulers of their own people. They were no longer representatives of the local people to the central government or its representative. In other words they became the government but with the mandatory power pulling the strings in order to secure European economic and political interests. This was clearly the case in Iraq. According to British government documents, the effectiveness of the Iraqi government under the leadership of King Faisal was a function of the airplanes of the Royal Air Force that were ready to bomb the malcontents into submission. The whole structure of government would collapse once these airplanes were removed.[22] In certain countries such as Iraq a class of landed aristocracy was directly established by the colonial power to provide political backing for the monarchy. Doreen Warriner observed that the foundation of the new kingdom in Iraq strengthened the position of the tribal sheiks by giving them legal ownership of land and representation in Parliament. Since settlement of tribal wars became a function of the army, the new landed aristocracy found itself secured in a position of privilege in the state without obligation to it. As oil money provided an alternative source of investment in agriculture and other sectors of the economy, the function of these large landowners became simply to preserve their position in the packed parliament and of resisting any change.[23] The change in the land-tenure system in Iraq was a part of region-wide change in the landownership system, which underwent drastic changes in the nineteenth and twentieth centuries and which in turn reflected the impact of the international economy on the agriculture-based Arab economies. According to Issawi:

The rise in the value of agricultural produce greatly strengthened the desire to own land outright. The government anxious to increase their revenues from taxes on such produce . . . abolished the *timars*, *iltizams* [tax farming], and other intermediary institutions. At the same time, the bonds tying the peasants to the land were snapped and those binding the village community together loosened; among the causes were greater security, increasing government centralization, growing population, and, above all integration in the market. . . . The result, all over the region was the development of a land tenure characterized by large estates . . . tilled by sharecroppers; a huge number of very small peasant proprietors, often with highly fragmented holdings; short and precarious leases; high rents; large debts; rising land values; and growing landless proletariat earning very low wages."[24]

In addition to the political-military backing that the mandatory system provided to the newly installed regimes, it helped to integrate the local economies into the international system directly without having to go through another layer of relationships—the Ottoman government. The removal of the Ottoman intermediary function not only facilitated such an integration but allowed the local elites and the dominant foreign interests to distribute among themselves the economic surplus. The removal of the Ottoman authority also provided Britain and France with direct access to the resources of the mandated areas and ample opportunities to exploit them. The granting of the oil concession by the newly established Iraqi government is a case in point.

The nature and implications of the mandatory system in Iraq were assessed by Peter Sluglett as follows:

In any balance sheet for the Mandate, the Iraq people outside the small circle of government . . . were the losers. The Government was not carried on for their benefit, but for the benefit of the Sunni urban political class within a framework created and supported by the British authorities. . . . When it was clear that British interests would no longer be at risk, and when the necessary mechanism to protect them had been perfected it was time to withdraw. . . . It is profitless to blame the British Mandatory authorities for failing to ensure that the Iraq Government concerned itself with the wider interests of the nation, or made efforts to reconcile rather than exacerbate the tensions within the state: to do so would be to misunderstand the nature of imperialism.[25]

The failure of the Arab revolt to achieve political and economic independence meant that the next phase in the evolution of Arab nationalism had to entail the elimination of European domination and its agents—the Arab governments that France and Britain had installed. Although Britain and France granted Iraq, Syria, and Lebanon, but not Palestine, formal independence through treaty arrangements, the independence was so constricted as to be meaningless. These new conditions forced the Arab nationalists into taking one step at a time. The first step called for the removal of foreign domination embodied in the treaties that granted independence, while the second entailed the transfer of political power through the removal of foreign-installed local elites. The efforts of the Arab nationalists did not show results, however, until after World War II because Arab governments of the interwar period were dominated by nationalists who had a very narrow agenda and who considered their association with European governments as not only unavoidable but also the natural thing to do.

Yet while the history of the interwar period was shaped by European colonialism and its local elites who succeeded in consolidating their positions of economic and political power, other forces that eventually undermined these positions were at work. In addition to changes in the agricultural sector outlined earlier, the industrial sector underwent important changes as well. These included the emergence of local industry to meet local demand, which could not be satisfied from traditional sources due to the Great Depression and/or war conditions. In the Ottoman era treaty impediments made it impossible to afford protection to local industry. Removal of these obstacles enabled governments to provide such protection to infant industry. Under such protective policies this period witnessed a considerable degree of import substitution in a wide range of light industries.[26]

As government functions expanded, so did its military and civilian bureaucracies and technocracies. This meant that new recruits from outside the ranks of traditional elites had to be drawn into the labor force. The emergence of these classes coincided also with the rise of two other classes—urban and rural proletariat—primarily because of changes in the pattern of landownership and import-substitution industrialization. As the structure of the economy changed, another class of petty bourgeoisie—bankers, shippers, exporters and importers, insurance agents, and so on—tied to the international economic system also emerged. As World War II came to an end, the configuration of social classes and their interests had undergone a major change since the establishment of governments in the Arab region. While economic and political power was concentrated in the hands of traditional elites—landed aristocracies, large industrialists, and Ottoman-trained military officers turned politicians—other newer classes with different aspirations and needs began to come to the fore. While the traditional elites had by the end of World War II associated their political and economic fortunes with imperialism, the new classes were challenging the status quo in search of new social and economic order. The opportunity to replace the old order forced itself upon the Arab region when the state of Israel was created in 1948 in Palestine. The creation of Israel turned out to be the most serious challenge to face the old order since it demonstrated its unwillingness and inability to preserve an Arab Palestine. This failure exposed the bankruptcy and destroyed the political legitimacy of the first generation of Arab nationalist regimes.

It goes without saying that the failure of the Arabs and Pan-Arabism in 1948 was one of historic proportion from which Arab nationalism has never recovered. Explanations and rationalizations abound, ranging from collusion between imperial powers, Arab regime bankruptcy, superior enemy technology, and others.[27]

The old nationalist order that came to power in the aftermath of the Arab Revolt and the imposition of the mandate system was displaced by a new, younger generation of nationalists in a succession of military takeovers in the core Arab countries of Syria (1949), Egypt (1952), and Iraq (1958). These regimes succeeded in destroying the economic power base of landed aristocracy through enactment of land redistribution laws, which limited the size of landholdings. The new regimes expanded the public sector and absorbed large domestic enterprises and nationalized foreign enterprise when such nationalization was feasible. Their pronounced failure, however, may be found in at least five areas. First, they failed to help the Palestinians achieve their national aspirations in self-determination, not to mention their failure to curb Israeli expansionism. Second, they opted to adopt and implement paternalistic, nonparticipatory, and repressive systems of government. This system of government was an unavoidable outcome of their unwillingness to broaden the base of their political support. This unwillingness may be seen in the assertion, for example, that the well-informed Arab cannot be Communist without giving up Arabism, since the two are mutually exclusive and communism is alien to everything Arab and is the greatest danger to Arab nationalism. Third, they chose not to develop the economies in a manner that would reduce dependency on the international capitalist system. To do otherwise would have meant a recognition of classes, and class conflict was something that the new generation of nationalists chose to reject. Fourth, they failed to move along the path of Arab unity, which was supposed to be their most immediate and most important objective. Last but by no means least, these nationalist regimes drifted into a number of policy arrangements and understandings with the oil regimes of Saudi Arabia and the smaller Gulf states, a subject that merits a few words at this juncture.

One of the most important developments in the twentieth-century Arab world and Arab nationalism has been the rise of the importance of oil as a source of income, wealth, and political power. In turn, as was noted earlier, this led to a shift in the leadership of the Arab world from the core countries of Egypt, Syria, and Iraq to the family regimes of the oil states. This shift, which became evident in the aftermath of the 1967 Arab defeat, was accelerated and dramatized after the 1973 October war, which was supposed to end the occupation of the Arab territories of the Sinai, East Jerusalem, the Golan Heights, the West Bank, and Gaza, which Israel had captured in the 1967 war. History will show that the decision by the Arab oil states to reduce their output and place selective embargo measures on their oil exports for a few months in the name of the Palestinian cause was a brilliant, profitable act that increased dramatically their income, wealth, and political power within the Arab world. History will also show that Arab nationalism has never given nor will it ever likely give so much power and wealth to so few in such a short period of time. Let us remember that the combined population of Saudi Arabia and the other family regimes in the Gulf is less than 10 million or less than 5 percent of the combined Arab population. Let us also remember that it was only a few short years before his death that Jamal Abdel Nasser was engaged in a bitter political and sometimes even military confrontation with the family regime of Saudi Arabia and its supporters in the Arab region.

The 1967 defeat and the October war changed all that when these family regimes established their nationalist credentials, quadrupled their national incomes, and became the arbiters of many Arab issues. The rise in oil income created a huge gap in the distribution of income and wealth between these family regimes and other Arab states, distorted economic development in many Arab countries, helped create patterns of consumption totally insupportable by local resources, and increased Arab dependency on the West. The move also derailed many issues from their Pan-Arab path while reducing others to money matters.

In short it can be said that the oil states, thanks to their oil wealth, succeeded in what might be called the denationalization of Arab nationalism. This process was culminated and found its clearest expression in the formation of the club of the petro-rich known as the Gulf Cooperation Council (GCC).

The GCC under the leadership of Saudi Arabia, it should be remembered, has an entirely different agenda from those who were hoping for a more equitable distribution of Arab national resources among the Arab countries. Saudi Arabia, which became the undisputed financial power in the Arab world after the oil price revolution, took the lead in rallying Muslim governments to form the Islamic Organization Conference under its leadership, thus creating a countervailing power to the forces of Arab nationalism. It was Saudi Arabia, in cooperation with Kuwait and pre-Qaddafi Libya, that created the Organization of Arab Petroleum Exporting Countries (OAPEC) in order to remove oil from the Pan-Arab agenda. It was Saudi Arabia that prevailed in the aftermath of the 1967 defeat to move the Palestine question to the sphere of American diplomacy. And last but not least, it was Saudi Arabia that led the forces of capitalist market-oriented development in pressuring aid-receiving Arab states to reorient their economies in favor of the domestic private sector and international capitalism. The point to be remembered is that given their wealth, income, and intimate economic, political, and military dependency on the United States, it would be unrealistic to expect the GCC governments to embrace the goals of Pan-Arabism in unity and nonalignment.

It is important to point out that the dramatic increase in oil wealth and income destroyed whatever prospects there might have been for some meaningful economic achievements at the Pan-Arab level. The decisions of the 1980 Arab Summit Conference provide a good illustration. At that conference it was agreed among other things to adopt and fund a Joint Arab Development Decade. Yet this joint program was funded to the tune of only $5 billion, or $500 million per year. One need not point out how inadequate this amount of funding is relative to the massive needs of the Arab countries and their combined population of 200 million. Yet it should be pointed out that the combined military spending of the Arab states in 1984 amounted to more than $61 billion with the GCC states alone spending $28 billion.

It would be no exaggeration to say that petromoney brought into being classes whose economic and political prosperity had become dependent on this distorted pattern of wasteful spending. These classes include military and civilian bureaucracies, beneficiaries from contracts, commissions, agencies, transactions, recruiting, land speculation, construction of infrastructure, industrialists, importers and exporters, among others, all of whom have become increasingly dependent on the international capitalist system. Given this system of relations and given the vast amount of resources at the disposal of the state, the state itself had become a formidable force in each and every Arab society while the role of intellectuals and nationalist thinkers was eroded and marginalized.

It is obvious from the changes that were brought about by the oil wealth that the concomitant rise of the influence of family regimes requires that the whole concept of Arab nationalism be revisited for rigorous analysis to see whether it can be salvaged and restored to the unifying role it was once thought it could play. It is very difficult to envisage any serious change in the present thrust of Arab nationalism, which at the current phase of Arab political history is anchored on the premise that the sovereignty of the state takes precedence over Pan-Arab issues and on the central importance of petromoney in Arab economies. The present impotence of Arab nationalism as a force of change is made worse so long as the Arab regimes continue to commit their societies to the capitalist path to development and continue to strengthen their linkages of dependence with the international capitalist system. The examination of this two-tier issue of Arab nationalism and capitalism and Arab economic dependence will face Arab nationalists with their most intellectual challenge.

IDEOLOGICAL CONTENT OF ARAB NATIONALISM

There is no one generally accepted source or authority that would define Arab nationalism and its ideological content. Variability in the historical contexts that gave rise to movements such as Arab nationalism, the particular epoch that engendered a given type of struggle, the forces that presented challenges to Arab nationalism (be it foreign but Muslim, or foreign and non-Muslim, or local but foreign-dependent) are some of the laments that gave rise to various interpretations of ideological contents and goals of Arab nationalism. Indigenous factors such as the nature of class and power structure, land tenure, cultural heritage, and distribution of income and wealth are some of the other elements that affected the evolution of national movements such as Arab nationalism.

It can be said that the rise of Arab nationalism in the modern era is associated with European expansion in the region. The invasion of Egypt by Napoleon in 1798 and his expulsion from it by Britain three years later brought the Arab region directly within the sphere of imperialist world domination. At another level the evolution and the thoughts of Arab nationalism in the last century were affected by the rise of European nationalism and the theories that attempted to explain their evolution. Thus from European theories of the nation modern Arab nationalists borrowed the idea of defending and extolling common language and history as factors on which they placed greater stress than they did on territorial ties. For the Arab nationalists it is the Arab nation that must take precedence in determining the moving force behind Arab nationalism rather than the particular piece of Arab land where a person was born. In other words, the Arab nation constitutes the main distinguishing and unifying characteristic of the Arabs rather than the place of birth or residence and in which the territorial factor is of paramount importance. In this context regional divisions are perceived to be artificial, since they were imposed by foreign rule and domination and are being continued by the narrow national (provincial) interests of Arab states. The ideas and values of modern Arab nationalism have one objective: the establishment or the reestablishment of a strong Arab nation.[28] Sati al-Husri, who is considered to be the main theoretician of Arabism, spoke of the Arabs as constituting a single *Umma*, or nation, regardless of their domicile in any one Arab country or their religion. The single most important criterion is that they speak Arabic and live in one of the Arab countries, which are nothing but branches of the Arab nation after all. He goes on to highlight the fact that the present Arabic state system is nothing but a legacy of the period of foreign occupation and that these states were born out of haggling between imperialist powers.[29] For al-Husri, in other words, an Arab nation is something that exists and has an objective basis, which is its language. This nation, however, was divided into a number of states, each with its own boundaries, government and other requisites of a modern state. And since this division was externally imposed, it became incumbent upon Arab nationalists to remove these artificial barriers and reconstruct a unitary state for an already unified Arab nation.[30]

Given the foreign-imposed conditions that had to be overcome—from Ottoman control to European colonialism and imperialism—the rhetoric of Arab nationalism tended to have revolutionary overtones. This was particularly the case in the post–World War II period when nationalist movements throughout the Third World sought political independence and the removal of the conditions that allowed certain social strata to profit from their ties with Western economies. Yet it is important to note that Arab nationalism from its very inception to the present is a middle-class political movement that influenced all other classes. Although Arab nationalism did not have a unified organization or a unified political leadership, its underlying sentiments and aspirations have been strong enough to permit at certain junctures mass mobilizations on behalf of its objectives and ideals as well as to compel conservatives to accept at least temporarily some of its aims.[31]

These aspirations and sentiments were articulated through two main political movements that came to power, as was mentioned earlier, in a number of Arab countries in the second half of the twentieth century. One movement was led by Jamal Abdel Nasser while the other was led by the Arab Baath Socialist party. When Nasser and his fellow army officers succeeded in overthrowing the monarchy in Egypt in 1952, their interests in furthering the goal of a Pan-Arab movement were unclear at best. Instead their focus was to rid Egypt of some of the more flagrant economic injustices and waste that the monarchy had imposed on the Egyptian people. Yet in the pursuit of its own policy Egypt was looked at to play a major role in shaping the forces and the direction of Arab nationalism. Egypt's willingness to purchase arms from the Soviet bloc in 1955, after having been refused such arms by the West, represented a significant step on the road to political independence. This exercise of sovereignty rights by an Arab government, which was construed as an unprecedented act of defiance of the dominant Western power, enhanced the leadership position of Egypt and Nasser in the Arab region. A year later, Egypt's position was further enhanced when Nasser decided to nationalize the Suez Canal. The 1956 nationalization of the Suez, which was the first such act by any Arab government, had several important implications for the forces of Arab nationalism. It symbolized the willingness and the determination of a poor country like Egypt to challenge the domination of foreign powers that had shaped the economic and political evolution of the Arab region. Given the strategic importance of the Suez Canal, its successful nationalization proved to the Arabs that a country like Egypt, contrary to what was then conventional wisdom, could successfully operate the complicated workings of a major international waterway such as the Suez Canal. The importance of the Suez nationalization prepared the ground for the debate regarding the validity of the oil concessions and the need to restructure if not nationalize these foreign-held concessions. But for the time being the Suez nationalization established Nasser and Egypt as the standard by which the performance of other Arab leaders and countries had to be judged.

This position of leadership was, paradoxically, further enhanced when in November 1956 Egypt was invaded by forces of Israel, Britain, and France to overthrow Nasser's regime and to return the Suez Canal to foreign control. The invasion of Egypt in the aftermath of the Suez nationalization demonstrated to the Arabs and to the Third World in general the extent to which foreign powers were willing to go to hold on to their economic and strategic position. Political independence obtained after World War II and membership in the United Nations provided no assurances that national boundaries and territorial integrity could not be violated at will by a superior military power bent on preserving its economic and political privileges.

The failure of the invasion to accomplish its objectives had the effect of strengthening the forces of Arab nationalism in general and the position of Nasser both in Egypt and in the Arab world in particular as a leader of these forces. In challenging foreign domination and surviving the tripartite invasion of his country by Israel, France, and Britain, Nasser set a standard of legitimacy for other Arab leaders and regimes. Arab nationalism under Nasser took as its point of departure the liquidation of Western economic domination or at least its gradual phasing out. The failure of other regimes to embark upon similar policies brought into question their legitimacy. Iraq is a good case in point.

The Iraqi regime under the monarchy had opted to associate itself more closely with the West when it agreed in 1955 to join the United States–sponsored Baghdad Pact (later to be called the Central Treaty Organization). In addition to Iraq the pact comprised Iran, Turkey, Pakistan, and Britain, ostensibly to strengthen the region's security vis-à-vis the Soviet Union. But for the Arab nationalists the threat to their security and aspirations had come and would continue to come from Israel and its Western allies. The invasion of Egypt was a powerful demonstration of this belief. From this perspective the Baghdad Pact was looked upon as a means to contain and weaken the forces of Arab nationalism. But the ability of Nasser's regime to survive the invasion strengthened the forces of opposition in Iraq to the point that by July 1958 the monarchy was overthrown and was replaced by a nationalist regime. No sooner had the new regime established itself than it decided to withdraw from the Baghdad Pact and to open negotiations with the oil companies to change some of the terms of the oil-concession agreement.

The rise of Arab nationalism also manifested itself in 1958 when Egypt and Syria decided to unite and form the United Arab Republic under Nasser's leadership. The experiment lasted until 1961 when Syria decided to regain its independence.

The rise of the tide of Arab nationalism under the leadership of Nasser and Egypt was paralleled by the emergence of another similar political movement. Its philosophy was articulated by the Arab Baath Socialist party, which made its debut in Syria in the 1940s. The core of Baathist ideology is the quest for Arab nationalism and unity. For the Baath one of the objectives of imperialism is to retard and prevent Arab unity. It follows that existing political divisions and fragmentation must be removed if the Arabs are to overcome stagnation and backwardness. In order not to confuse its own socialism with that of Communists or Marxists, the Baath not only rejects the concept of class struggle as the driving force in historical development but also asserts that the well-informed Arab cannot be communist without giving up Arabism, since according to the Baath the two are mutually exclusive. Indeed, the Baath goes so far as to assert that communism is alien to everything Arab and it will remain the greatest danger to Arab nationalism so long as the latter is unable to give a systematic, coherent, overall definition of its aims.[32]

Since the Baath asserted the supremacy of Arab nationalism and Arab unity and rejected communism, Marxism, and non-Arab socialism, one would have expected an articulation of an alternative outline of an ideology. Such an alternate is not to be found. Instead, the emphasis continues to be on the importance of Arab nationalism and Arab unity, an emphasis that is characterized by a high degree of circularity. Thus in stressing the paramount importance of Arab unity one of the founders and the leading theoretician of the Baath party had this to say:

Starting from our unitary conception of the Arab cause, we do not believe that it is possible to separate Arab unity from socialism. Arab unity is a higher value than socialism and is more advanced, but the demand for Arab unity will remain an abstract and theological notion, and in some cases a harmful delusion, if it is not put in its real context. That context is the sentiments of the people; the Arab people are, after all, the only force capable of making Arab unity a reality.[33]

As to the meaning of Arab socialism, Michel Aflaq's understanding of the concept seems to have little if any relevance to economic policy. Thus, he stated, "When I am asked to give a definition of socialism, I can say that it is not to be found in the works of Marx and Lenin. I say: *socialism is the religion of life and of its victory over death* [emphasis added]." Aflaq went on to say that the Arabs should "take care not to lose their nationalism nor to confuse it with the felonious notion of class interests, so as not to endanger national unity."[34]

The outright rejection of Marxian analysis of class interests and conflicts and the irrelevance of their socialism to objective economic realities such as problems of income and wealth distribution and questions of resource allocation forced the Baathists to acknowledge the debt of intellectual Arab life to Marxism. The intellectual challenge that Marxism presented in the areas of social justice and a more equitable pattern of income distribution forced the Baath to include such goals in its economic and social program.[35] The most serious challenge to the very essence of the Baath ideological main constituency came from the party's own left wing, which claimed that the party was out of touch with the needs of the people. This was attributed not only to the flawed policies of the party but also to its very traditional ideology. Aflaq's ideology in particular was singled out for criticism on the grounds that it is based on the thesis that the aim of the Arabs' struggle is to restore the past and that according to him progress is a backward step into the past and the future for him consists of nothing more than making contact with the souls of the ancestors.[36]

In reflecting on the evolution of Arab nationalism, one is struck by the impact of foreign military and/or political influence and the Arab world's commitment to and belief in a market-based economic system and international capitalism. Foreign political influence refers here to the impact on Arab nationalism of the political and military presence or intrusion of foreign powers such as the Ottoman Empire, France, Britain, or the United States as well as movements such as Zionism. Thus while one can trace early Arab nationalist thoughts and sentiments in the modern era to an attempt by Arab elites to loosen the grip of the Ottoman hold on the Arab provinces, one cannot separate the outcome of such attempts from the manipulation of and alliances with European powers. It was the French foreign ministry, for instance, that promoted the convening of the First Arab Congress in Paris in 1913. It is significant to note that as late as that year the Arab delegates maintained that they did not wish to secede from the ailing empire and that they wanted only a larger share of power. It is worth noting also that these pioneering nationalists who came from so-called "respectable" families referred to themselves as Turkish Arabs or Ottoman Arabs and stressed that they wanted to remain Ottomans. During World War I Britain, through its dealings with Sharif Hussain of Mecca, displaced France as the patron of Arab nationalism and the Arab revolution.

The second major set of forces that shaped the evolution of Arab nationalism was the economic interests of the ruling groups in the Arab world. Local Arab elites who controlled the trade, agricultural, and industrial sectors soon realized that the coincidence of their economic and business interests with the forces of international capitalism, imperialism, colonialism, and occupation was very rewarding. But this coincidence of interests in the context of the international capitalist order meant nothing but dependency in which Arab economies were made to respond to the imperatives of the international market and not to the needs of Arab societies.

The first generation of Arab nationalists who governed the Arab countries in the first half of this century was driven out of power by an alliance of a wide range of small middle classes under the leadership of the military. This was especially the case in the core Arab countries of Egypt, Syria, and Iraq. Although the new generation of nationalists advocated its own brand of Arab socialism, this socialism in practice was similar to development policies in most countries of the Third World where the public sector had to assume responsibilities that the private sector was either unwilling or unable to tackle.

Although the concept of Arab unity is central to the political thought of both the Baathists and the Nasserites, neither political movement was successful in attaining such unity. On the contrary the experiment with unity between Syria and Egypt proved to be transitory. Even when the Baath party succeeded in obtaining and retaining power for decades, in Syria and Iraq political fragmentation remained as strong as ever. Furthermore, the tendency has been to refocus political attention and economic resources away from the interests of Pan-Arabism to regional and narrow local interests.[37] This trend was strengthened dramatically in the course of the oil boom, which engulfed the Arab region in the last quarter century.

THE ECONOMICS OF ARAB NATIONALISM

One of the most glaring gaps in the ideological content of Arab nationalism is the virtual absence of economic analysis articulating the economic dimensions and objectives of the Arab nation. Aside from general demands such as the desire to be free from foreign economic domination and exploitation, twentieth-century Arab nationalists, like their predecessors, ignored the economic dimension of their movement.

There are several explanations for this conspicuous absence of economics. Arab nationalism arose as a political response to foreign domination—first Ottoman, then European. The overriding objective of the movement was the establishment or the reestablishment of an Arab nation-state. In their quest for independence from the Ottomans and in the course of their interaction with Europe, Arab nationalists came to believe that the political ideas and institutions of Western Europe were not only the necessary basis of national strength but the best in themselves. Furthermore, it was taken for granted that independent Arab states should adopt the characteristic institutions of European liberal society.[38] This meant that private enterprise and the institutions of a market-based economy, which had been prevalent in the Arab region prior to independence, would be retained after independence. There was, in other words, a coincidence of interests and compatibility of views between the nationalists and the European powers that controlled the Arab region. It could not have been otherwise, given the political and military control that France and Britain had exerted over the Arab states. Moreover, foreign domination lasted in certain parts of the Arab region well into the second half of the twentieth century. For instance, not until 1968 did Britain declare that it would leave the Persian Gulf by 1971. Furthermore, the other Arab states also went through constant political changes after they became independent.

But the most important explanation for the lack of economic analysis seems to be the disdain and indifference with which some of the important writers and thinkers on Arab nationalism viewed economics. Thus Sati al-Husri went so far as to deny the importance of economic forces and interests to the evolution of Arab nationalism. According to him, even to consider economic interests as one of the foundations of Arab nationalism is contrary to intelligence and logic. Another theoretician of Arab nationalism, Abdel Rahman al-Bazzaz, who has served as secretary general of OPEC and became Iraq's prime minister in the 1960s, echoed al-Husri's views when he said that it is possible for nationalism to arise among people who are aware of their national existence, their national language, and the spiritual values that are given to them by their common history without the need for a materialistic economic unity to hold the group together.[39] It is possible that in ignoring the importance of economic forces in shaping events, theoreticians of Arab nationalism may have set the stage for the general neglect of economic analysis by Arab nationalists in general. It is also conceivable that in the historic rivalry between Arab Marxists and Arab nationalists the latter may have chosen to distinguish themselves from the former by downgrading the importance of economic factors.

Another explanation may be found in the nature of economic development in the Arab region in the nineteenth century. Issawi maintains that the Arab region experienced much less industrialization than either East Asia or Latin America.[40] To the extent that the Arab region suffered from economic stagnation under the Ottomans and from de-industrialization due to European penetration, a case can be made for the lack of economic analysis that would be relevant to the region. Yet another factor may be that levels of education outside traditional religion-oriented systems were limited at best and economics was a relatively young discipline in its own place of birth, Europe. It could not have been expected that Arab intellectuals would pay attention to such a field of inquiry when their most important and immediate objective was to rid themselves of foreign domination or at least loosen its grip on their lives. It can also be said that the general level of illiteracy, which was very high during the Ottoman centuries in both Arab and non-Arab provinces, did not make economics a coveted field of study. Even in the twentieth century when a number of Arab countries emerged as independent states, the emphasis of their education tended to be on the humanities and law rather than on the social sciences. Another explanation for the lack of interest may be found in the nature of the leadership of Arab nationalism. From the early stages of the Arab nationalist movement to the present, the military component of its leadership had been decisive with political parties and movements playing a subordinate role. In those instances when a civilian leadership assumed power, it did so with the support of the military. This meant that intellectual discourse was of marginal importance to the army officers, who were most interested in diverting as much of the country's resources as possible to the armed forces. The central question of economics, the devising of a rational system for the allocation of scarce resources, was of little importance to the military.

Although interest in economics increased in this century and especially in its second half, there is still an obvious lack of a system or systems of economic thought that can be described as Arab. Arab nationalism continues to lack economic content. As the well-known Arab economist Yusif Sayigh observed, Arab thinkers, whether they are in power or not, or whether they were in positions of intellectual or ideological or party leadership, have so far failed to produce a comprehensive system of thought that could constitute the social and economic content of Arab nationalism.[41] In the absence of emerging schools of Arab economic thought, Arab economists found themselves engaged in a process of knowledge transfer that entailed the introduction of Western economic thought—classical and neo-classical economics, Keynesian and Marxian economics, and more recently economic thought of some Latin American schools of dependency.

After having studied modern Arab economic writing and thought, Mahmoud Abdel-Fadil concluded that Arab economists had failed to make serious contributions similar to those of Latin American or Indian economists.[42] While this assessment is correct, it should be stressed that economic thought and policies in the Arab region and at the Pan-Arab level were influenced by three important developments.

The first was the experiment by Jamal Abdel Nasser of Egypt to restructure the Egyptian economy by introducing measures that expanded the public sector considerably. For several years Nasser's has been the only Third World experiment in state-building and economic development along socialist lines outside the Marxist-Leninist model.[43]

The second was the battle over oil. Arab nationalists and thinkers had always viewed oil as the symbol of continued foreign domination over Arab resources, economies, and therefore political independence. The nationalization of the Iranian oil concession in 1951 was an important historical turning point in spite of the fact that the nationalization failed and Mossadegh's government was overthrown. The successful nationalization of the Suez Canal was another turning point for oil watchers. In time nationalization of Arab oil became a central issue that joined the economic history of the region with its political history. Abdullah Tariki, who held the position of oil minister in Saudi Arabia and was one of the founders of OPEC, held the view that oil should be placed at the service of the Arab nation as a whole and not be confined to Saudi Arabia alone. In the early 1960s his slogan that Arab oil belongs to the Arabs set the stage for the eventual use of oil as an instrument of foreign policy in 1973. In the interim he actively sought to demystify the intricacies of oil economics. He eventually advocated the nationalization of oil concessions and the use of oil and its revenue for Pan-Arab causes and objectives both political and economic.[44] While the struggle to free Arab oil resources from the control of multinational capital has eventually succeeded, such success proved to be detrimental to the evolution of an independent Arab economic thought. The oil boom that engulfed the Arab region in the 1970s seemed to have swept in its affluence the independence of Arab economists as well. In other words, Arab economic thought in the 1970s moved much closer to the official Arab government or establishment position. In addition, in the period 1965–1980 the expanding demand by the League of Arab States and its specialized agencies for economists created a bureaucracy that had the effect of removing a relatively large number of economists from individual countries and placing them at the service of the Arab state official position.[45]

CURRENT ARAB ECONOMIC THOUGHT AND WRITINGS

Although theorists and ideologues of Arab nationalism did not distinguish themselves for their economic theories or writings, the same cannot be said about the large number of Arab economists who attempted to fill the gap. Arab economic writing is a recent phenomenon, which can be said to date from the postwar period. The dearth of economic writings may be explained by two factors. First, there was, as indicated earlier, a dearth of economists. Second, most Arab states were not in the position prior to World War II to exercise independent economic policies, since most of them were not politically independent. Economic policies were determined either directly by a colonial power or indirectly through a colonial power–approved local regime.

The forces of nationalism and independence that gathered momentum in the 1950s, both in the Arab region and in the Third World in general, encouraged Arab economists to provide a framework for analysis and policy to meet the needs of emerging nations. Thus the nationalization of the Suez Canal in 1956, the tripartite attack against Egypt of the same year, and the rise of Nasserism in Egypt and the rest of the Arab world were some of the more prominent changes that stimulated economic writing. The Algerian war of national liberation, which joined the movement for national independence and the struggle against colonialism and imperialism with the movement of Arab nationalism, provided another source of stimulus for economic analysis that sought to articulate policies for the newly independent states and the measures that they may take to assert their sovereignty over natural resources and national wealth.

In his *Arab Economic Thought and Issues of Liberation, Development and Unity* Mahmoud Abdel-Fadil delineated four major areas of contribution by Arab economists, reflecting the changing Arab political, social, and economic context.[46] In the first place the Arab struggle against imperialism and its control of national resources moved Arab economists to study and attempt to apply to the Arab world some of the contributions to development economics by Latin American economists. Theories of dependency and center-periphery theories received considerable attention from Arab economists.[47] Arab economists discovered that the process of integrating Arab economies into the international economic system, whether under the Ottoman rule or Western rule, provided many similarities with the evolution of many Latin American economies. Foreign investment in Arab economies, especially in the oil sector, led many Arab economists to examine the validity of oil concessions and weigh the benefits that would accrue to the state should the terms of an oil concession be restructured or nationalized. Nor did Arab economists fail to point to the distortive effects on national economies of the rising dependence on the oil sector.[48]

Another area of inquiry that interested Arab economists was the debate concerning the call by the Third World for the establishment of a new international economic order (NIEO). The debate concerning the NIEO, which gathered momentum in the 1970s, was of particular importance to the Arabs, since it coincided with the rising importance of Arab oil and financial resources in the world economy. Many Arab economists attempted to develop a general Arab economic perspective within the context of NIEO that would help the Third World correct some of the inequalities in the patterns of economic relations between the countries of the center and the periphery. Given the particularly dominant role of foreign oil companies, it was only natural that Arab economists would find themselves paying special attention to the damage that the activities of multinational corporations could inflict on the prospects of Arab economic development.[49]

The second area of inquiry that interested Arab economists was centered on problems of economic development and planning. Arab economists were found to lack originality in their contribution in comparison to those of their colleagues in India or Latin America. Instead most Arab economists tended to confine their contribution to translating and summarizing ideas that were prevalent in Western academic circles regarding economic growth, development, and planning. These ideas, which gave rise to most economic policies in the Third World, including the Arab countries, emphasized the importance of capital, technology, import-substitution policy of industrialization, market economy, and international trade as the forces that would push the economies of developing countries along the path of development and growth. When conventional development theories came under attack in the 1970s for being irrelevant to the problems of economic underdevelopment, Arab economists took up the attack as well. Yet a distinguishing feature of Arab economic thinking has been the realization that, in order to sustain itself, an Arab economy must rely on a Pan-Arab market rather than on world demand. But since political division and fragmentation resulted in an unequal pattern of distribution of resources, it followed that development could not be achieved in any one country. This fact made it imperative that the process of economic development had to be considered in a Pan-Arab context if it were to succeed. In other words, there has to be an integrated development in all Arab countries if the process were to be self-sustaining. From this perspective Arab economic integration becomes not only a Pan-Arab political objective but an economic imperative as well.[50]

A third area of inquiry that interested Arab economists was socialism. As was indicated earlier, Arab nationalists have considered Marxism and communism and their derivatives as alien ideologies that were incompatible with the Arab scene. This viewpoint, it should be stressed, did not mean that there were no Arab thinkers who thought that the attainment of Arab nationalism's goals could not be attained through a Marxist path. Maxime Rodinson noted, for example, that Arab unity in its broadest form encompassing all Arab countries was first formulated around 1930 by the tiny Communist parties of the Arab countries.[51] The general suppression in all Arab states of political ideologies that fell outside the boundaries of official tolerance crippled the prospects for the emergence and acceptance of alternative ideology or ideologies articulating alternative approaches to the problems of economic development in the Arab region. Instead, most economic policies carried out in most Arab states were described as having been based on the tenets of Arab socialism.

The main tenets of Arab socialism, as can be gleaned from the writings of Arab economists who dealt with the subject, include the following:

1. Arab socialism allows a high degree of private property and consequently a high degree of income inequality.
2. Arab socialism sanctions private ownership of means of production and therefore allows considerable room in the economy for a national bourgeoisie.
3. The sanctioning of private property and the right to inherit wealth are rooted in the teaching of Islam, which must be respected.
4. Arab socialism aims to have a high level of output and an equitable distribution of such output.
5. Arab socialism believes in the economic progress of future generations, but such progress cannot be undertaken at the expense of the present generation whose needs should not be sacrificed.

Arab socialism, in other words, must be able to strike a balance between the needs of the present generation and the aspirations of future ones.[52]

These principles of Arab socialism were influenced by the thoughts of Nasser, who stressed the importance of the principle of nonexploitive private property and the principle of equitable distribution of national output. Arab economists' views of Arab socialism were determined to a considerable extent by economic policies and measures adopted by governments in Egypt, Iraq, Syria, and Algeria. In all these countries certain economic activities were either reserved for the public sector or were transferred to this sector through nationalization. Public sector activities in these four leading Arab countries are in line with economic practices in most Third World countries where private capital had shown reluctance to commit itself to risky or long-term undertakings such as industrial production. These measures tend also to reflect the rising political power of the national bourgeoisie and its interest in having a larger share of economic activity at the expense of the larger and usually foreign-dominated or foreign-linked enterprises. In his extensive study of writings on Arab socialism in the 1960s, Abdel-Fadil found himself reaching the conclusion that most of these writings were restatements of official ideological documents, that many tended to rationalize public policies that were already in place, and that such writings had failed to pay minimum attention to the problems associated with transition to socialism and the contradictions that manifest themselves in any serious process of such transformation.[53]

The fourth area of inquiry that interested Arab economists were the issues of Arab economic integration and Arab economic unity. Although the League for Nationalist Action advocated as early as 1933 that Arab economies should be developed in the direction of Arab economic unity, not until the 1950s was the issue of economic unity seriously discussed by Arab economists.[54] The creation of the League of Arab States in 1945 gave impetus to the study of the feasibility of some forms of Arab economic integration. But it has been observed that several economic unity agreements that were concluded under the auspices of the Arab League turned out to be no more than mere attempts to remove trade barriers among economies that were to develop independent of each other.[55] The onset of the oil era in the 1970s, which widened the economic gap between oil- and non-oil-producing states, had the effect of making the quest for Arab economic unity even less appealing to the richer oil states than it had ever been.

NOTES

1. For a detailed analysis of these points see Maxime Rodinson, *The Arabs* (Chicago: University of Chicago Press, 1981), 89–90.

2. Ibid, 23 and 33.

3. See Mujdi Hammad, *The Arab Military and the Unity Question* (in Arabic), (Beirut: Centre for Arab Unity Studies, 1987), 59.

4. See Albert Hourani, *Arabic Thought in the Liberal Age, 1798–1939* (London: Oxford University Press, 1962), 31–35.

5. See Bassam Tibi, *Arab Nationalism: A Critical Enquiry* (New York: St. Martin's Press, 1981), 51.

6. Hourani, *Arab Thought in the Liberal Age*, 260.

7. Ibid.

8. Rodinson, *The Arabs*, 24–25.

9. Tibi, *Arab Nationalism*, 72–77.

10. Hourani, *Arab Thought in the Liberal Age*, 262.

11. For a detailed analysis of the various currents of thought see Hourani, *Arab Thought in the Liberal Age*, chapter 11, and Tibi, *Arab Nationalism*, chapter 5.

12. Hourani, *Arab Thought in the Liberal Age*, 278–282.

13. See Rodinson, *The Arabs*, 93.

14. See Walid Kazeeha, "The Concept of Arab Unity in the Early Twentieth Century" (in Arabic), *Al Mustaqbal Al Arabi*, No. 4 (November 1978): 12–26, especially p. 18.

15. Maxime Rodinson, *Marxism and the Muslim World* (New York: Monthly Review Press, 1981), 163.

16. Hourani, *Arab Thought in the Liberal Age*, 287–290.

17. Tibi, *Arab Nationalism*, 88.

18. For a detailed analysis of the role of these officers in the revolt as well as their motives see Hammad, *The Arab Military*, 75–81.

19. Hourani, *Arab Thought in the Liberal Age*, 289–290.

20. Ibid, 290.

21. Anis al-Sayigh, *The Hashimites and the Great Arab Revolt* (in Arabic) (Beirut: 1966), 277. Quoted in Tibi, *Arab Nationalism*, 89–90.

22. L. S. Stavrianos, *Global Rift: The Third World Comes of Age* (New York: Morrow, 1981), 535.

23. Doreen Warriner, *Land Reform and Development in the Middle East: A Study of Egypt, Syria and Iraq* (London: Royal Institute of International Affairs, 1957), 137–138. According to Samir Amin, landed aristocracy was directly established as such by imperialism during the 1920s in Iraq, Morocco, and the Sudanese Gezireh. See Samir Amin, *The Arab Nation: Nationalism and Class Struggles* (London: Zed Press, 1978), 29.

24. Charles Issawi, *An Economic History of the Middle East and North Africa* (New York: Columbia University Press, 1982), 138–139.

25. Peter Sluglett, *Britain in Iraq 1914–1922* (London: Ithaca Press, 1976), 297–298. Quoted in Stavrianos, *Global Rift*, 535.

26. Issawi, *Economic History*, 158–162.

27. See Muhammad A. Shuraydi, "Pan Arabism: A Theory in Practice," in Hani A. Faris (ed.), *Arab Nationalism and the Future of the Arab World* (Belmont, Mass.: AAUG [Association of Arab-American University Graduates] Press, 1987), 95–114.

28. See Rodinson, *The Arabs*, 100–103.

29. See his "The Primacy of Arabism" in Anouar abdel-Malek (ed.), *Contemporary Arab Political Thought* (London: Zed Books, 1983), 139–140.

30. For a good discussion of al-Husri's views see Tibi, *Arab Nationalism*, 90–132. See also Wamidh Jamal Omar Nadhmi, "The Nationalist Thought of Sati al Husri," in Centre for Arab Unity Studies, *The Evolution of Arab Nationalist Thought* (in Arabic) (Beirut: Centre for Arab Unity Studies, 1986), 201–224.

31. See Anouar abdel-Malek (ed.), *Contemporary Arab Political Thought* (London: Zed Books, 1983), 1–14.

32. For a good outline of the main points of the Baath's program see J. M. Abdulghani, *Iraq and Iran: The Years of Crisis* (Baltimore, Md.: Johns Hopkins University Press, 1984), 30–33.

33. See Michel Aflaq, "Arab Unity Above Socialism," in abdel-Malek, *Contemporary Arab Political Thought*, 148–149.

34. Cited by Tibi, *Arab Nationalism*, 175.

35. See Sadoon Hammadi, "Arab Nationalism and Contemporary Challenges," in Centre for Arab Unity Studies, *The Evolution of Arab Nationalist Thought* (in Arabic) (Beirut, 1986), 344.

36. See Tibi, *Arab Nationalism*, 178.

37. See Hanna Batatu, *The Old Social Classes and the Revolutionary Movements of Iraq: A Study of Iraq's Old Landed and Commercial Classes and of its Communists, Ba'thists, and Free Officers* (Princeton, N.J.: Princeton University Press, 1982), 1088–1093.

38. See Hourani, *Arab Thought*, 298.

39. See Mohammad Labeeb Shuquair, "The Economic Dimension in Arab Unity Thought: The First Stage, from the Beginning of Arab National Thought to the Mid Fifties" (in Arabic), *Al Mustaqbal Al Arabi*, No. 3 (September 1978): 76–85.

40. Issawi, *An Economic History*, 155.

41. Cited by Mahmoud Abdel-Fadil, *Arab Economic Thought and Issues of Liberation, Development and Unity* (in Arabic) (Beirut: Centre for Arab Unity Studies, 1982), 87.

42. Ibid, 178.

43. Rodinson, *Marxism and the Muslim World*, 268.

44. Ibid, 34–38. See also Pierre Terzian, *OPEC: The Inside Story* (London: Zed Books, 1985), 92–95.

45. Abdel-Fadil, *Arab Economic Thought*, 179.

46. Ibid.

47. For a good survey of these theories see Ronald H. Chilcote, *Theories of Development and Underdevelopment* (Boulder, Colo.: Westview Press, 1984).

48. See Abdel-Fadil, *Arab Economic Thought*, 33–42.

49. Ibid, 43–47.

50. Ibid, 53–81, especially p. 66.

51. See Rodinson, *The Arabs*, 98.

52. See Abdel-Fadil, *Arab Economic Thought*, 91. See also Tareq Y. Ismael, *The Arab Left* (Syracuse, N.Y.: Syracuse University Press, 1976).

53. Abdel-Fadil, *Arab Economic Thought*, 90–93.

54. For a brief outline of the views of the League for National Action see Walid Kazeeha, "The Social-Political Foundations of the Growth of Contemporary Nationalist Movement in the Arab East" (in Arabic), *Al Mustaqbal Al Arabi*, No. 6 (March 1979): 63–75.

55. Abdel-Fadil, *Arab Economic Thought*, 117–118.

3

ARAB NATIONALISM AND ARAB ECONOMIC UNITY

The issue of Arab unity and Arab economic unity became an integral part of the debate over the objectives of Arab nationalism in the post–World War II period. The interwar period saw, as was noted in the previous chapter, the emergence of several Arab states that were at various stages of formal political independence and economic development. These states, given the political and economic control exerted over them by Britain and France, developed their economies in both their internal as well as external dimensions under the guidance and influence of the European powers. As time went on, particular patterns of trade, banking, investment, and monetary blocs had developed not between these states but between each one of them and France or Britain. This in turn created and fostered economic interests in Arab countries that had become part of the economic sphere of influence of European economies. Concomitant with these economic, trade, and financial linkages there developed local interests, which benefited from the international economic system. This meant that the general framework of Arab nationalist ideology during the interwar period had become a function of the relationship between the imperial authorities and the local elites, who had become increasingly dependent on those authorities for their political survival and economic interests. In turn, as Walid Kazeeha observed, alternative radical leadership that might attempt to destabilize this pattern of relations had to be curbed. He went on to conclude that Arab nationalist thought during this period was used to serve the interests of the local elites and to avoid dealing with issues such as independence and unity, which might jeopardize these interests.[1]

Changes in the world economy, such as the Great Depression and the war itself, succeeded in overcoming local and foreign resistance to the establishment of local industries. This import-substitution industrialization created new and more vested economic interests, which succeeded in creating protective shields for their infant industries and strengthened the sanctity of the concept of the sovereignty of the state, the boundaries of the state, and the political divisions that had been created and imposed by Britain and France.[2]

Two other important changes proved to be of crucial importance in shaping the history of the Arab world in the postwar period. The first was the creation of the state of Israel in Palestine, which broke the geographic unity of the Arab world. The second was the emergence of oil, which proved to be one of the most serious dividing factors in the fortunes of Arab states and also a powerful force that intensified the dependency of the economies of the entire Arab region on the world capitalist system.

The nationalists who were in power in the Arab countries found themselves unprepared to deal with these developments at both analytical and policy levels. The analysis in the following pages will be confined to addressing the question as to why, after forty years of attempting to achieve some form of economic unity among the Arab states, such a goal remains as illusive today as it was when the League of Arab States was created in 1945.

SOCIOPOLITICAL BASES OF ARAB NATIONALISM

The question of some form of Arab economic unity goes back to the 1930s when the League for National Action asserted that Arab economies should be developed along lines that would ultimately lead to the attainment of Arab economic unity.[3] The difficulty with this and other similar expressions is that they presuppose the existence of certain commonality of interests among those whose interests are to be affected. Another difficulty is that they also presuppose the existence of the political will and the necessary mechanisms and institutions that would translate a nationalist objective into an integrated and functioning economy.

But the most serious flaw in these arguments is that they tend to overlook the fact that in the interwar period political and economic developments in each Arab country took place more or less in isolation from similar developments in other countries. An important feature of these developments, as was noted earlier, was the rise to positions of political and economic leadership of local elites who were supported by the presence of foreign powers—Britain in the case of Iraq, Egypt, and Palestine; and France in the case of Syria and Lebanon. These local elites were drawn from the ranks of the same old class of notables who served as agents of Ottoman rule. During the Ottoman period the notables acted in the name of the Ottoman Empire in exploiting the resources of the provinces and in transferring the revenue to the central government. In return for their services the notables became in time large landowners thanks to a complicated Ottoman land-tenure system. When Britain and France acquired mandate authority over Arab countries, they found it in their interest not only to keep this particular class but also to strengthen it through the transfer of ownership of more state land to them. Government spending on irrigation, administration, and marketing as well as the taxation system had the effect of reinforcing the privileged position of these groups. The transfer of ownership of state-owned land to tribal heads and leaders for the purpose of settling their followers was another means that helped in the consolidation of the power of these elites.[4]

In addition to large landowners there were two other classes who cooperated with European colonial powers. Also inherited from the Ottoman era, they were the military and the *ulama* (clergy). The functions of each of these two classes were complementary to those of the others in that they played the role of the middlemen and enforcers of the political and economic policies of the Ottoman rulers. These functions continued to be performed by the same groups under the direct or the indirect rule of the Europeans. But the relationship between local elites and European colonial powers could not remain unchanged, since the Arab states as colonies of European advanced capitalist economies were expected to play a different role from the one that was assigned to them under Ottoman rule. Under Ottoman rule the primary function of Arab provinces was to generate revenue. However, under European-dominated international capitalism Arab economies were regarded as markets for European goods and as sources of raw materials for and outlets for European capital investment. These new linkages, which accelerated the process of integrating Arab economies in the international economic system, had the effect of creating important stakes in the existing political arrangements both internally and externally for those local elites who derived economic and political benefits from these arrangements. Given the close identification of economic and political interests between the local ruling elites and foreign colonial powers, it was very difficult to challenge the position of dominance of foreign influence. Under these conditions Arab nationalism was at a dead end.

Arab nationalism found itself caught in a contradiction of major proportion. Its failure to challenge the position of control of imperialism ran counter to the very essence of nationalism, Arab or not. A leading Arab nationalist thinker at the time such as Sati al-Husri found himself saying that the way to rid the Arab nation of imperialism is through improving educational institutions and curricula, which would in the long run enable the Arabs to challenge imperialism through their cultural and scientific achievements. It is clear that al-Husri's prescription entailed the acceptance of the principle of coexistence with imperialism for a long time to come, something that undoubtedly expressed the prevailing interests of ruling elites.[5] Under these conditions Arab economic unity was neither appealing nor feasible, given the political fragmentation of these countries. But with changing social and economic conditions the relative importance of various elites in the social order also had to change. The relative position of the *ulama*, for example, was weakened. Their usefulness to the new political order diminished from what it was in the Ottoman era, when the rulers stressed the role of Islam in the life of the state and therefore the role of the *ulama*, who were looked upon as religious agents of the state. Another important change was the rise of a class of national bourgeoisie, whose economic activities encompassed small-scale industry, banking, financial, and related services—a mercantile class that depended on foreign trade and thus was dependent on the international economic system. Professionals, bureaucrats and technocrats, and rising new cadres of military officers who were not drawn from the ranks of traditional elites were also part of this class. These social changes took place, however, in a rigid social and political order that did not have the flexibility to absorb the new entrants into the political system. Moreover, the identification of the older elites with European imperialism proved to be a political liability in the postwar period when many Third World countries were succeeding in gaining political independence from the European colonial powers.

What compounded the political weakness of the old elites and eroded their legitimacy was their unwillingness or inability to keep Palestine for the Palestinians. The creation of the state of Israel on Arab land exposed the bankruptcy of a political and social order that chose to tie its fortunes to colonial powers.

The rigidity of the political system, the political failure of traditional elites, and the emergence of a middle class composed of technocrats, the military, and national bourgeoisie that did not derive its legitimacy from a foreign power gave rise to new political and economic demands, which were articulated by a younger generation of Arab nationalists. The political demands centered on national independence, political and economic unity among Arab states, and the restoration to the Palestinians of their rights to self-determination. The economic demands centered on an expansion of the public sector, limiting landholdings, and reducing the size of the private sector in industry and foreign trade. Taken together these demands constituted the political and economic bases of Arab nationalism in the second half of this century. There are at least three features of twentieth-century Arab nationalism that differentiate it from Arab nationalism of earlier periods. First, there has been a clear break between Arab nationalism and Islam. While nineteenth-century Arab nationalism tended to associate itself with Islam as a way to reestablish Arab identity, Islam by the second half of this century ceased to be a necessary condition for Arab nationalism. In other words Arab identity and other prerequisites of nationalism were well established independent of the historical linkage between Islam and Arabism. Second, Arab nationalism in the second half of this century was propagated by an assortment of middle-class groups comprising intellectuals, bureaucrats, technocrats, military officers, petty bourgeoisie, writers, journalists, and other professionals. Third, while older advocates of Arab nationalism did not question the premises of the then-existing economic system, the younger advocates stressed the importance of economic issues in their declarations.

After overthrowing the old social and political regimes in Egypt, Iraq, and Syria, the new breed of Arab nationalists found themselves faced with the same imperatives of the international economic system that the old order had to contend with. At the national level the nationalists of the 1950s and the 1960s found themselves facing some of the most important questions relating to the size of the public sector, private property, ownership of means of production, land reform, class structure, the role of the national bourgeoisie in the economy, and a host of similar questions for which their charters and programs were ill equipped to deal in an implementable fashion.[6] Of particular importance to the evolution of thought and policy of these nationalists was the theoretical predicament in which the national bourgeoisie placed them.

As a nationalist, anti-imperialist segment of society, the national bourgeoisie was regarded as indispensable for the achievement of the broader objectives of Arab nationalism. Yet by its very nature the national bourgeoisie, regardless of its size and its political philosophy, is driven by the profit motive. To be otherwise is to cease to be bourgeois or capitalist. Given the fact that all Arab economies were open economies with foreign trade playing a large and important role, it was only natural that the national bourgeoisie was as influenced by the imperatives of the international economic system as its predecessor. What accentuated the predicament of the nationalists was the fact that their leadership was composed primarily of intellectuals and civilian and military bureaucrats and businessmen. In short the leadership was elitist. This narrow class base of the nationalists and the leadership role that the new elites played in shaping policies were recognized as factors responsible for the failure of the nationalists to attract a broad-based following. Thus at its sixth nationalist congress in 1963 the Baath party recognized this predicament and blamed the petty bourgeoisie for most of its difficulties and expressed the fear that once in power, the party would find itself transformed into a class of bureaucrats.[7] Yet this assessment failed to lead to a break with the bourgeoisie. This should not be surprising, since these nationalists were drawn by and large from the bourgeoisie itself, which tended to have these characteristics:

1. It was dominated by two interrelated groups: a political-military bureaucracy and a technocratic civilian bureaucracy.

2. The continued presence of this class in political power depended on an active and expanding public sector in industry, trade, and agriculture.

3. Given its place in the social spectrum, the Arab petty bourgeoisie tended to suffer from political, ideological, and social disarticulation or incoherence. This in turn explains its insecurity as well as its unpredictability in dealing with other social classes and groups both internally and regionally.

4. The inability or the unwillingness of the petty bourgeoisie to work within a genuinely democratic framework led it to take to itself the role of paternalistic guardianship over the people and to resort to extensive and elaborate security and administrative systems of repression and manipulation to preserve its positions of power.[8]

These characteristics were strengthened and reinforced by the blending of economic and political interests of public-sector managers and private-sector entrepreneurs and the formation of what had been described as a "new bourgeoisie."[9] The political fragmentation of Arab nationalism that manifested itself in the consolidation of separate political regimes in Egypt, Syria, and Iraq with each regime paying increasing attention to its own continuity had important implications for the quest for Arab economic unity as will be seen in the following section.

ARAB ECONOMIC UNITY

The question of economic unity among Arab countries, as noted earlier, goes back to the 1930s. Formal attempts in the direction of such unity were not initiated, however, until 1945 when the League of Arab States was established. The 1945 agreement created within the league a permanent committee for economic and fiscal affairs, which was charged with the task of formulating agreements, policies, and measures that would strengthen Arab economic cooperation. Yet the Arab League agreement contains a provision that a member is bound only by the agreements it ratifies. This provision, which respects the sovereignty of the state, had the effect of rendering any Pan-Arab agreement useless unless all member states ratify such an agreement and proceed to implement its provisions, since the league has no juridical power over noncomplying member states. But here also lies the central problem of any Arab League–sponsored agreements regarding Arab economic unity or any other agreement, for that matter. This is attested to by subsequent Arab economic agreements that went unfulfilled.[10]

In 1950 and after the defeat of the Arab states by Israel in 1948, the league adopted the Joint Defense and Economic Cooperation Treaty, which created a ministerial-level Arab Economic Council to promote economic cooperation and coordination in order to raise living standards in the Arab countries. In 1957, only a few months after the British-French-Israeli invasion of Egypt, the league and the Economic Council approved an Economic Unity Agreement, but members did not ratify it until 1964. It is interesting to note that the provisions of the Economic Unity Agreement surpassed those of the Economic Council in that they called for the free movement of goods, labor, and capital as well as the freedom to own and inherit property and the right to work and establish residence in Arab countries. In 1965 the league approved another agreement establishing the Arab Common Market. One of the notable aspects of these agreements is that while the Economic Council comprised all members of the league, the Economic Unity agreement was ratified by thirteen countries and the Arab Common Market received the ratification of only five countries.[11]

The rise of oil prices in the 1970s led to massive movements of labor, capital, and remittances among Arab countries. Yet these flows took place outside the framework of the league and its institutions. Development plans in Arab countries were uncoordinated, and individual country development plans did not have a Pan-Arab dimension to them. In other words, Arab countries continued to follow their own paths to development without paying attention to the implications for other Arab countries.

The league's numerous attempts to nudge Arab economies toward some form of coordination was an exercise in futility for at least three reasons. First, the structural weakness of the league's charter itself allows a member country the option of complying or not complying with ratified agreements and makes implementation subject to an individual country's perception of its own interests. Second, the vast increase in oil revenue provided the oil states with the opportunity and the financial resources to embark on all sorts of bilateral financial and economic arrangements with other countries regardless of their consequences to the league's decisions. Third, the sharp increase in the relative importance of the oil sector in the totality of combined Arab economies made any serious attempt at coordination subject to the consent and cooperation of the oil states. One of the paradoxes of the sudden increase in oil revenue was the concomitant proliferation in the number of specialized agencies created within the league's framework to facilitate integration among member states.[12] These agencies include, in addition to the ones mentioned earlier, the Arab Fund for Economic and Social Development, the Arab Organization for Agricultural Development, the Arab Organization for Industrial Development, the Arab Labor Organization, the Arab Monetary Fund, and the Arab Organization for Underwriting of Investment. Two other organizations that were formed outside the framework of the league deserve to be mentioned: the Organization of Arab Petroleum Exporting Countries (OAPEC) and the Arab Organization for Mineral Wealth.[13] In assessing the effectiveness of the Arab League and its specialized agencies Abdel Hasan Zalzala had the following verdict: But these achievements were not commensurate with the effort spent nor with the possibilities or with national aspirations. This is so because the achievements did not change either from an objective or practical perspective the existing conditions in the Arab world and failed to forge organic linkages between their economies. And most Arab economic cooperation remained marginal and inconsequential in its effect.[14] Zalzala went on to explain the reasons for this institutional failure: In trying to understand why after several decades of official Arab economic cooperation its results were so meager numerous ministerial and high-level technical experts studied the problem in light of changing Arab and international conditions. The reports diagnosed two structural defects in joint Arab economic effort. The first was the absence of a central authority that would be responsible for planning, execution and follow up of economic policies. The second was the multiplicity of specialized Arab organizations which led to overlapping and duplication and conflict in their activities, decisions and specializations.[15]

In order to overcome these defects, in 1977 the league decided to change the name of the Arab Economic Council to Arab Economic and Social Council and charge it with several tasks including the articulation of a strategy for joint Arab action, supervision over specialized Arab economic and social organizations, and evaluation of the performance of each Pan-Arab economic organization.[16]

The prospects for more serious Arab economic cooperation were supposed to be enhanced further at the 1980 Eleventh Arab Summit Conference held in Amman, Jordan. The Eleventh Summit ratified four major agreements: (1) Pact for Pan-Arab Economic Action, (2) Strategy for Joint Arab Economic Action, (3) Agreement on a Joint Arab Development Decade, and (4) Agreement on Investment of Arab Capital in Arab Countries.[17] The Strategy for Joint Arab Action agreement highlighted several goals relating to Arab economic unity. One such goal is economic integration as an important step for economic unity, something that calls for fundamental changes in Arab economies. Another goal of the strategy agreement was the establishment of a new Arab economic system that would serve the purposes of Arab economic development and would result in a satisfactory division of labor within the Arab world. A third objective would be narrowing the income gap between and within Arab countries. A fourth objective would be an acceleration in comprehensive Arab economic development to increase Arab national self-reliance.[18] The strategy agreement, which was to be in effect for the period 1981–2000, stressed several priorities. These include security of the Arab world, development of Arab human resources and labor in order to meet Arab economic development requirements and a reduction of dependence on foreign labor, acquisition of technology to serve the needs of national security and basic industry, expansion of agriculture to insure food security, optimal use of oil and other energy resources, and support for joint Arab action to lay the foundations for industrialization and to achieve industrial integration. Other priorities covered such areas as infrastructure; coordination of Arab economic, fiscal, trade, and monetary relations with the rest of the world to serve Arab objectives; and directing the financial sector to channel Arab savings for investment in Arab economic development to enhance Arab monetary and trade positions in accordance with the requirements of joint Arab action. The strategy also envisaged the initiation of planning at the Pan-Arab level to prepare and follow up the implementation of a joint Arab economic development plan that would entail five-year plans starting in 1981.[19]

Another document that the Amman summit ratified in November 1980 focused on what was called the Arab Development Decade (ADD). It should be stressed at the outset that this was not a development plan in the conventional sense of the term. There was no plan nor was there any linkage with individual country development plans. Upon close inspection the ADD turns out to be no more than a ten-year, $5 billion special account that was sponsored by five oil-producing states, Saudi Arabia, Iraq, Kuwait, Qatar, and the United Arab Emirates. The special account was slated to receive $500 million annually from the five states for ten years. The special account was to be administered by the Arab Fund for Economic and Social Development with the lending decisions being made by the five contributing states. The funds, which were to be lent to less-developed Arab states, were to be used to help finance large projects that would strengthen economic relations among Arab countries, help Arab economic integration, and raise economic and social standards in borrowing countries.[20]

The third agreement concerned itself with the investment of Arab capital in Arab countries and was designed to replace three standing agreements on the same general subjects that had been ratified in 1953, 1957, and 1963.[21] The central function of the new agreement is the enactment of a new legal framework to facilitate capital movement among Arab countries. In order to encourage Arab capital movement, host countries were expected to remove barriers to the free movement of such capital and to provide legal protection for the invested capital and its returns. The agreement went on to spell out a number of incentives to stimulate capital movement such as nondiscriminatory treatment, freedom to transfer capital and returns, and protection against nationalization except under very restricted conditions.[22]

ARAB ECONOMIC UNITY UNDER THE ARAB LEAGUE

The interaction between the League of Arab States and the objective of Arab economic unity is a prime illustration of the supremacy of individual state sovereignty over what is perceived to be a commonality of interests among member states. In this respect the league is no different from similar international and other intergovernmental organizations such as the United Nations and its specialized agencies. Yet there is a central difference between the league and its constituent members on the one hand and other organizations in that the league was established by a number of governments whose people share common language, history, and cultural heritage and who have long been driven by the aspirations of Arab nationalism and its advocacy of Arab unity. The preference for state sovereignty and narrow provincial interests was embodied in the very pact that created the league in 1945, which stipulated that all decisions must be unanimous and that the states are not obligated by any decision that may conflict with their own laws. This meant of course that any one country had a veto power over the deliberations of the group. The adherence to state sovereignty should not be surprising, as these states were administered by different elites who had acquired political and economic power and fortunes over a long period of time. Aspirations and ideals of Arab nationalism notwithstanding, it was simply not feasible to expect ruling elites in these states to act differently.

Another explanation for the lack of commitment to Pan-Arab policy objectives may be found in the way political systems in these states evolved. When Britain and France divided up the Arab east under a mandatory system, they retained to themselves all the necessary governing powers and privileges. The creation of modern governments in the countries under their mandate meant that the economic evolution of these states was to be shaped by the needs of the world economy. Economic linkages and relations were developed with the industrialized countries rather than among the Arab states themselves. It was not surprising, therefore, that whenever there was a conflict between the interests of an individual Arab state and those of the Arab countries as a group, the interests of the single country were given priority over the broader Pan-Arab interests. Indeed it can be said that during most of the league's life most Arab governments were not even thinking in a Pan-Arab framework. Their most important task as they saw it was to create political and economic institutions that were responsive to the-interests of local elites and also acceptable to Britain and France. It can also be said that neither Britain nor France would have allowed the establishment of the Arab League had they considered it to be a threat to their economic and political interests in the Arab region. This convergence of interests between local elites and imperial powers at the Pan-Arab level was a logical extension of the coincidence of their interests at the country level. Although narrow political and economic interests and considerations played a major role in the marginalization of the Arab League, the nature of economic development in each country made the potential for a serious attempt at economic unity or integration less promising. Thus several decades after the creation of the league and the establishment of the Council for Arab Economic Unity and the common market agreement, only thirteen member states (out of twenty-two members) opted to ratify the former and only eight members joined the latter.

This lack of seriousness toward Arab economic unity or any other form of real economic integration on the part of the Arab states must lead to the conclusion that league member states had no intention of moving along the path of economic unity in the first place.[23] In addition to the vested political interests of local elites Yusif Sayigh points to three other groups whose interests were at variance with the objective of economic unity. Arab industrialists who advocate removal of trade barriers on their exports have also advocated that their own markets be protected from competing imports from other Arab countries. The same can be said about the mercantile class, which always called for measures to facilitate trade but opposed measures that would affect the structures of individual Arab economies. The third group is the technocrats and bureaucrats, who play an important role in state decision making. Although politicians, bureaucrats, and technocrats tend to serve the interests of local business communities, they have also acquired positions of interest independent of those of other groups.[24] In supporting this contention Sayigh points to the many Arab economists who would advocate unity and integration when they are not in power but turn their backs against integration when they move to the corridors of power as consultants or policymakers.[25]

Yet another pretext that was employed to blunt the effort toward integration revolves around the perceived differences between the so-called "socialist" and "capitalist" economic systems in the Arab region. It was argued that economic unity could not be attained given the nature of the process of decision making in both groups of countries and given also the purposes of these economic systems and the interest groups they serve. Yet close inspection of the structures of Arab economies would reveal that such differences have been exaggerated. The so-called socialist economies have failed, for example, to expand public ownership of means of production. Instead they narrowed the range of such ownership and turned the economies to systems of state capitalism. Similarly the so-called capitalist system could not be said to be without a significant public sector or important welfare programs. The differences between the two systems are too narrow to be considered serious obstacles to economic unity.[26]

If differences in the organization of economic systems could not be construed as serious stumbling blocks for economic unity, the same cannot be said for the marked differences in national and per capita incomes that the oil price increases brought about in the 1970s. These differences dichotomized the Arab states into oil- and non-oil-producing states with marked qualitative and quantitative differences in economic interest, orientation, outlook, linkages with the West and its multinational corporations, and above all in the course of future economic development. The sudden increase in oil prices and revenues and the emergence of balance-of-payments surpluses provide oil-producing states with political and economic advantage to shape the outcomes of the debate over Pan-Arab issues including economic unity. The policy thrust of the oil states turned immediately not on how to use these resources to advance economic integration but rather on what mechanisms need to be adopted to recycle balance-of-payments surpluses to capital and financial markets in industrialized countries.

It is true that there have been massive movements of labor and financial resources between oil and nonoil states following the oil price increases in the 1970s. These movements cannot be said, as some Arab economists maintain, to have accomplished by way of economic integration in a few years far more than all the agreements among the Arab states in the period 1945 to 1973.[27] It is difficult to see how these flows could have contributed to Arab economic integration when they were neither planned nor permanent. Moreover, the flow of labor from Arab countries had to be reversed once the oil boom conditions gave way to the new realities, which dictated contraction in public- and private-sector spending.

It is also relevant to indicate that naturalization policies of labor-importing countries run counter to the objectives of Arab unity. With the notable exception of Iraq, which grants other Arab citizens freedom of entry, work, and residency, labor-importing countries follow very strict policies toward the employment of Arab workers. Arab workers, like all other foreign workers, must obtain a work permit prior to their entry to an Arab labor-importing country. Arab workers are also required to leave the host country once their contracts end. Arab workers, like most other foreign workers, are barred from bringing their families with them, nor are they allowed to form or join labor unions. These workers are also barred from owning stocks, bonds, or real estate, and their wages and salaries tend to be lower than those of their resident counterparts who are on the same skills scale. In short Arab workers do not receive any preferential treatment over non-Arab foreign workers in that the pattern of restrictions and discrimination is essentially the same.[28] In certain cases the restrictions extended even to purely personal matters.[29]

Far more significant than the differences in the nature of various Arab economic systems—differences that in the last analysis rest on the size of the public sector—is the fact that balance-of-payments-surplus oil states found themselves focusing their attention on the management of their portfolios and not on Pan-Arab economic issues. Nonoil Arab states and other Third World states were to be dealt with through loans, in other words, a portfolio approach, and not through economic integration. Retrospectively the differences in economic systems argument was one of several used to explain political conflict or lack of political cooperation between a nationalist regime such as Nasser's Egypt and Faisal's Saudi Arabia. By the time of the oil price increase in 1973 political differences had long vanished as a result of the accommodating policies of Sadat's Egypt to Faisal's Saudi Arabia. The point at issue here is that by becoming the major dispensers of funds on bilateral, regional, and multilateral levels, the oil states succeeded in determining the pace of action regarding the prospects for Arab economic integration. The influence that these states were able to wield in Pan-Arab organizations such as the Arab League and its specialized agencies, by virtue of their financial contribution and fiscal resources, insured that whatever joint Arab economic action was to be undertaken would remain within the parameters set by these states. The 1980 Arab summit's decisions outlined earlier provide clear indication of the virtual absence of serious interest in Arab economic unity. Equally important is the contribution of Arab economic thought to the debate on economic unity in the era of petrofunds.

Two trends dominate the debate on the question of Arab economic unity or economic integration in the decade of the 1970s. The first trend tended to stress the importance of Arab petrofunds and the role that these funds could play in bringing about closer economic relations between the Arab countries. The starting point of this thesis is the assertion that Arab thought in the 1950s and the 1960s regarding economic unity tended to be idealistic and manifested lack of understanding of individual country economic problems. This in turn led advocates of economic unity to underestimate the difficulties that had to be surmounted in order to achieve economic integration. Instead, what was needed was more realism and gradualism and a minimum level of agreement on what could be realistically attained. From this perspective Arab petrofunds become central in that their unfettered deployment and employment throughout the Arab region should become the first priority of those with the capital to export and those who need the capital to develop their economies. And relative to this goal everything else should be considered of secondary importance including ideologies and political considerations. What should be stressed instead is the role of the private sector and the importance of the profit motive in both capital-exporting and capital-importing countries. The advocates of this approach expected Arab funds to be invested in joint projects, which were thought to serve as instruments for development and use of resources throughout the Arab region.

The joint projects approach is, according to its advocates, superior to other approaches to economic integration such as free trade areas, customs unions, and common markets because it gets around the thorny issues of sovereignty, political differences, and other sources of conflict. A joint project is by its very nature narrowly defined and is confined to the production of a specific good or service.[30] To provide a Pan-Arab sanction for this approach, the Arab League convened in 1977 a twenty-member committee of experts to write a working paper on a strategy for joint Arab economic action. The committee's paper, which was presented at a 1978 special conference sponsored by the league and the Union of Arab Economists, identified several constraints on joint Arab economic action. These include insistence on state sovereignty, protectionist policies, and dominant financial and trade interests that were directed more toward international rather than toward regional linkages, bureaucratic interests that lack the necessary commitment to Pan-Arab economic policies, and the reorganization of individual economies along Pan-Arab lines, which will be bound to be to the disadvantage of certain groups.[31] Having outlined the constraints, the committee stressed three new avenues or points of departure for joint Arab economic action:

1. Joint Arab economic action should be considered as an extension of individual country development effort and should be encompassed within the framework of their development plans.
2. Petrofunds should play a leadership role in joint projects, and the responsibility of the oil states should not end at the point where funds are provided. The oil states should attempt to create an environment that would insure the realization of the benefits of capital movements in the receiving countries.
3. Economic incentive, that is, profit motive, should replace political factors as incentive for capital movement.

It was also postulated that Arab capital movements that were not prompted by profit incentives would shrink and eventually cease.[32] The view that joint economic action should be market-related and private sector–dominated was challenged by another approach, which saw economic calculations as but one aspect of the overall development process.

In commenting on the same report, Ismail Sabri Abdalla examined the concept of joint economic action as a way to reconcile the needs of individual country development and the requirements of Arab economic integration. His thesis was that the report of the committee was guilty of overstressing the role of economic growth in the general process of development. An understanding of the broader requirements of the latter would remove any contradiction between regional and Pan-Arab interests because development entails delinking dependency relations—economic, social, cultural, and technological—with the industrialized countries and replacing them with self-reliance. The real choice facing Arab countries, according to Abdallah, is not between individual country development and Pan-Arab development. It is instead between an integrated dependency on the international capitalist system and integration with equality among Arab countries.[33]

It is clear from this brief outline that the difference between the two approaches is fundamental and derives from an ideological chasm between their proponents. On the one hand there are those who would like to see the pattern of economic relations between individual Arab countries and the international economic system preserved. Petrofunds can act as an important force to strengthen this pattern for both oil- and non-oil-producing countries. Experiments in joint Arab action in the 1950s and the 1960s were found wanting because of their potential for infringement on an individual state's political and economic institutions or in short its sovereignty. Capital movement and joint projects were thought to be politically neutral. This, of course, is not true. Foreign investment has never been known to be neutral. It is true, of course, that the independence of the organs of the states may be preserved, but the same cannot be said about the general orientation and direction of a country's political and economic life. The strengthening of economic linkages with an international economic system dominated by few industrialized countries can in no way be viewed as neutral. And it is precisely this supposed neutrality that the exponents of the other approach wanted to change. To be self-reliant and less dependent on the international economic system meant that the Arab states had to adopt and implement a Pan-Arab integrative development process with economic unity being only one of its components. But by the nature of the case such a Pan-Arab development process would have to result in far-reaching structural social, political, and economic changes. It could not and should not be expected to come from existing Arab states and regimes. There seems to be no way out of this deadlock except by breaking it. Unity in the last analysis is a political decision with the economists playing an important but secondary role.

Assessing the role of economics in the whole process of Arab unity, Nadeem al-Bitar warned in 1978 that when action for Arab unity is bogged down by economic models and measures that are unrelated to their surrounding social, political, and ideological relations without any dynamic or revolutionary understanding of these relations, the action is bound to concentrate on the narrowest outcomes and to forget the higher purposes that they were supposed to serve. Moreover, the kind of Arab unity that is promoted through economic coordination will by definition mean political and ideological unity among the Arab countries. Yet the advocates of economic integration and unity are silent when it comes to political and ideological contradictions among Arab states and seem to assume that these contradictions will somehow disappear as a result of economic integration. An Arab unity-oriented process of economic development will not succeed without a radical change of the ownership and the distribution of economic resources, a change that will have to be confronted politically. Otherwise existing economic contradictions will not allow the development process to evolve toward Arab unity.[34] Regardless of how one may approach the issue of the feasibility of Arab economic unity, there are several important considerations that have to be taken into account.

As Ibrahim Kubba wrote in the 1950s, a strong case can be made for Arab unity given the Arabs' history, cultural heritage, geographical unity, and comparable stage of economic development. Since the present state of political division and fragmentation was imposed by foreigners—Ottomans and Europeans—it is important that these artificial barriers be removed in order to achieve Arab political unity. But this political unity will have to be the outcome of long-range planning, since without such planning one should not expect such unity to materialize. An important prerequisite of this unity is its ideological content, which will have to be socialist if the needs of the people are to be met. Moreover, Arab unity will have to be realized in stages and may have to take different forms in different participating countries. In this scheme of things economic unity becomes the cornerstone of political unity.

Kubba distinguishes between three approaches to economic unity. The first approach is the formal or legalistic or the decreed approach to unity whose advocates think that economic unity can be attained by merely signing a piece of legislation or treaty. Such an approach ignores the fact that unity means the unification of several economies each with its resource endowment, units of production, and its own unique social and class relations. It may be useful to indicate that the Arab League's attempts at unity represent a clear application of the legislative or treaty approach.

The second approach maintains that each country should concentrate on its own economy and leave the realization of unity to future conditions.[35] The second approach seems to have predicted the preferences and the practices of the oil era and balance-of-payments-surplus oil states.

The third approach is what Kubba calls the "scientific" approach to unity. The thrust of the approach is that since unity is a giant undertaking, it must be pursued according to two principles: (1) that economic unity must take place between countries that share common political orientation, and (2) that it requires for its achievement long-range planning with clearly defined stages. For such economic planning to succeed it must take several considerations into account. These include (1) economic coordination among individual country economies in order to avoid duplication, waste, and fragmentation; (2) coequality among countries in order to avoid the exploitation of one country by another; (3) a minimum degree of self-sufficiency to avoid dependency; and (4) economic integration to avoid monopoly, competition, and conflicts between Arab economies.

Looking back at what has taken place over the last four decades under the rubric of Arab economic integration or economic unity, one is compelled to draw several conclusions. All the projects that were formalized by the Arab League remained by and large paper projects. Economic planning and decision making remain a matter for the individual state with Pan-Arab economic planning remaining an illusive goal. One by-product of the activities of the Arab League was the proliferation of its specialized agencies. This proliferation did not prove conducive to economic unity. The failure of Arab League effort is rooted in the fact that none of its plans and decisions are binding upon member states. State sovereignty takes precedence over collective interstate decisions.

Any explanation of the failure of attempts for Arab economic integration must take into consideration factors other than the structure of the Arab League and the importance of the concept of sovereignty. According to Abdel Hamid Brahimi there are several important factors that may explain the failed attempts for Arab economic integration. One such factor may be found in the contradiction between the desired common objective of integration and the multiplicity of decision-making centers. Such contradiction may be seen when certain Arab states agreed on some form of political union without taking into consideration whether their economies had sufficient complementarities to move along the path of economic integration. Another factor that contributed to the failure of economic integration was the absence of sectoral transnational planning among Arab countries. A related explanation in this regard is that market mechanisms rather than structural reorganizations of the economies had been regarded as the preferred instrument for integration. Economic and financial dependency on the industrialized countries is another impediment to economic integration.[36]

The inability of the Arab states system and the Arab League to attain the objective of economic unity was underlined by the advent of the sharp oil price increases in the 1970s. The gap between oil and nonoil states, which the oil price increases widened sharply, was superimposed on a system of states that has not been known for its collective commitment to economic unity. The thrust of the oil era as well as the Arab League and its thinkers and economists tended to abandon the lofty goals of integration and unity that characterized the 1950s and the 1960s and concentrate instead on the virtues of profit incentives for capital movement and Arab joint projects. This in effect was a throwback not only to the preoil era but one may say to the pre–Arab League era.

NOTES

1. See Walid Kazeeha, ''Arab Nationalism in the Stage Between the Two World Wars'' (in Arabic), *Al Mustaqbal Al Arabi*, No. 5 (January 1979): 60.

2. For a discussion of some of the economic factors at work in the interwar period see Muhammad Labeeb Shuqair, *Arab Economic Unity: Its Experiences and Expectations* (Beirut: Centre for Arab Unity Studies, 1986), Vol. 1, 274–280.

3. Mahmoud Abdel-Fadil, *Arab Economic Thought and the Issues of Liberation, Development and Unity* (in Arabic) (Beirut: Centre for Arab Unity Studies, 1982), 117–118.

4. See Kazeeha, ''Arab Nationalism,'' 55–66. Suffice it to say that in an agriculture-based society such as Iraq close to 12 percent of cultivated land was owned by thirteen families only. See Mohammad Salman Hasan, *Studies in the Iraqi Economy* (in Arabic) (Beirut: Dar Al Taliaa, 1966), 22–46.

5. For al-Husri's views on this point see Kazeeha, ''Arab Nationalism,'' 63–65.

6. For some of the economic views of the Baath party and Nasser see Tareq Ismael, *The Arab Left* (Syracuse, N.Y.: Syracuse University Press, 1976), Appendices A and C.

7. Walid Kazeeha, ''Socio-Political Foundations of the Growth of Contemporary Nationalist Movement in the Arab East,'' *Al Mustaqbal Al Arabi*, (March 1979): 63–75.

8. Ibid, 69–70.

9. See Yahya Sadowski, ''Patronage and the Ba'th: Corruption and Control in Contemporary Syria,'' *Arab Studies Quarterly* 9, No. 4 (Fall 1987): 442–461, especially p. 449.

10. For a good outline of Arab League economic agreements see Abdel Hasan Zalzala,

"The Challenges Facing Arab Economic Integration" (in Arabic), *Al Mustaqbal Al Arabi*, No. 21 (November 10, 1980): 6–21.

11. Ibid, 8.

12. According to Zalzala 60 percent of Arab League specialized agencies were created in the 1970s. Ibid, 9.

13. For detailed description of these and other Arab League specialized agencies see League of Arab States, *Specialized Arab Organizations: Basic Information and Founding Document* (in Arabic) (Tunis, 1984).

14. See Zalzala, "The Challenges," 9. This assessment is particularly important, since it comes from the league's assistant secretary for economic affairs, who like all international civil servants has a tendency to be gentle in his criticism of his employers.

15. Ibid.

16. See League of Arab States, *Toward Joint Arab Economic Action (Main Paper): Document presented to the Eleventh Arab Summit Conference, Amman, Hashemite Kingdom of Jordan, 1980* (Tunis, n.d.). Henceforth referred to as Joint Arab Action I. The second volume in this series of three volumes deals with Arab Economic Relations with the rest of the world and will be cited as *Joint Arab Economic Action II* while the third volume, to be cited *Joint Arab Economic Action III*, covers Arab economic matters. All three volumes are in Arabic.

17. Burhan al-Dajani, "The Economic Dimensions of the Eleventh Arab Summit Conference," in Centre for Arab Unity Studies, *Studies in Arab Economic Development and Integration* (in Arabic) (Beirut, 1982), 197–230.

18. See *Joint Arab Economic Action I*, 7–12.

19. Ibid, 13–15.

20. See al-Dajani, "The Economic Dimensions," 209.

21. For more details on the three agreements in question see Abdel Hasan Zalzala, "The Economic Role of the League of Arab States" (in Arabic), *Al Mustaqbal Al Arabi*, Nos. 42, 43, and 44 (August–October 1982): 147–165.

22. For a more detailed treatment of this agreement see al-Dajani, "The Economic Dimensions," 205–209.

23. On this point see Yusif A. Sayigh, "Arab Economic Integration and the Pretext of National Sovereignty" (in Arabic), *Al Mustaqbal Al Arabi*, No. 6 (March 1979): 23–41.

24. Ibid, 26–27.

25. Ibid, 27.

26. Ibid, 27–28.

27. See George Qurm, "The Pretext of the Conflict Between Arab Economic Systems and the Evolution of National Development" (in Arabic), *Al Mustaqbal Al Arabi*, No. 30 (August 1981): 143–150.

28. For a more detailed analysis of these and other related issues see Ibrahim Saad el-Deen and Mahmoud Abdel-Fadil, *Movement of Arab Employment: Problems, Effects and Policies* (Beirut: Centre for Arab Unity Studies, 1983), chapter 4, especially 201–203.

29. According to Burhan al-Dajani some labor-importing countries in the Gulf extended their restrictive policies to personal matters such as marriage, a practice that runs counter to the teaching of Islam. See his "The Woes of Arab Economic Development in Time of Oil States' Financial Surplus," *Al Mustaqbal Al Arabi*, no. 8 (July 1979): 6–22, especially p. 16.

30. Abdel-Fadil, *Arab Economic Thought*, 120.

31. See Sayigh, "Arab Economic Integration," 31–33.

32. Abdel-Fadil, *Arab Economic Thought*, 120–121.

33. See Ismail Sabri Abdalla, "Observations on the Strategy for Joint Arab Action, *Studies in Arab Development and Economic Integration*, 189–196, especially p. 195.

34. Abdel-Fadil, *Arab Economic Thought*, 123.

35. Ibrahim Kubba, *This Is the Path of July 14: Defense Before the Revolution's Court* (Beirut: Dar Al Taliaa, 1969), 119–121.

36. Abdel Hamid Brahimi, *Dimensions of Arab Economic Integration and Future Possibilities*, 4th ed. (Beirut: Centre for Arab Unity Studies, 1986), 204–223.

4

MULTINATIONAL OIL AND THE DEEPENING OF ARAB DEPENDENCY

One of the most important and lasting developments in the Arab world during the interwar period was the entry of multinational capital into a number of Arab countries to develop oil resources for the purpose of exporting oil and thus creating new linkages between Arab economies and the international economic system. This chapter will focus on the evolution of these linkages and the dependency to which they gave rise through an examination of the rise of special patterns of relationships between oil companies and oil-producing countries and the role that the oil sector came to play in shaping economic and political change in the Arab world.

CONCESSIONS, CARTELS, AND CHANGE

Until 1961 the Iraq Petroleum Company (IPC), which was owned by a consortium of five multinational oil corporations, had exclusive oil rights covering an area that virtually coincided with the whole territory of the country.[1] These five corporations were British Petroleum (BP), Exxon, Mobil, Shell, and Compagnie Française des Petroles (CFP). In addition to these corporations there were three other multinational enterprises that played pivotal roles in the Middle East oil industry. These were Texaco, Gulf, and Standard Oil of California (Socal). While Socal, Texaco, Exxon, and Mobil obtained the Saudi oil concession, Kuwait's oil concession went to Gulf and BP. It should be added that the IPC owners obtained also the oil concessions in Qatar and the United Arab Emirates while BP was, until 1951, the sole holder of the Iranian concession.

The concession system had certain unique characteristics, which tended to solidify the control of these multinational oil firms over the oil sectors of producing countries. The most pronounced features of the system are the following:

1. The duration of the concession was to last several decades—sixty years in the case of the Saudi concession and seventy-five years in the case of the concessions of Iraq and Kuwait.

2. Another important feature of the concession was its coverage that, as was indicated earlier, tended to coincide with the entire territory of the concession country. This feature gave the companies monopoly power over the development of a country's oil resources.

3. The companies had the sole power to determine output and export levels and to set prices. In other words the governments were excluded from participating in making decisions relating to what became the most important sector of the economy.

4. In exchange for these privileges that were exacted by the oil companies the governments of oil-producing countries were reduced to mere recipients of a fixed amount of revenue, set by the companies on a per unit of output basis.

In commenting on this imbalance in company-government pattern relationships, George W. Stocking was moved to state that "never in modern times have governments granted so much to so few for so long."[2]

The asymmetry in the respective positions of governments and companies may be explained by several historical factors. In the first place governments in the Arab world were either created or controlled by Britain or France at the time the concession agreements were signed in the 1920s and the 1930s. Thus the concessions in Iraq were obtained when Iraq was under direct British rule. The situation was essentially the same in Kuwait, Qatar, and Abu-Dhabi, since these sheikdoms were British protectorates.

A second factor was the sheer ignorance on the part of governments of the importance of oil and the oil industry. Thus in Saudi Arabia the concession was granted by a ruler who was described as not a modern or medieval man but the last of the great figures of the Old Testament. And in Iran the concession was obtained from a monarchy that was described as an old, long-mismanaged estate, ready to be knocked down at once to whatever foreign power bid highest or threatened most loudly its degenerate and defenseless rulers.[3] Even as late as 1951 the Iraqi officials who were negotiating with IPC certain modifications in the concession confessed their ignorance of the existence of posted prices—the prices at which oil was traded in open world markets.[4]

Third, the asymmetry in power relations between governments and companies was built into the concession system itself because every operating company was owned by more than one multinational oil corporation. These companies were in turn backed by their home governments. Moreover, these major oil firms had by 1928 entered into cartel arrangements to eliminate competitive pricing by fixing market shares, controlling output growth from various sources, exchanging oil to lessen transportation costs, and ultimately fixing prices of crude oil and products regardless of source or cost of production.[5]

THE INTEGRATING OF ARAB OIL INTO THE WORLD ECONOMY

One of the most outstanding features of the international oil industry during the interwar period was its ability to set prices under a single basing point system, which covered oil traded internationally. Under this system prices for both crude oil and products were set as though there were only one center of oil production— the Gulf Coast of the United States. According to this system a buyer anywhere in the world paid the United States Gulf price plus freight from the Gulf of Mexico even though the oil actually was shipped from a closer field.[6]

The subordination to and the integration of Arab oil into the multinational oil company cartel may be seen in the anomalous situation where oil consumers in Iraq were charged prices based upon quotations at the United States Gulf Coast, regardless of the facts that (1) the crude oil was produced in Iraq, (2) it was produced at low cost, (3) it was refined in a nearby refinery, and (4) the products were marketed by a local company.[7]

The single basing point system of pricing could have been maintained had the dominant position of the United States oil industry remained unchallenged. The emergence of the Middle East as a new production center and the special transportation conditions during World War II persuaded the British government to insist that oil needs of consumption centers in the Eastern Hemisphere should be met from the nearest source of supply. The British government also insisted that actual freight cost should be charged instead of the much higher freight charges from the United States Gulf Coast to these same consumption centers. The companies, however, succeeded in setting the price of the low-cost Middle East oil at the same level as that of the high-cost American oil, thus not only ensuring the continuity of their monopoly position in the world oil markets in both hemispheres but also allowing them to increase their profits as they expanded their sales of Middle East oil.[8]

As World War II was coming to an end, it became clear that the United States would no longer continue to be a major oil exporter. It also became clear that Europe's increasing need for oil in the postwar period had to be met primarily from the Middle East, while Japan's anticipated phenomenal increase in demand for oil had to be met entirely from Middle Eastern sources.

In order to avoid flooding the world oil market with low-cost Middle Eastern oil, the American and British governments concluded in 1944 the Anglo-American Oil Agreement, which had two prime objectives: (1) to enable American oil companies to have more access to Middle East oil, and (2) to regulate supply in the face of rising demand in order to ensure the orderly evolution of international petroleum trade in the postwar period. As the U.S. Senate Committee on Foreign Relations noted:

Given the fact that there was more Middle East oil than there were markets for it, it was obvious that production allocations were going to be made. The problem, therefore, was not whether but who would control that international allocation mechanism. As it turned out, the failure of the Anglo-American Oil Agreement delegated this global function to the major international oil companies.[9]

This delegation to the major multinational oil companies of the function of regulating global supply to meet rising demand led to several changes in the structure of the oil industry in the Middle East and had several important implications for the pattern of power relations between the governments and the companies.

In the early postwar period Exxon concluded that its sources of crude oil in the United States, Venezuela, and the Middle East would not be sufficient to meet its market needs throughout the world. At the same time the owner of the Saudi concession, Aramco (Arabian-American Oil Company), had access to vast reserves of low-cost crude oil. Yet the owners of Aramco (Texaco and Socal) did not have the marketing facilities that they needed if they were to deliver Saudi oil to the world market. By 1947 a major restructuring of the ownership of Aramco was completed, which resulted in the purchase by Exxon of 30 percent and Mobil of 10 percent interest in Aramco for a mere $102 million. A few years after the restructuring of Aramco the four owners and the other majors were given access to Iran's oil resources in the aftermath of the failure of the 1951 nationalization measures and the restructuring of Iran's oil sector in 1954. Thus by 1954 the seven majors and CFP in one combination or another had virtually all the oil produced in the Middle East under their direct control—95 percent of Iran's oil resources and 100 percent of the oil resources in Iraq, Saudi Arabia, Kuwait, Qatar, and Abu-Dhabi.

This position of collusive control by few multinational oil companies gave them the power to regulate output in each and every country where they were operating. Such regulation was not only intended to meet corporate commercial interests throughout the world, but it gave them the power to influence economic and political developments in oil-producing countries and to ensure compliance with corporate plans. The ability of companies to ensure country compliance may be explained by at least three considerations.

First, as time went by during the postwar period, governments of oil-producing countries became increasingly dependent on the oil sector as the primary source of budget revenue and foreign exchange earnings to finance ordinary expenditure such as defense, health, education, and housing as well as development spending. Dependence on oil revenue increased sharply starting in the early 1950s when the method of calculating government revenue was changed from a flat rate of 25 cents per barrel to 50 percent of the difference between production cost and posted price. This change had the effect of tripling government per barrel revenue. Coupled with the rise in oil output and export in the decade of the 1950s, it had the effect of raising government revenue sharply. Thus in 1949 total payments to governments of oil-producing countries amounted to $149 million. By 1959 payments increased more than eightfold, to $1.3 billion. The other side of this rise in government income was the rise in dependency on changes in world demand for oil and the policies of the companies over which governments had no influence. The extent of dependency on the oil sector was made clear in the aftermath of Iran's nationalization of its oil sector and the plunge in its output from 700,000 barrels a day in 1950 to a mere 28,000 barrels per day after the 1951 nationalization. The primary explanation for this drop was Iran's inability to sell its oil because companies boycotted the nationalized oil. Iran's ensuing economic difficulties set the stage for the CIA-backed coup, which overthrew the elected government of Mohammad Mossadegh and prepared the way for the reentry of multinational oil companies in Iran.

The second explanation for company power was the nature of corporate joint ownership of operating companies in different countries. Exxon, for example, had access to oil resources in all the Arab countries and Iran. BP, by the same token, had oil interests in Iran and all the Arab countries except Saudi Arabia. This joint ownership gave oil companies the flexibility to increase output in one country at the expense of another without affecting their worldwide interests. This flexibility was demonstrated after Iran nationalized its oil when the companies increased output in Kuwait, Saudi Arabia, and Iraq to offset the decline in Iran's oil output. It was demonstrated again after 1954 when Iran's oil had to be reintroduced into the world market, which meant that the rate of production growth in the other countries had to be lowered.

The third explanation for the power of the companies may be found in the pattern of relationships between these companies and their home governments, which used their positions of power in the world to enable these oil firms to obtain concessions, to penetrate markets and to back them in their dealings with the host governments. A few examples will illustrate this point. As was indicated earlier, the British government, as the mandatory power, played a crucial role in securing Iraq's oil for the majors. Similarly the French and American governments made certain that their own corporate citizens had access to that oil. Another example relates to the decision by the United States government to provide financial subsidy to Saudi Arabia in the 1940s. During World War II when conditions were not conducive for Aramco to expand its output, the United States government, urged by the oil companies, stepped in to provide financial assistance directly to the Saudi government. A directive issued by President Franklin D. Roosevelt in 1943 to the Lend-Lease administrator stated, ''In order to enable you to arrange Lend-Lease aid to the government of Saudi Arabia, I hereby find that the defense of Saudi Arabia is vital to the defense of the United States.''[10] Again, in the aftermath of the Iranian nationalization, the United States played an active role to insure that American oil companies had a major share of the Iranian concession. Thus on January 14, 1954, the National Security Council decided that ''the security interests of the United States require United States petroleum companies to participate in the international consortium.''[11]

Again, when the monarchy in Iraq was overthrown in July 1958, the United States government considered military intervention in Iraq to undo the newly established republican regime. But a decision was reached that military action could not be justified as long as the new government respected Western oil interests, which it did. The near military invasion of Iraq led Robert Engler to observe that this "gunboat diplomacy was clearly in line with the State Department's commitment to pipelines and profits."[12]

In assessing the triangular relationship between the oil companies, governments of oil-producing countries, and the United States government, the Senate Committee on Foreign Relations stated that the system of allocation of output between various oil-producing countries was administered by the multinational oil firms with the help of the United States government. The committee went on to say that the system was premised on two basic assumptions: (1) that the companies were instruments of United States foreign policy, and (2) that the interests of the companies were basically identical with the United States national interests. Furthermore, the committee identified United States foreign policy objectives as: (1) that the United States provide a steady supply of oil to Europe and Japan at reasonable prices for post–World War II recovery and to sustain economic growth, (2) that stable governments be maintained in pro-Western oil-producing countries, and (3) that American-based firms be a dominant force in world oil trade. The committee concluded that these three objectives were largely attained during the decades of the 1950s and 1960s.[13]

OPEC, OIL NATIONALISM, AND CHANGING CIRCUMSTANCES

In the decade of the 1950s several important events forced oil-producing countries to reexamine the terms of concession agreements. One of the most important forces of change was Arab nationalism, which greatly affected the political configurations of the Arab region.

In 1952 a group of Egyptian army officers under the leadership of Jamal Abdel Nasser succeeded in overthrowing the British-backed royal dynasty and establishing a republican regime with Pan-Arab orientation. Nasser's position as a nationalist independent Arab leader was strengthened in 1954 when he negotiated an agreement by which the British withdrew their troops from the Suez Canal Zone, which they had occupied since 1882. Nasser's position as an anti-imperialist Arab nationalist was reinforced when he successfully challenged the dominant position of Britain and France by nationalizing the Suez Canal in 1956. The failure of the October 1956 tripartite—British, French, and Israeli—invasion of Egypt to unseat Nasser and return the administration of the Suez Canal to British and French hands provided Nasser with his greatest triumph against the colonial powers that had ruled the Arab world for decades.[14] In February 1958 Egypt and Syria united to form the United Arab Republic, thus realizing the Arab nationalists' hope for Arab unity. The forces of nationalism were further strengthened when the British-backed Iraqi monarchy was overthrown in July 1958. These political developments had the effect of strengthening the forces that advocated a reexamination of the concession system that had governed the pattern of relationships between companies and governments for decades.

As was indicated earlier in this chapter, the concession system emerged at a time when governments had neither the political power nor the knowledge to determine terms more favorable to them than the ones that they had to accept. In short, the very nature of the concession system contained within it inevitable points of conflict, which emerged over time, The conflict centered among other things on the duration of the concession, the relinquishment of areas unused by the companies, settlement of disputes, power to tax, the disposal of associated natural gas, managerial functions, employment of nationals, production cost elements, and price-setting power.

This asymmetry, which reflected in the helplessness of the governments, became more pronounced as the importance of the oil sector and oil revenues increased. This importance was articulated by a former minister of the economy in Iraq when he said, "Our whole economic development is geared to the revenues from the flow . . . of oil. Our whole political stability depends on the flow . . . of oil. It is not just a private matter involving a private company's profits. It is a matter that affects the whole state of Iraq."[15]

The difficulties of oil-producing countries were compounded by the fact that each one of them had no choice but to face alone a cartel or a consortium of major oil companies operating in their territories. Memories of what happened to Iran's nationalized oil were fresh in the minds of policymakers in Arab oil-producing countries. Thus when the Venezuelan oil ministers approached oil policymakers in the Middle East with proposals for cooperation and coordination of oil policy objectives, the opportunity was eagerly seized. The leading proponent of the Venezuelan connection was Abdullah al-Tariki, the director general (later minister from December 1960 to March 1962 when he was replaced by Ahmad Zaki Yamani) of petroleum and mineral affairs in Saudi Arabia.

Tariki had several concerns and a number of objectives. He complained bitterly that the companies did not want the governments to have anything to do with oil and that in order for the government to improve the lot of the people, oil revenue must be increased. Since decisions affecting revenue were the exclusive prerogative of the companies, the terms of the concession accordingly had to be changed. Moreover, governments had to engage in vertical integration in order to benefit from the value added instead of being passive recipients of certain revenue. No less important was Tariki's advocacy of cooperation with other oil-producing countries in policies that would regulate production to meet the world's rising demand for oil. He also advocated an upper ceiling on company rate of return on investment in oil-producing countries.[16]

In addition to the rising sentiment of oil nationalism and the desire to restructure the terms of the concessions, oil-producing countries were concerned that the oil companies were in a position to reduce Middle East oil prices in order to widen its markets. With the new fifty-fifty profit sharing system, which was adopted in the 1950s, however, any reduction in the price would lower government revenue by one-half of the reduction in the price. Oil companies actually did exactly that as they gradually lowered the official setting price of Arabian Light from $2.18 per barrel in 1948 to $1.80 in 1960 while at the same time allowing domestic American prices to increase from $2.68 to $3.28 during the same period.

THE EMERGENCE OF A COUNTERVAILING POWER: OPEC

In September 1960 three Arab (Saudi Arabia, Iraq, Kuwait) and two non-Arab (Iran and Venezuela) oil-producing countries agreed to form the Organization of Petroleum Exporting Countries (OPEC).[17] The decision to form OPEC was a natural outcome of the imbalance in the bargaining power between the companies and the governments. This imbalance and its threat to political and economic stability gained in strength as the economies of the oil-producing countries have become more dependent on oil revenue. The power of the companies to set price levels and output volumes unilaterally exposed the weakness and the vulnerability of the governments at a time when the tide of nationalism was on the rise in the Arab region and throughout the Third World.

As was indicated earlier, the prices of Middle East oil were reduced in the decade of the 1950s by the oil companies in order to enable oil to penetrate world markets. And when prices were unilaterally reduced by the companies in 1959 and again in 1960, thus inflicting a revenue loss of some 15 percent on the oil-exporting countries, the governments of these countries were forced to act by forming OPEC. As Ian Seymour noted, the reductions (especially the one in 1960) served to awaken the actual owners of the oil resources from their inaction and provided the spark for the emergence of a governmental counterforce—OPEC.[18]

The formation of OPEC failed, however, to change the traditional imbalance in power relations. Although the founding members of the new organization declared that they could no longer remain indifferent to the unilateral power of the companies in effecting price changes and that the 1960 price reduction should be rescinded, they failed to take the necessary political and economic decisions to enforce their declared policies. Instead they allowed themselves to engage in the pursuit of those policies that would maximize their revenue without coordination with other member countries of OPEC. In other words, the determination of price levels and output volumes remained a corporate matter until 1971 when OPEC finally succeeded in negotiating collectively with the companies. The result was the Tehran Price Agreement, which set prices for a five-year period. The major exception to this generalization and the one that encouraged OPEC to move toward the 1971 collective negotiations was the success in 1970 of the Libyan government in forcing the companies to raise prices.[19]

Only a few months after the conclusion of the Tehran Agreement on prices, the Bretton Woods international monetary system, which had been constructed by the industrialized countries under the leadership of the United States, suffered its most severe crisis since its inception. In August of that year the United States government declared that it would no longer convert foreign-held dollar balances into gold at the fixed price of $35 per ounce of gold. The suspension of dollar convertibility into gold led to a decline in its value vis-à-vis other major currencies. Since the dollar was the currency in which posted prices were expressed and revenues were calculated, governments asked that prices be adjusted upward to reflect the depreciation of the dollar. Instead, they had to settle for partial compensation.[20]

The collapse of the Bretton Woods system illustrates the inability of oil-producing countries to protect their interests in the international economic system. No less important than the effects of the instability in the international monetary system was the effect of rising imports prices at a time when the cost of imported oil in real terms had actually declined. There are three elements in this relationship: revenue per barrel received by producing countries, cost of goods imported by producing countries, and the delivered price of imported oil paid by major oil-consuming countries. First, as was indicated earlier, revenue per unit of oil output remained constant and in some instances declined in the period 1950 to 1970 due to the series of price cuts that oil companies introduced in order to expand their markets. Thus the per barrel revenue in the Middle East, which was 81 cents in 1955, declined to 76 cents in 1961, but increased to 86 cents in 1970.[21] By contrast the prices of goods imported by oil-producing countries continued to increase during the same period. This is reflected in the upward movement of the prices of goods exported from industrial countries, which increased by 22 percent in the United States, 14 percent in Canada, 17 percent in the United Kingdom, 14 percent in France, 21 percent in Germany, and 4 percent in Japan—the main trading partners of Arab oil-producing countries.[22] The third element relates to changes in the delivered prices that oil-consuming countries actually pay for their imported oil. According to an index of three cost components—price of crude oil, tanker freights, and currency valuations—between 1957 and 1970 the cost of imported oil in Germany had declined by 40 percent, in the Netherlands by 35 percent, in Japan by 31 percent, and in Italy by 30 percent.[23] It is very clear from the data that the working of the international economic system was such that the terms of trade had moved in favor of industrial countries and resulted in the transfer of resources from oil-producing to major oil-consuming countries.

OIL SUPPLY/DEMAND IMBALANCE AND THE OIL PRICE EXPLOSION

One of the most important turning points in contemporary political economy of the Arab countries, both oil- and non-oil-producing, was the series of events that led to the October 1973 oil price explosion and the consequences of that for Arab nationalism, the more marked division between the oil haves and have-nots among the Arab countries, and the reinforcement of the forces of dependency that resulted from that explosion. Before dealing with these issues, a brief outline of developments in the world oil market is in order.

The United States oil industry and oil market have always played a pivotal role in the international oil industry. As was indicated earlier, prices at the United States Gulf Coast terminals constituted the basis for price quotations throughout the world. And in order to protect the American oil industry from potential disruptive effects of competition, a system of output prorationing was devised to regulate output and maintain price stability. This was done by oil-producing states, which took upon themselves the task of prorating the estimated demand for crude among producing fields and wells. The United States government enforced the states' regulatory power by prohibiting interstate sales of crude oil produced in violation of state prorationing measures.[24]

The United States oil industry could have the benefits of prorationing and price stability so long as there were no other competing sources of oil or so long as such sources were also regulated. The international petroleum cartel provided the necessary regulating mechanism for foreign oil until the postwar period when the Middle East emerged as a low-cost oil-producing region with vast reserves to develop. In order to insulate the American oil industry from the price-depressing effects of imported oil, an import quota system was adopted in the 1950s. But as demand for oil continued to rise and as the American industry was producing at full capacity, the quota system became unnecessary and was formally removed in 1973 as more oil had to be imported to meet the rising demand. The sustained economic growth in industrialized countries, the entry of the United States in the world market as a major oil importer, and the interest of certain oil-producing countries in conservation caused by the early 1970s an upward pressure on prices. Thus according to OPEC estimates product prices charged by oil companies increased from an average of $21 per ton in 1970 to $52 per ton in 1973—an increase of $31—whereas the average increase in government revenue was $6 per ton, from $7 to $13, during the same period.[25]

The rise in company profits relative to member country revenue, the supply/demand imbalance in the oil market, the continued erosion in oil revenue purchasing power due to inflation in industrial countries prompted a number of oil-producing countries to call for the abrogation of the Tehran Agreement in favor of setting prices unilaterally by producing countries. By September 1973 OPEC, however, decided to enter into negotiations with the oil companies to raise oil prices by revising the terms of the Tehran Agreement. The negotiations started on October 8, two days after the Arab-Israeli war broke out.

ARAB NATIONALISM, OIL, AND THE OCTOBER WAR

October 1973 will be remembered as a major turning point in the modern history of the Arab world and the international oil industry. October 1973 witnessed the successful coordination of policies between the governments of Egypt and Syria to initiate military action in order to liberate the territories occupied by Israel in 1967. For Egypt the main objective of the October War was the recovery of Sinai and for Syria it was the recovery of the Golan Heights. Neither country had any illusions about driving the Israeli forces of occupation back to the 1967 borders. The undertaking was nonetheless something of a feat for Arab armies, which had suffered repeated defeats by the Israeli armed forces.

The second force that gave October 1973 special historical significance in Arab modern history was the use of oil as an instrument of foreign policy. Within the context of the October war Arab oil-producing states agreed to restrict oil output and to embargo their exports to aid in the attainment of the objectives of the war.

Behind the immediate attempt to recover the Sinai and the Golan Heights was the central and more critical issue of the Palestine question. The assumption was that the October war was initiated with the ultimate objective of solving the Palestine problem, which had become an integral part of Arab political life throughout the twentieth century. Arab governments had already reconciled themselves prior to the outbreak of the October war to an overall settlement of the Arab-Israeli conflict under which Israel would withdraw from all the territories it occupied in 1967: Sinai, Golan Heights, the West Bank, Gaza, and East Jerusalem, in exchange for a peace agreement.

The understanding among Arab governments had been that a resolution to the Palestine question was the ultimate goal of any settlement of their conflict with Israel. This understanding was to be reflected in certain policy positions that the oil-producing countries decided to adopt in order to provide some complementarity to the war effort undertaken by Syria and Egypt.

The failure of diplomacy between 1967 and 1973 to settle the Arab-Israeli conflict and to resolve the Palestine question convinced Egypt and Syria that military action was necessary if a political settlement with Israel were to be reached. The mere fact that the armies of the two countries were able to initiate joint military action against a military power thought to be invincible was a major accomplishment. Moreover, success in actually achieving certain military advances meant that with proper training, equipment, and leadership the Arab soldier should be able to achieve military parity with his Israeli counterpart. The shocking realization of this fact was described as an earthquake; it marked a fundamental shift, at Israel's expense, in the Middle East balance of power. For the first time in the history of Zionism, the Arabs had attempted, and partially succeeded, in imposing a fait accompli by force of arms. The setback was not just military; it affected all those factors—psychological, ideological, diplomatic, and economic—that make up the strength and vigor of a nation. The Israelis had paid a heavy price for merely holding their attackers to an inconclusive draw.[26]

In initiating action against the forces of occupation, the governments of Egypt and Syria made it abundantly clear that the liberation of their occupied territories was only one of two objectives. The other objective was an equitable solution to the Palestinian question through the recognition of the historical and natural rights of the Palestinian people to self-determination and without this recognition no peaceful solution to the Middle East conflict could be fashioned.

OIL DIPLOMACY AND THE OCTOBER WAR

Two days after the war broke out on October 6, 1973, Arab oil-producing countries started, through the Organization of Petroleum Exporting Countries (OPEC), negotiations with the major oil companies for the purpose of setting higher prices for their oil. The gap between what the OPEC negotiators were asking for (an increase in the price of crude oil from $3 to $6 per barrel) and what the companies were offering (45 cents) prompted the multinational oil companies to ask their home governments if they should "offer to sweeten the deal to the point where it had a reasonable chance of being accepted by the producing countries."[27] The virtually unanimous reaction of the governments of the industrialized countries was that the companies should not improve their offer.

Faced with this rejection, OPEC Arab and non-Arab member countries decided on October 16 to raise the price of crude oil by 70 percent from $3 to $5.11 per barrel. The significance of this decision was as much its magnitude as the fact that it was taken unilaterally by a group of Third World countries for whom oil was the primary source of national income and in some cases the only source of foreign exchange earnings. Given the fact that over their long petroleum history Arab governments had no say in how prices were determined and given the observed pattern of company-government negotiations since the concession system came into being in the 1920s, it is very difficult to avoid the conclusion that the October war provided the context and the impetus for the unilateral decision of OPEC member countries to raise oil prices.

More significant than the increase in the price of oil was the decision by Arab oil-producing countries to impose output cutbacks and embargo measures on the exports of crude oil to certain countries. Although the Arabs attempted to use oil as a political instrument in 1956 when Israel together with Britain and France invaded Egypt and again in 1967 when Israel invaded and occupied the Sinai, the Golan Heights, the West Bank, and Gaza, the 1973 oil decisions were different from earlier ones both qualitatively and quantitatively.

The 1956 interruption was effected by the demolition of one of the pumping stations carrying Iraqi oil to the Mediterranean through Syria. The attempt was ineffective and had no impact on the international supply of oil. The 1967 embargo imposed by several Arab states failed to affect the oil market conditions due to the availability of excess capacity output in the Western Hemisphere. The 1973 oil measures, by contrast, were different because they (1) had a declared political objective, (2) established certain quantitative reductions, and (3) enjoyed a consensus among the participants.

The idea that oil could be used as an instrument of foreign policy assumed an important dimension for the first time in 1967 when the Conference of Arab

Finance, Economy, and Oil Ministers met in Baghdad on August 15–20 and decided to adopt the following resolution: "The conference . . . was of the opinion that the stoppage of the oil flow would constitute an effective economic weapon on condition that such stoppage should not be of a partial nature or subject to any time-limit."[28]

The ministers' resolution, however, was rejected later in the month by the Arab Summit Conference in Khartoum. In its rejection of the ministers' recommendation the Khartoum conference made the following statement: "The Summit Conference concluded that the oil flow could itself be used as a positive weapon in that Arab oil represents an Arab asset which could be used to strengthen the economies of those Arab states which were directly affected by the aggression, thereby enabling them to stand firm in the battle. The Conference therefore decided to resume oil pumping operations."[29]

Although the 1967 Arab Summit Conference sanctioned the resumption of oil shipments, it did so in exchange for a financial subsidy to be provided by Saudi Arabia and other Arab Gulf states to Egypt, Jordan, and Syria. The conference also decided to engage in political action on the international and diplomatic levels in order to eliminate the effects of the aggression and ensure the withdrawal of Israeli forces from Arab territory that they occupied after June 5.[30]

This rejection of the use of oil as a political weapon was reaffirmed at the December 1969 Arab Summit Conference held in Rabat. The position of the Arab states was based on the premise that by appealing to the United States to exert pressure on Israel, a general settlement of the conflict and the recovery of occupied territory could be obtained. President Jamal Abdel Nasser signaled the readiness of the Arab states to reach a settlement when he appealed to President Richard Nixon in May 1970 to help the Arab countries recover their occupied lands. Following the public appeal by Nasser, Secretary of State William Rogers floated a plan in June 1970 that called for Israeli withdrawal from the occupied areas as part of an overall settlement of the Arab-Israeli conflict. Jordan and Egypt readily accepted the Rogers plan over the objections of the Palestinian community. The objection of the Palestinians to the Rogers Plan (which was based on United Nations Security Council Resolution 242) was rooted in the resolution's failure to mention the inalienable rights of the Palestinians to self-determination. Indeed the resolution failed to make any mention of the Palestinians, save for its reference to "achieving a just settlement of the refugee problem."[31] The decision to accept the Rogers plan and to have the United States act as the primary broker in reaching a settlement between the Arab governments and the government of Israel meant that Arab oil policy had to be accommodative rather than confrontational. It also meant that Arab oil had to continue to flow in even larger volumes to meet the needs of the industrialized economies. But such an oil policy has its own built-in limitation in that it was based on the belief that an American-sponsored diplomatic solution to the conflict was possible. When it became clear two years after the announcement of the Rogers plan that the American government was unwilling to pursue its own plan, the idea of using oil as a political instrument was revived. There were several important changes between 1970 and 1972 that enhanced the importance of oil as an instrument of political pressure.

One of the most outstanding achievements of that period was the success in 1970 of the new republican regime in Libya in raising the price of crude oil as well as the tax rate on the profits of the oil companies. The success of the Libyan government led oil-producing countries in OPEC to engage in collective negotiation with the oil companies for the purpose of adjusting prices and tax rates. This exercise in collective bargaining led to the conclusion of the famous Tehran Agreement in February 1971, which stipulated certain price increases and fiscal adjustments over a period of five years. It should be noted that the OPEC countries found it necessary to resort to the threat of nationalization to prod the companies to reach agreement within a given period of time.

The United States by the early 1970s had become a major oil-importing country with an increasing dependence on Arab oil. The rising international dependence on Arab oil led to a resurgence of Arab interest in seeing the United States reexamine its policy of total support for Israel's continued occupation of Arab lands. The belief that this American policy had to be confronted by some kind of Arab economic challenge found an expression when, during an interview, President Anwar al-Sadat of Egypt alluded to the linkage between Arab oil and American interest in the Arab world:

Q: There is talk of a partial Arab oil boycott—the Arabs only selling enough oil to cover their immediate expenses. Do you think this is a practical possibility? How soon? And with what effect?

A: I have never asked for a boycott. But I have spoken about US interests in the area as a whole. When Nixon gives Israel $70 million for the settlement of new refugees from Russia and when the US Senate, a day or two before, votes another $300 million for Israel, I tell other Arab leaders that the US is getting a lot of money from its investments and revenue in the Arab world. All I can tell you is that US interests will shortly become part of the battle for the recovery of our land. An oil boycott is feasible but it's a very complex problem. We are not hysterical and there is no need for hysteria. But I can assure you that US interests in the Middle East are in for a long hot autumn, and if Mr. Nixon thinks he is going to have a quiet time in the area as he is running for reelection, he has another surprise coming.[32]

Sadat's prodding of Arab oil-producing countries seemed to have fallen on deaf ears as the following exchange with King Faisal of Saudi Arabia shows:

Q: Some circles are advocating the use of oil as a weapon to bring pressure on the US to modify its hostile attitude towards the Arabs. What is your view on this matter?

A: I recall that such a suggestion was made by some at the Rabat [Arab Summit] Conference but it was opposed by Gamal Abdel-Nasser on the grounds that it would affect the economies of the Arab countries and interfere with their ability to support Arab staying power; at the same time such a measure would not affect America

because America does not need any of our oil or other Arab Gulf oil before 1985.
Therefore my opinion is that this proposal should be ruled out, and I see no benefit
in reviving its discussion at this time.[33]

But Saudi Arabia could not ignore for long the disturbing stagnation of the
Arab-Israeli conflict and its implications for the stability of political life in the
region. It is important to stress that by 1972 the Libyan government under the
leadership of Colonel Muammar Qaddafi had become well entrenched in power,
the Palestinian nationalist movement under the leadership of the Palestine Liberation Organization (PLO) had become an important Arab, regional, and international force; and the Iraqi and the Syrian governments were uncompromising
in their political pronouncements on the Arab-Israeli conflict and Palestinian
national rights.

It should be added that the Saudis' own assessment of political currents in the
Arab world led them to believe that unless the Arab-Israeli conflict was moved
off dead center, the forces of destabilization would get the upper hand in any
confrontation. Should that happen, not only would American interests be jeop-
ardized but the whole system of Arab regimes could collapse under the weight
of its dependence on the United States. This realization as well as the special
position that Saudi Arabia has in the Arab and the Islamic worlds made it
extremely difficult for the Saudis not to reexamine their position vis-à-vis the
question of oil as an instrument of foreign policy.

The Saudis, in other words, found themselves in a predicament that was not
of their own making. Indeed the predicament was created by policies of the
United States, which endorsed and financed Israeli occupation and policies in
the Arab region. An insight into the thinking of King Faisal comes through his
conversation in May 1973 with American oil executives when he tried to impress
upon them the gravity of the situation in the Middle East. The oil executives
reported that the king "went to great length to explain his predicament in the
Middle East as a staunch friend of the U.S.A." and that it was absolutely
mandatory that the United States government do something to change the direction of events taking place in the region. A simple "disavowal of Israeli
policies and actions by the United States government would go a long way
toward overcoming the current anti-American feeling." The king was of the
opinion that the combination of Zionist policies and the activities of the communists in the region was on the verge of having American interests thrown out
of the area and that he was not able to stand alone much longer against the
currents that were overtaking the region.[34]

The Saudi monarch's apprehension was understandable in light of the United
States' unwillingness to carry out its own policy regarding the resolution of the
Arab-Israeli conflict. This failure disillusioned its supporters in the Arab world
and exposed their vulnerability to the politics and policies of their less conservative contemporaries who were becoming more vocal in their calls for the use
of oil as an instrument of foreign policy. In addition, Faisal's position was further

pressured by the successful nationalization of the Iraq Petroleum Country (IPC) in May 1972 and a pronouncement by Iraq's president Ahmad Hasan al-Bakr at the Baghdad Seminar of 1972: "It is now in our power to use Arab oil as a weapon against our imperialist enemies in all our battles of liberation and particularly in our battle of a destiny in Palestine."[35]

Not only were the Saudis pressured by President Bakr of Iraq, President Sadat of Egypt, and the events of the IPC nationalization, but the call for the use of oil as a policy instrument came also from other quarters. The International Conference of Arab Trade Unions in December 1972 called for complete economic boycott of the United States and urged Arab governments to begin destroying and striking at American interests throughout the Arab world.[36] In a similar vein the Economic Council of the Arab League met in Cairo in December 1972 to discuss the possibilities of using Arab oil to pressure the United States to change its policies.

These emerging pressures in the Arab region led the Saudi government to reach the following conclusions:

1. If United States policies relative to the Middle East conflict remained unchanged, American interests in the Arab world would be in jeopardy.

2. That the government of Saudi Arabia was being isolated in the Arab world, and its ability to preserve American interests in the region was being undermined.

3. The unequivocal support of Israel by the United States was allowing communist and radical elements in the Arab world to take over and sway Arab public opinion against the United States.[37]

These assessments by the government of Saudi Arabia were communicated by American oil executives representing the four owners of Arabian-American Oil Company (Aramco): Exxon, Texaco, Mobil, and Standard Oil of California (Socal) in May 1973 to the relevant bureaucratic hierarchies and policymakers in the Defense Department, the State Department, and the White House. The reaction of the United States government to these warnings was to dismiss them. Government officials thought that no change in the course of American policy in the Arab region was necessary. Indeed, official Washington thought that King Faisal was crying wolf when no wolf existed except in his imagination and that there was little or nothing the United States government could or would do on an urgent basis to affect the Arab-Israeli issue.[38] Simply put, King Faisal was not able to get even a simple statement from the United States government to shore up his position in the Arab world.

Faisal's feeling of isolation was now complete and resulted in his public pleading with the United States to show some understanding for his position. He stated his case in an interview on the National Broadcasting Corporation's program "Meet the Press" on the eve of the October war in these terms:

NBC: Your Majesty's remarks on this subject in the past have been interpreted to mean that Saudi Arabia might restrict its shipments of oil particularly to the United States, is that a correct interpretation?

Faisal: We do not wish to place any restrictions on our oil exports to the United States, but, as I mentioned, America's complete support of Zionism against the Arabs makes it extremely difficult for us to continue to supply the U.S. petroleum needs and to even maintain our friendship with the U.S.

As friends of the U.S. and in the interest of maintaining and cementing this friendship, we counsel the U.S. to change its one-sided policy of favoritism to Zionism and support against the Arabs.

NBC: If I am correct, His Majesty at one time said that oil and politics did not mix. Has something occurred in the last several months to change your thinking on these lines?

Faisal: Undoubtedly, we are under attack from the Arabs themselves because of our friendship with the U.S., and we are accused of being in collusion with Zionism and American imperialism against the Arabs.

NBC: And it is in response to those attacks that His Majesty has felt called upon to speak out on this subject?

Faisal: I want to draw attention of my American friends to this serious situation so that we would not reach the point where we would be compelled to take other measures.[39]

To recapitulate, the defeat of the Arab regimes and the occupation of Arab territories by Israel in the June 1967 war propelled most of the Arab governments into seeking an American solution to the conflict. However, the accommodationist policies of these regimes failed to persuade the United States to change its support of the Israeli policies of occupation. The success of some Arab governments such as Algeria and Iraq in the nationalization of oil companies operating in their countries created a new set of conditions that gave rise to the belief that oil could be used as a political instrument.

Although the Saudis opposed and quieted calls for the political use of oil, by 1973 it was extremely difficult for them to continue to ignore such voices. By that time it became clear to the Saudis and other Arab governments that the United States foreign policy in the Arab region had only one thrust: total support of Israeli action.

NOTES

1. Technically speaking, there were two other companies in Iraq, the Mosul Petroleum Company and the Basra Oil Company. These two companies were subsidiaries of IPC and were owned by the same parent companies.

2. George W. Stocking, *Middle East Oil: A Study in Political and Economic Controversy* (Nashville, Tenn.: Vanderbilt University Press, 1970), 130.

3. Ibid, 123–126.

4. See Nadim al-Pachachi, "The Development of Concession Agreements and Taxation in the Middle East," *Middle East Economic Survey (MEES)*, March 29, 1968.

5. John M. Blair, *The Control of Oil* (New York: Pantheon Books, 1976), 54–56.

6. For an elaboration of the working of this form of pricing see Wayne A. Leeman, *The Price of Middle East Oil: An Essay in Political Economy* (Ithaca, N.Y.: Cornell University Press, 1962), 89–98. See also Abbas Alnasrawi, *OPEC in a Changing World Economy* (Baltimore, Md.: Johns Hopkins University Press, 1985), 45–51.

7. See U.S. Senate Select Committee on Small Business, *The International Petroleum Cartel* (Washington, D.C.: Government Printing Office, 1952), 95. This study was prepared for the Subcommittee on Monopoly by the staff of the Federal Trade Commission. Henceforth will be referred to as *FTC Report*.

8. The profitability of the concession system may be appreciated by comparing company and government receipts. According to Issawi and Yeganeh, Middle East oil operations for the period 1913–1947 gave the companies a total net income of $2.1 billion while the governments (Iraq, Saudi Arabia, Kuwait, Bahrain, Qatar, and Iran) received only $510 million. See Charles Issawi and Mohammed Yeganeh, *The Economics of Middle Eastern Oil* (New York: Frederick A. Praeger, 1962), 183–189. It is worth noting in this context that government revenue was fixed at 25 cents per barrel of oil produced. See *FTC Report*, p. 96.

9. See U.S. Senate Committee on Foreign Relations, Subcommittee on Multinational Oil Corporations, *Multinational Oil Corporations and U.S. Foreign Policy* (Washington, D.C.: Government Printing Office, 1975), 42–43. Henceforth *MNC Report*.

10. Ibid, 38–39.

11. See U.S. Senate Committee on Foreign Relations, Subcommittee on Multinational Corporations, *The International Petroleum Cartel, the Iranian Consortium and U.S. National Security* (Washington, D.C.: Government Printing Office, 1974), vii. It should be added that in compliance with this decision the attorney general rendered an opinion to the president that the proposed consortium plan, when viewed in connection with the security requirements of the United States as determined by the National Security Council, would not in itself constitute an unreasonable restraint on trade. See Ibid.

12. See Robert Engler, *The Politics of Oil: A Study of the Private Power and Democratic Directions* (Chicago: University of Chicago Press, 1961), 264.

13. *Multinational Oil Companies*, 2.

14. For a brief outline of the sequence of events that culminated in the 1956 invasion of Egypt see L. S. Stavrianos, *Global Rift: The Third World Comes of Age* (New York: Morrow, 1981), 646–650.

15. Quoted in Stocking, *Middle East Oil*, 141.

16. For more of Tariki's views see Ian Seymour, *OPEC: An Instrument of Change* (London: Macmillan Press, 1980), 30–36, and Stocking, *Middle East Oil*, 316–321.

17. In addition to the five founding members nine additional members were admitted: Qatar joined OPEC in 1961, Indonesia and Libya in 1962, Abu-Dhabi in 1967, Algeria in 1969, Nigeria in 1971, Ecuador in 1973, and Gabon in 1974. In 1971 Abu-Dhabi's membership was transferred to the United Arab Emirates as the former became part of the latter.

18. See Seymour, *OPEC*, 19. See also Fuad Rouhani, *A History of O.P.E.C.* (New York: Praeger Publishers, 1971), 75–82.

19. For a detailed history of the evolution of OPEC's policies during this period see Seymour, *OPEC*, chapters 3 and 4. See also Abbas Alnasrawi, "Collective Bargaining Power in OPEC," *Journal of World Trade Law* 7, no. 2 (1973): 188–207.

20. Ibid.

21. *MEES*, various issues.

22. See *Economic Report of the President, 1974* (Washington, D.C.: Government Printing Office, 1974), 93.

23. See *Petroleum Intelligence Weekly (PIW)*, March 27, 1972, p. 2.

24. For a detailed discussion of these policies see Blair, *The Control of Oil*, chapters 6 and 7.

25. *MEES*, September 21, 1973.

26. David Hirst, *The Gun and the Olive Branch: The Roots of Violence in the Middle East* (London: Futura Publications, 1978), 259.

27. *MNC Report*, p. 149.

28. *MEES* (Supplement), September 8, 1967, p. 6.

29. Ibid, 3.

30. Ibid.

31. For the text of Resolution 242 see *Journal of Palestine Studies* 8, no. 2 (Winter 1979): 210–211.

32. *MEES*, August 4, 1972, 1–2.

33. Ibid, 1.

34. U.S. Senate Committee on Foreign Relations, Subcommittee on Multinational Corporations, *Multinational Corporations and United States Foreign Policy*, pt. 7 (Washington, D.C.: Government Printing Office, 1974), 506. Henceforth *MNC Hearings*.

35. *The International Seminar on Oil As a Weapon*, Baghdad, November 11–14, 1972. (Cairo: Afro-Asian Peoples' Solidarity Organization, 1974), 700.

36. *MNC Hearings*, Pt. 7, 534–536.

37. Ibid, 509.

38. Ibid.

39. *Arab Oil & Gas*, September 16, 1973.

5

ARAB NATIONALISM AND THE ARAB OIL "WEAPON": THE BUILT-IN FAILURE

The decision by Arab oil-producing states to reduce output and place an embargo on oil exports to the United States and the Netherlands during the October 1973 war came to be known as the "Arab oil weapon." It should be noted that the use of oil as an instrument of economic and diplomatic pressure was the result of a number of decisions taken at different times during the war and implemented in a manner that revealed a considerable lack of planning. In the following pages these decisions will be analyzed.

On the eve of the October war, the position of the United States vis-à-vis the Israeli occupation of Arab territories was conveyed to President Sadat as follows: "The drift of what Kissinger said . . . was the United States regrettably could do nothing to help so long as we [Egypt] were the defeated party and Israel maintained her superiority."[1]

This attitude, which made the United States position indistinguishable from that of Israel, gave rise to calls that American economic interests, mainly oil, in the Arab region should be targeted for nationalization or disruption in order to force a change in policy toward Israeli occupation. The Saudis came to the conclusion that the rising tide of Pan-Arab sentiment for the Israeli withdrawal from the territories it occupied in the 1967 war and United States indifference toward such withdrawal were jeopardizing their own political and economic interests in addition to those of the United States. The Saudis came to the realization that if they were to fail to take some action, another Arab government might assume the position of leadership and determine the terms of the debate and the specific policy actions within Arab oil councils. In other words, it was thought that the movement toward nationalization of foreign oil companies operating in the Arab world, a movement that had been advocated by Iraq, Algeria, and Libya, might acquire serious momentum. Since the Saudis were opposed to nationalization, it was important for them to determine the nature and scope of any joint Arab oil policy actions. The Saudis had already decided in August 1973 to use some form of oil pressure should another war with Israel break out.[2] The real issue was what kind of measures would be appropriate from Saudi perspective and interests.

THE OIL WEAPON: PRODUCTION CUTBACK AND EMBARGO

When the October war broke out, Iraq hastened to nationalize the remaining American, British, and Dutch interests in the remaining oil concession, the Basra Oil Company. Algeria, Libya, and Iraq took the position that the nationalization of American interests in the Arab region would be the most effective means of forcing a change in American foreign policy toward the conflict. The Kuwaiti National Assembly in the meantime voted soon after the October war broke out for the government to consider the withdrawal of Kuwaiti funds from United States banks and to reexamine its oil export policy toward the United States.

The position of the Saudi government, on the other hand, was not to resort to nationalization or an oil embargo or the withdrawal of funds as policy measures. Instead, a reduction in oil output by all Arab countries should be considered as an effective means in helping the war effort.

The contemplated Saudi cutback had been anticipated by the owners of Aramco, and they reported it to the White House. The Aramco owners indicated also that the Saudi room for maneuverability in inter-Arab politics had been narrowed by the public position of the United States government toward the October war when it called upon the combatants to retire to their positions prior to the outbreak of the war. This policy statement was taken by the Arabs as one more demonstration of United States endorsement of Israeli occupation of Arab lands. The United States government reiterated its endorsement of Israel's occupation of Arab territories when it asked King Faisal to use his offices to prevail upon Egypt and Syria to withdraw their armies to the cease-fire line of October 6. Once again the Saudis felt that the United States had failed to appreciate the gravity of what was taking place or the historical importance of the October war. In the context of this continued American endorsement of Israeli policies the Saudis informed Aramco that they might be forced to resort to production cutbacks if the United States government increased its support to Israel. It was the fear of such a cutback that led the owners of Aramco to appeal to President Nixon not to increase United States military support to Israel.[3]

While the Aramco owners were appealing to the president, the United States government was deliberating sending military supplies to Israel to replenish losses on the battlefield. An announcement by the State Department on October 15 affirmed that the United States had begun to resupply Israel with aircraft and equipment. This decision left the Saudis with no option but to bend to Arab pressure and to agree to use oil as an instrument of foreign policy.

The Saudi plan, which was adopted on October 17, 1973, by the oil ministers of Arab oil-producing countries (with the exception of Iraq), called for a reduction in oil output until such time as: (1) total evacuation of Israeli forces from all Arab territories occupied during the June 1967 war was completed, and (2) the legitimate rights of the Palestinian people were restored. Because of its historical significance the text of the October 17 ministerial declaration is quoted below in full:

The Arab oil exporting countries contribute to the prosperity of the world and the growth of its economy through their exports of this wasting natural resource. And in spite of the fact that the production of many of these countries has exceeded the levels required by their domestic economies and the energy and revenue needs of their future generations, they have continued to increase their production, sacrificing their own interests in the service of international cooperation and the interests of the consumers.

It is known that huge portions of the territories of three Arab states were forcibly occupied by Israel in the June 1967 war, and it has continued to occupy them in defiance of UN resolutions and various calls for peace from the Arab countries and peace-loving nations.

And although the international community is under an obligation to implement UN resolutions and to prevent the aggressor from reaping the fruits of this aggression and occupation of the territories of other by force, most of the major industrialized countries which are consumers of Arab oil have failed to take measures or to act in such a way as might indicate their awareness of this public international obligation. Indeed, the actions of some countries have tended to support and reinforce the occupation.

Before and during the present war, the United States has been active in supplying Israel with all the means of power which have served to exacerbate its arrogance and enable it to challenge the legitimate rights of others and the unequivocal principles of the public international law.

In 1967, Israel was instrumental in closing the Suez Canal and burdening the European economy with the consequences of this action. In the current war, it hit East Mediterranean oil export terminals, causing Europe another shortfall in supplies. This is the third such occurrence resulting from Israel's disregard of our legitimate rights with US backing and support. The Arabs have therefore been induced to take a decision to discontinue their economic sacrifices in producing quantities of their wasting oil assets in excess of what would be justified by domestic economic considerations, unless the international community hastens to rectify matters by compelling Israel to withdraw from our occupied territory, as well as letting the US know the heavy price which the big industrial countries are having to pay as a result of America's blind and unlimited support for Israel.

Therefore, the Arab oil ministers meeting in Kuwait today have decided to reduce their oil production forthwith by not less than 5 percent of the September (1973) level of output in each Arab oil exporting country, with a similar reduction to be applied each successive month, computed on the basis of the previous month's production until such time as total evacuation of Israeli forces from all Arab territory occupied during the June 1967 war is completed and the legitimate rights of the Palestinian people are restored.

The conferees took care to ensure that reductions in output should not affect any friendly state which has extended or may in the future extend effective concrete assistance to the Arabs. Oil supplies to any such state will be maintained in the same quantities as it was receiving before the reduction. The same exceptional treatment will be extended to any state which takes a significant measure against Israel with a view to obliging it to end its occupation of usurped Arab territories.

The Arab ministers appeal to all the peoples of the world, and particularly the American people, to support the Arab nation in its struggle against imperialism and Israeli occupation. They reaffirm to them the sincere desire of the Arab nation to cooperate fully with all the peoples of the world and their readiness to supply the world with its oil needs as soon as the world shows its sympathy with us and denounces the aggression against us.[4]

Although many countries were in favor of halting oil exports to the United States, the Saudi government prevailed upon other governments to give the United States time to change its policy. The Saudi perception that American foreign policy that was committed to Israel and its occupation of Arab territories could change was proven to be embarrassingly naive when President Nixon forwarded to the Congress a request for $2.2 billion in additional military assistance to Israel only two days after the Kuwait Declaration.

Once again the Saudis had no choice but to go along with those who had already imposed embargoes on oil shipments to the United States. Oil shipments to Holland, Portugal, and South Africa were also embargoed because of these countries' support for Israel. The cutback and embargo measures were accompanied by a classification of oil-importing countries in the following groups: (1) preferred—countries receiving 100 percent of their September 1973 oil imports or their average imports of the first nine months of 1973, whichever was greater, (2) neutral—countries receiving Arab oil imports reduced by the across-the-board output cut, and (3) embargoed—countries that were denied Arab oil. In December 1973 Arab oil-producing countries introduced a fourth category called "most favored," composed of those countries that were to receive current demand requirements as distinguished from the historical demand limitation applied to the preferred list of countries.[5]

One major Arab oil-producing country, Iraq, opted not to join the decision to reduce output but observed the embargo decision against the United States and other embargoed countries. Iraq explained its position in the following terms:

Iraq had not signed the decision cutting back exports by 5 percent, which was taken by the meeting of Arab Oil Ministers held in Kuwait . . . the attitude of the Iraqi delegation to the meeting can be summarized in the following three-point proposal (1) The complete liquidation of US economic interests particularly oil interest, by nationalizing all US companies operating in the Arab homeland. These companies represent US oil interests in the Arab states and were in control of over 63 percent of total Arab crude oil production during the first six months of 1973. Furthermore, they control about 100 percent of the production of certain Arab states possessing vast oil reserves, which fact would increase their control over Arab oil in future. (2) The withdrawal of all funds invested by the Arab states in the United States. These funds are so large that their withdrawal would constitute a blow to American economic interests and weaken the American economy, particularly insofar as the US balance of payments is concerned. (3) Breaking off diplomatic and economic relations between all the Arab oil producing countries and the United States of America.[6]

AN ASSESSMENT OF THE OIL MEASURES

The October 1973 output and embargo measures adopted by Arab oil-producing countries were described in these words: "The overall system of oil embargoes and cutbacks in production was elaborated and proposed by Saudi Arabia through its oil minister, Mr. Ahmad Zaki Yamani. In conception and application it is both simple and effective."[7]

While the system may have been simple, it was far from effective. Before analyzing the reasons for the failure of the system, it would be useful to record the modifications that Arab governments introduced on the embargo measures during the remainder of 1973.

1. A meeting of nine Arab oil ministers in Vienna on November 18 decided to exempt the nine-nation European Economic Community (EEC) from the 5 percent reduction in Arab oil supplies scheduled for December 1973.

2. The Arab Summit Conference, held in Algiers from November 26 to 28, confirmed that the Arab oil embargo and production cutback measures would continue until Israel withdrew from the occupied Arab territories and the national rights of the Palestinian people were restored. The conference also decided that, in recognition of their recent declarations of policy in favor of the Arabs, Japan and the Philippines would be exempted from the effects of the 5 percent cutback in Arab oil production scheduled for December.

3. A meeting of Arab oil ministers held in Kuwait on December 8 issued a resolution stating that "if agreement is reached on withdrawal from all the territories occupied since 1967, foremost amongst them Jerusalem, in accordance with a timetable, which Israel agrees to and whose implementation is guaranteed by the United States, the embargo on exports to the United States will be lifted as soon as the withdrawal programme begins."

4. A meeting of Arab oil ministers held in Kuwait on December 24 and 25 decided to raise the level of Arab oil production by 10 percent with effect from January 1, 1974, thereby reducing the overall cutback in Arab oil exports from its December rate of 25 percent to 15 percent, calculated on the basis of September 1973 production. This decision superseded the earlier one taken on December 8 providing for a further 5 percent cutback in Arab production effective from January 1, 1974. The effect of the latest decision was to decrease the shortfall in Arab oil cutbacks from their December level of about 4.5 million barrels per day to approximately 2.7 million barrels per day as of January 1, 1974.[8]

It can be seen from these changes that the commitment of Arab oil-producing countries to attain certain political goals began to falter and lose credibility soon after the celebrated embargo measures were adopted.

Another aspect of the embargo and cutback measures that weakened their effectiveness was the shuffling of countries between categories. An example of this is the position of the Saudis vis-à-vis Japan. The Saudi government demanded that Japan break off all economic, trade, and diplomatic ties with Israel to ensure full resumption of Arab oil supplies. Japan's response, however, was that it did not have sufficient reason to break ties with Israel. Yet despite the absence of reversal in policy, Japan was elevated from the "neutral" category to the "preferred" category. Nor was Japan the only country that received more oil in exchange for some ineffectual statement. The countries of the European Economic Community represent another case in point. These countries, except for the Netherlands, had been exempted as was noted earlier from the projected December 5 percent reduction. The reason for the exemption was an EEC statement recognizing the desirability of implementing United Nations resolutions on the Arab-Israeli conflict.

A more serious and significant change in Arab oil strategy was the December 8 resolution by the oil ministers that, as was mentioned earlier, committed the oil-producing countries to lift the embargo measures in exchange for an announced program of withdrawal of Israeli forces from occupied Arab territories. The resolution, in other words, made it clear that restoration of the national rights of the Palestinian people ceased to be an objective of the oil strategy. The only focus of policy now was the withdrawal of Israeli forces from occupied territories. Even the withdrawal did not have to take place for the oil measures to be removed. Instead, the Arab governments would be satisfied with a promised phased withdrawal of Israeli forces to be guaranteed by the United States. A few weeks after the December 8 meeting Arab oil ministers met again and decided to introduce more modifications of their oil policies, which in turn diluted the effectiveness of the embargo measures by enabling oil companies to ship more non-Arab oil to the American market.

The change in the Arab position could not have been independent from what Secretary of State Henry Kissinger had to say about United States foreign policy in the Middle East in the period following the October 22 cease-fire. At that time he made it clear that it was inappropriate for Arab leaders to expect the United States to play a major role in arriving at a settlement to the Middle East conflict and to put it under economic pressure at the same time. The Arab leaders, according to Kissinger,

can either give us a reasonable opportunity, once the negotiating process is under way, to see what we can do to make our contribution to bringing about the just and lasting peace to which we have committed ourselves, and which they affirm is their goal as well. Or they can attempt to deal with us by making a series of specific demands backed up by economic pressures. We would not be able to accede to that second procedure. And we believe that for the sake of our future relationships, for the sake of making clear that we conduct our policy for the interests of the general peace, that the first course is by far the more advisable for the Arab leaders. And the decision, of course, is up to them.[9]

In this statement, Kissinger made it clear that the United States government would refuse to engage in a process of a Middle East settlement if the Arab leaders were to continue to make specific demands (Israeli withdrawal from occupied territories and the restoration of Palestinian rights) backed by economic pressures (oil cutbacks and embargo). Although he said that the decision was for the Arab leaders to make, in fact he made the decision for them when he stated that there was only one procedure that he could follow and the Arabs were "advised" to accept.

It should be pointed out that Kissinger's demand was an accurate reflection of the contradictory position of Arab leaders. It was totally inconsistent of the Arab governments to ask the United States to mediate a settlement with Israel while at the same time exerting economic pressures against the "mediator." Those leaders had to choose between American mediation, an effort that would have required the removal of economic sanctions, or the retention of the sanctions and the foregoing of United States mediation.

In January 1974 the United States government succeeded in having Egypt and Israel reach an agreement on the disengagement of their forces. This agreement was viewed by many Arab states, especially Egypt, as evidence that the United States had sufficiently changed its policy toward the conflict to warrant the removal of the embargo. This new stance was reflected in a statement made by Secretary of State Kissinger on January 22 to the effect that the embargo would be lifted before the end of the forty-day period required for the completion of the disengagement. Kissinger went on to say,

We have had every reason to believe that success in the negotiations would mark a major step toward ending the oil embargo. We would therefore think that failure to end the embargo in a reasonable time would be highly inappropriate, and would raise serious questions of confidence in our minds with respect to the Arab nations with whom we have dealt on this issue.[10]

This position statement was echoed on the same day by President Sadat when he asserted that the United States had indeed changed its policy toward the Arab cause:

There is an undertaking on the part of the US to maintain what is called the balance of power in the Middle East and the US is maintaining this commitment in Israel's favor. However on the basis of the experience of the last three months and since Dr. Kissinger's successive trips I can now say that the United States is following a new policy.[11]

As to the ban on Arab oil exports to the United States, Sadat made this observation: "There is a principle that requires the Arabs to match any change in U.S. attitude with a similar change in their policy toward the U.S."[12]

In the following weeks statements by Arab officials indicated that the oil embargo should be lifted and oil cutback measures be removed. The views of

Arab governments were summarized in the following statement by the Saudi oil minister Ahmad Zaki Yamani:

The oil weapon has produced its desired effect—that is, it has stimulated a political change towards the Arabs. . . . There has been a real change in US policy towards the Arab problem for the first time in 25 years. . . . There are now clear political moves on the part of the US, which is the only country with the means to put pressure on Israel.[13]

Although most Arab oil-producing countries were in favor of the removal of the ban on exports, they thought it should be contingent upon sufficient progress toward an Israeli-Syrian disengagement agreement, and that the United States should continue to play an active role in an overall settlement. To underscore this position, most of these governments agreed to a provisional lifting of the ban pending the achievement of satisfactory progress in the Syrian-Israeli disengagement agreement. The main explanation of the decision for a provisional lifting was the perception of the Arab oil producing countries that:

1. The October oil measures proved to be a resounding success in that they brought about the most significant change in U.S. foreign policy vis-à-vis the Arabs in twenty-five years.
2. The Arabs were assured by the United States government that it would continue its effort toward the ultimate objective of the withdrawal of Israel from all occupied territories.
3. The Arab governments thought that if their expectations with respect to the withdrawal and a just settlement of the Palestine question were disappointed, they could always reimpose the oil measures.[14]

But no sooner had the Arab governments agreed to the provisional lifting of the ban than President Nixon made it clear that no strings should be attached to the removal of the embargo, since conditional removal would be counterproductive to future United States peace efforts. This public American position caused the Arab governments to reexamine their decision. When they met in Vienna on March 17–18, the majority decided to lift the embargo unconditionally and indefinitely with Syria and Libya dissenting.[15] And so the five-month period of oil cutback and embargo measures came to an unceremonious end without having accomplished their declared policy objectives of Israeli withdrawal from territories it had occupied in 1967 and the restoration of Palestinian rights.

The economic consequences of the oil measures were also not noted for their effectiveness. The country that was supposed to be affected the most, the United States, was dependent on Arab oil imports for 5 percent of its energy consumption. The indirect impact on the American economy was insignificant, since the oil cutback measures did not last long enough to affect the economies of the industrialized countries that were dependent on the Arab region for their oil imports.

Indeed the "effectiveness" of these measures was summed up by the Saudi minister of state for foreign affairs in the following exchange:

Q: Do you think you have achieved anything with this weapon?

A: Yes, we have achieved a lot. We have received thousands of letters which were neither critical nor insulting to us but which discussed the subject from a positive point of view and expressed satisfaction with what we have achieved.[16]

Ten years after the imposition of the oil measures the Organization of Arab Petroleum Exporting Countries (OAPEC) asked the rhetorical question whether the measures accomplished their objectives. OAPEC's answer was a simple no, since neither comprehensive Israeli withdrawal nor restoration of Palestinian rights was achieved.[17]

While OAPEC's assessment of the 1973 oil measures is correct in that they failed to achieve their objectives, it failed to ask the more important question: "Why did the policy fail to achieve its goals?" In evaluating Arab oil production and embargo measures as a foreign policy instrument to attain certain defined objectives, one is compelled to conclude that the policy contained within it the seeds of its own failure. Arab oil-producing countries agreed to use oil as a political instrument without having devised in advance a plan for such use. The measures to reduce oil output and impose a ban on oil exports were taken on an ad hoc basis and in response to unfolding developments during the war itself. No sooner had a cease-fire been announced between the combatants than the Arab states started to waver on their commitment. The Arab oil-producing countries then found themselves engaged in a series of decisions that diluted the effectiveness of the original oil measures.

More important, the Arab position was one of contradiction. While the declared objective of the oil policy was to force a change in United States policy toward Israeli occupation and the Palestine question, the Arab states placed their confidence in the United States as a mediator. Given the long history of the American-Israeli alliance, one is compelled to conclude that the governments of Arab oil-producing countries were either naive in their understanding of American objectives in the region, or they lacked the seriousness of purpose when they resorted to oil cutbacks and embargo measures. Given the long and complex history of interaction between Arab governments and United States foreign policy practices in the Middle East, one could not, by any stretch of the imagination, say that policymakers in the Arab region are either naive or uninformed with respect to United States foreign policy objectives in the Arab region. This leaves the second explanation, that is, that foreign and oil policymakers were not serious when they announced to the world that their oil measures would remain in effect until the goals of the policy were achieved.

Another factor that explains the lack of seriousness of Arab oil measures is that, as was noted earlier, the oil producers were divided as to the kind of economic response that should be used in the prevailing conditions. Given the position of Saudi Arabia as the most important oil-producing country, however, no policy could have been successful without the endorsement of the Saudis. In other words, it was Saudi Arabia's policy that had to be observed by the other producers. Given the close ideological, political, and economic identification of Saudi Arabia with the United States, it could not have been expected that the Saudi government would do anything that would harm the long-term economic and political interests of the United States in the region. This was evident by the reluctance of the Saudis to join other producers in any action until United States policy toward the conflict gave the Saudis no choice but to adopt temporarily the output reduction and embargo measures outlined above.

At a broader and more realistic level it can be said that any punitive oil policy could not have been sustained for any long period of time given the nature of Arab economic and political systems. In the Arab world of 1973 the bulk of the oil was produced by seven countries—Algeria, Iraq, Libya, Qatar, Saudi Arabia, United Arab Emirates, and Kuwait. Most of these countries, especially the Gulf states, were so deeply integrated in the international economic system and dependent—in political, security, military, and economic terms—on the United States and Britain that it would have been inconceivable for them to sustain their oil embargo. And since Iraq opted not to go along with the embargo, only Algeria and Libya, whose oil exports in 1973 amounted to no more than 11 percent of total OPEC exports, were left. Given the fact that the economies of all Arab oil-producing countries had become by 1973 so dependent on their oil export earnings, it would not be realistic to expect governments to endanger the viability of the political and economic systems of their individual countries for the sake of broader Pan-Arab objectives. This is true whether one speaks of Algeria, Libya, Saudi Arabia, or Kuwait.

In retrospect, the most notable achievements of the October war Arab oil measures turned out to be not the withdrawal of Israel's military forces from Arab lands occupied in 1967 or the restoration to the Palestinians of their national rights. Instead the war and the oil measures led to some far-reaching changes in the international oil industry. These included the oil price explosion of 1973–1974, the transfer of controlling power over national oil sectors to the governments of oil-producing countries, the emergence of balance-of-payments surpluses, the acceleration of spending on development projects in oil-producing countries, and the accentuating of the dichotomy between Arab oil and nonoil states. The war and its related measures also had a far-reaching impact on the political and economic direction of the Arab world as a whole due to the rise in the relative importance of the Gulf states, which reflected the rise in their economic and political power, thanks to the sharp increase in oil revenue. In addition, the October 1973 changes in the oil industry led to the formation under the leadership of the United States of the International Energy Agency (IEA), which sought to coordinate energy policies of the industrial countries.

THE OIL PRICE REVOLUTION

In addressing the oil price revolution, one has to deal with the pricing behavior of the Organization of Petroleum Exporting Countries (OPEC).[18] There were two major changes in the price of crude oil as a result of the October war. The first change was effected by OPEC on October 16, 1973. The other was made effective January 1, 1974. While the first price change can be explained to a considerable extent by the changing market conditions at the time, as well as the events of the war, the second change resulted directly from the October war itself. This is so because the oil measures adopted by Arab oil countries created the market conditions that made it possible for OPEC to decide on the second price change. The section assesses the impact of the various forces on the behavior of the price of crude oil.

As mentioned earlier, OPEC and the oil companies had scheduled oil price negotiations to start on October 8. The decision to negotiate a change in the price was dictated by the fact that the concession agreements were still in effect and the OPEC countries and oil companies were bound by the five-year price agreement that had been negotiated in Tehran in February 1971. Yet as soon as the Tehran Agreement was concluded, certain important changes in the world economy and the energy market combined to render the provisions of the agreement obsolete from the perspective of producing countries. These changes, as explained in the previous chapter, include the collapse of the Bretton Woods international monetary system, the devaluation of the dollar, continued rise in prices of goods imported by oil-producing countries, the entry of the United States in the world market as a major oil importer, conservation policies adopted by certain oil-producing countries, the emergence of oil supply/demand imbalance in the world market, and the continued rise in company profits.

Under these conditions OPEC decided that the terms of the Tehran Agreement were no longer acceptable and that negotiations with the oil companies had to be initiated for the purpose of raising the posted price of Arabian Light, the benchmark price, by $2 per barrel to $5. This OPEC-wide decision to enter into negotiations with the companies was announced on September 16, and the date for the negotiations was set by OPEC to be October 8, 1973. But the outbreak of war on October 6 had the effect of stiffening the position of the OPEC negotiators. The refusal of the oil companies to accede to the $2 price increase, which would have raised government revenue by $1.28 (to $3 per barrel under the then prevailing tax and royalty rates) led OPEC member countries to set the new price unilaterally, effective October 16, 1973, at $5.12 per barrel of Arabian Light. The new price yielded government revenue of $3.04 per barrel.

On October 17, as was indicated earlier, the Arab member governments of OPEC (with the exception of Iraq) decided to reduce their output by 5 percent per month from its September 1973 level. A week later the embargo measures were put into effect.

The impact of the oil cutback measures by the Arab countries on the availability of oil and its price in the international market was what came to be known as the energy or oil crisis. The artificial oil shortage which resulted from the Arab oil measures led to sharp increases in the price of oil in the open market. Iranian oil, for example, was traded at $17 per barrel compared to the $5 official price.

This gap between official and market prices prompted Iran to play a price leadership role at the December 1973 meeting of OPEC by getting other OPEC member countries to agree to raise the benchmark price from $5.11 per barrel (set on October 16, 1973) to $11.65 per barrel effective January 1, 1974. The new price yielded a government revenue of $7 per barrel.[19]

THE OIL CONCESSION SYSTEM AND THE OIL PRICE REVOLUTION

In January 1974 the Arab world found itself in a very strange and new position. These countries together with other OPEC member countries were able to change the distribution of world income in their favor by changing the terms of trade in a unilateral action. Arab governments together with other OPEC member countries found themselves more intimately involved in the international financial system as lenders, foreign aid donors, and recyclers of funds they could not use for the development of their domestic economies.

Suffice it to say, in 1974 alone Saudi Arabia's revenue from oil was $22.6 billion compared with an accumulated total revenue of $15.7 billion for the years 1955 to 1973 and that the same 1974 revenue from oil was over five times its 1973 level. Such sharp increases created considerable opportunities and many problems. One of the major opportunities was the removal of capital as a constraint on economic development, a factor much emphasized in economic literature on development in academic journals, textbooks, and policy recommendations.

In short, the sudden increase in economic power and wealth of a handful of Arab oil-producing countries made it appear as if the entire Arab region was on the verge of real economic change that would help break the intolerable cycle of poverty, underdevelopment, and maldistribution of income and wealth. Such a change, it was thought, could propel the entire Arab region into a new era of progress through a new structure of economic relations and new distribution of human and financial resources among all Arab countries.

Not only were Arab oil-producing countries garnering considerable revenue from oil, but they were also thought of by other developing countries as having engaged in a serious historical experiment that might lead to change in the pattern of relationships between Third World countries and multinational corporations. The decision of October 16, 1973 to set the prices unilaterally and to regulate output resulted in the transfer to the producing countries of two important instruments of control over their economies. This was not merely a change in the distribution of profits and economic rent; it was also a restructuring of power relations away from oil companies and their home governments and in favor of oil-producing countries.

Historically all developing countries have struggled to change to their advantage terms of agreements that had been concluded with multinational corporations to develop natural resources. Invariably when the initial agreements were signed, the bargaining power was one-sided in favor of foreign capital. The concession agreements to explore for and exploit oil resources in the Arab region are an outstanding illustration of this fact. These concessions were either taken from or given by governments that were simply unaware of the potential of oil wealth and were concluded at a time when these governments were either part of an empire or under the political and/or military control of the home government of the multinational enterprise.

While the few Arab oil-producing countries were enjoying the financial benefits of the oil price revolution, the Arab world as a whole was still far from achieving any success on the important issues of Israeli withdrawal from occupied territories and the Palestine question. The beginning of 1974 also witnessed some important changes in inter-Arab affairs that made the attainment of the twin political objectives of the October war and the oil policy measures even more difficult to realize.

In the first place, the Israeli-Egyptian disengagement agreement of January 1974 was not accompanied by a similar agreement between Syria and Israel until oil-producing countries agreed to increase their oil output without having received any indication, formal or informal, that the United States government was about to initiate the necessary policy changes that would make it possible to meet the minimum acceptable demands. On the contrary there was every indication that the United States government was not going to effect any change in policy that would ultimately lead to a comprehensive solution to the Arab-Israeli conflict.[20] Moreover, whatever residue of resistance some Arab governments might have had toward the lifting of the oil embargo and output cutback measures, such resistance was too weak to withstand the combined pressure exerted by the president of Egypt, the president of the United States, and the king of Saudi Arabia.[21]

More important, the Arab governments accepted as early as October 1973 the thrust of the American approach toward dealing with the Arab-Israeli conflict. Secretary of State Henry Kissinger never hesitated to tell any Arab leader that the Middle East and its conflict was only one of the world problems that the United States government as a superpower had to deal with. Nor did he tell Arab governments that the United States government was in favor of a comprehensive settlement approach. On the contrary the United States government was very clear on this issue. As former Secretary of State Henry Kissinger put it, "The step-by-step approach pursued by the United States attempted to separate the Middle East problem into individual and therefore manageable segments. With respect to frontiers and all other issues, our policy up to now has been to try to segment them into as many individual issues as we can, because we thought this was more manageable."[22] To accept the segmented approach implied that any party to the conflict might exercise a veto power over a proposed settlement.

As to the Arab oil-producing countries, the impact of the higher oil prices and revenue shifted their attention almost totally from the Arab-Israeli conflict and the Palestine question to matters of managing money, petrodollars, infrastructures, and similar financial and economic concerns. Thus the importance and the declared objectives of the October war, which contributed so much to the creation of wealth and income for the oil-producing countries, was lost in the euphoria of high prices and petrodollar surpluses that the war created. It is important to stress in this connection that once the oil measures were removed, there was no way to reimpose them.

PETROFUNDS AND INTERNATIONAL FINANCE

One of the more important consequences of the oil price revolution for Arab oil-producing countries was the emergence of significant balance-of-payments surpluses. Oil export earnings in the aftermath of the price increases were in excess of expenditures on foreign goods and services. This phenomenon was neither surprising nor new. Countries such as Kuwait, Saudi Arabia, United Arab Emirates, and Libya were already accumulating assets in the money and capital markets of the industrialized countries, and the sudden increase in income that could not be matched immediately by a corresponding increase in expenditures on imports resulted in an acceleration in the accumulation process. Surpluses that were attributed to the oil price revolution came to be known as the OPEC surplus or OPEC funds or OPEC petrodollars or petrofunds, although most such funds were being accumulated by Saudi Arabia and Kuwait and to a lesser extent by the United Arab Emirates and Qatar. It should be noted that the second increase in the price of crude oil, which occurred at a time when the world economy and oil-importing countries were trying to adjust to the first increase, added a new dimension of urgency to the question of balance-of-payments surpluses. This in turn gave rise to discussion of the effects of these surpluses on the stability of the international financial system. Most of the concerns were either speculative, wrong, or prejudicial.

One of the wildest speculative forecasts of OPEC surplus came from none other than the World Bank, which estimated that OPEC-accumulated external assets would reach $659 billion in 1980 and $1.2 trillion in 1985.[23] Other organizations such as Morgan Guaranty Trust Company and the Organization for Economic Cooperation and Development (OECD) published estimates of OPEC surpluses that were far more realistic than the grossly exaggerated World Bank guesses. According to OECD forecasts, OPEC surplus was estimated to decline to a mere $15 billion by 1980. Morgan Guaranty's own estimate of 1975 indicated that the OPEC surplus would decline to $17 billion in 1978, from its $68 billion level in 1974, with total accumulation of assets of $178 billion by 1980.[24] Interestingly enough, the estimates made by Morgan Guaranty turned out to be the closest to what actually took place. Data for 1978 show that OPEC surplus declined to $3 billion and the surplus would have actually turned into deficit in the following year had the second oil price jump of 1979–1980 not occurred. According to data released by the International Monetary Fund, current account surplus of all OPEC member countries declined from a peak of $68 billion in 1974, the first full year of the new prices, to only $3 billion in 1978 with a total accumulation of $177 billion. The six major Arab oil-exporting countries' share of this total was 92 percent, or $168 billion. The countries responsible for this surplus were Saudi Arabia, Kuwait, the United Arab Emirates, Qatar, Libya, and Iraq.[25]

THE DISPOSITION OF THE SURPLUS

One of the most important considerations to dominate discussions in the wake of the oil price increase was the mechanism for the disposition of the OPEC surplus or the recycling of oil revenue. Since most of the OPEC surplus was owned by the six major oil-exporting countries (especially Saudi Arabia followed by Kuwait), the problem was reduced to how should these countries dispose of their surplus. The question had several nonfinancial dimensions. In the first place, industrialized countries were not accustomed to having balance-of-payments deficits with Third World countries, who traditionally were the ones to have chronic balance-of-payments deficits. The fact that there were sizable funds available to be recycled and owned by developing countries gave rise to unwarranted concern, real or imaginary, over actions that these countries might take and that may have some destabilizing effects on the international financial system. This unfounded concern was given credence by pronouncements of certain political figures and the mass media in the West, who engaged in speculative rhetoric over the danger of having so much money at the disposal of Arab money managers.

The disposition of the surplus took several forms, the most important of which was the placement of funds in the money and capital markets of industrialized countries. According to Jahangir Amuzegar, the disposition of the surplus took place under four main considerations: safety and liquidity of invested assets; preservation of the assets' purchasing power; placement of the surplus under the oil-exporting countries' limited human and institutional resources; and the need to help other nonoil developing countries. Given these considerations, it was not surprising that close to 84 percent of the surplus found its way to industrial economies in the form of financial investment in Eurocurrency markets, bank deposits, and government securities. Another 13 percent of the surplus went to developing countries in the form of loans and grants, with the balance being channeled to the World Bank and International Monetary Fund (IMF) to be used in the lending operations of these institutions.[26]

What about economic assistance to oil-poor Arab countries? The record indicates that most of the aid that Arab oil-producing countries provided did indeed go to other Arab countries. This is shown by the fact that during the period 1974–1981 between 64 percent and 92 percent of Arab official development assistance, which ranged between $4.5 billion and $9 billion, went to Arab countries. Looking at the data from a different angle, we find that total Arab official development assistance in this period amounted to $53 billion at a time when cumulative Arab oil revenue amounted to $875 billion. In other words, Arab development assistance to all countries, both Arab and non-Arab, amounted to only 6 percent of their oil revenue.[27]

Investing the bulk of the surplus in Western capital and financial markets was only logical, given the nature of economic and political dependency of most Arab regimes as well as the nature of monetary and financial arrangements between the Arab oil-producing countries and the industrialized countries. Leaving political considerations aside, it can be said that the nature of the international financial system was such that no other outcome could have occurred.

Arab oil-producing countries like most countries of the Third World evolved their monetary and financial network not among themselves but rather with industrial countries. This was due primarily to the colonial heritage of these countries. Their monetary systems and central banks were created, developed, and staffed by personnel from industrial countries: Britain, France, and the United States. Arab money managers and bankers were trained in the money, academic, and financial institutions of industrial countries. This identification with the Western system of finance insured the placement of Arab funds in this system. To do otherwise would have required comprehensive political and ideological reorientation, for which Arab regimes and Arab government money managers were neither willing nor prepared. The central force in all Arab economies as they are currently organized is the fact that they function at the periphery of the major economic centers—Western Europe, the United States, and Japan.

Investing Arab surplus in the West raised a host of other problems and issues that Arab governments chose not to tackle at the Pan-Arab level. One such issue, for instance, was the cost of imported oil to nonoil Arab countries. Like all other developing countries, nonoil Arab countries had to divert a larger portion of their foreign exchange earnings to pay for imported oil. The resulting balance-of-payments deficit meant that these countries had to increase their external debt, which in turn meant they had to resort to borrowing in the same money and capital markets where Arab oil surplus countries placed their petrofunds. Borrowing governments had to pay a higher interest rate on their borrowed funds than the surplus countries were receiving. This was to be expected, since the financial system must levy a charge for its services and profits. Arab oil-importing countries were in effect supplying a portion of the interest earnings of the surplus countries. More significantly, by forcing Arab oil-importing countries to resort to the international financial system, oil-producing countries in effect increased the dependency of borrowing countries on the international financial system.

The traditional reliance of Arab money managers on the Western banking system was so strong that even when a network of Arab international financial institutions emerged, it could not compete with the old system of placing funds in American and European banks, which continued almost unabated. This practice of discrimination by Arab governments against Arab banks elicited the following criticism from the Arab international banking community:

By 1979, however, although Arab banks and consortia had become well established in international centers like Paris and London, several of the original objectives conceived by Arab shareholders in the early consortia banks remained elusive. In particular, Arab banks were still not managing a significant proportion of their own funds. . . . Arab banks had yet to convince their own finance ministers that they offered as secure and well managed a portfolio deposit outlet for OPEC surplus funds as the large U.S. and European banks.[28]

THE FIRST NINETY DAYS AFTER THE OCTOBER WAR

In retrospect, the first ninety days following the outbreak of the October war were of crucial importance in setting the stage for the kind of Arab world that emerged in the following decade and for the successive failures—both political and economic—of Arab governments since then. Why? Although the full answer to this question must await subsequent analysis, some preliminary observations can be made at this stage.

Given the centrality of oil for the economies of both oil-producing and oil-importing countries, any attempt to use oil as an instrument of political pressure should not be undertaken lightly. Opportunities for the effective use of oil as a tool of foreign policy are rare. Indeed they must be. Such an opportunity did present itself in October 1973. But once oil was considered essential for the attainment of the objectives of the war effort, then the economic consequences had to be accepted. But to do that would have required a meaningful Pan-Arab unified political and economic decision-making process. Such a process was conspicuous by its absence.

Politically, Arab oil-producing countries were not prepared to use their only instrument of economic pressure. The sweeping commitment that output would be reduced monthly until such time as Arab territories were evacuated and Palestinian rights were recognized was violated shortly after it was made. Oil output was raised before the conclusion of the disengagement agreement between Israel and Egypt. Once the solemn commitment was broken, it was clear that Arab governments were not serious in their political and economic decisions. The Palestinians were excluded from political and diplomatic deliberations although the measures were supposedly taken in their behalf. Major decisions were made by Saudi Arabia and Egypt. The Saudis were only too happy to accept Egypt's verdict that the United States government had changed its policy toward the region in order for them to relax the oil restriction. In this way the whole question of the oil weapon ceased to be an Arab instrument of economic pressure to attain certain political ends. Instead Arab oil measures were reduced to being a bilateral arrangement between President Sadat and King Faisal. Since both leaders were anxious to have the United States government play the role of mediator in the conflict between the government of Egypt and the government of Israel, it was very clear that they had no choice but to agree to relax and/or remove the oil restrictions as soon as the United States demanded that they be relaxed.

The relaxation of the oil measures under United States government threats that it would not involve itself in the dispute between Israel and Egypt proved to be the first in a series of threats that influenced oil and nonoil policy deliberations and decisions. Once the initial demands of the United States were complied with, it turned out to be only a few weeks when the whole edifice of output cutback and embargo measures was abandoned without accomplishing any of their stated objectives.

Once the political issues were abandoned, Arab oil-producing countries turned their attention to the management of the sharp increase in oil revenues and the balance-of-payments surpluses that had to emerge, since their economies did not have the capacity to absorb all oil export earnings that the oil price revolution produced. Given the nature of the political and economic systems of the Arab countries and their historical evolution, it was not surprising that the governments of oil-producing countries turned their attention to the industrial countries for goods and services to import and for outlets for their balance-of-payments surplus. The rise in oil exports, oil revenues, and the emergence of balance-of-payments surpluses had the effect of deepening Arab dependency on the international economic systems along three distinct lines. First, the mere quantitative rise in oil exports and oil export earnings caused the economies of these countries to be more dependent on one sector to the exclusion of other goods-producing sectors. Yet the oil sector, although formally now under the control of governments, was in the last analysis subject to fluctuations in world demand for oil. Thus efficiency and conservation in consuming countries, emergence of new sources of oil, and interfuel substitution away from oil were factors over which producing countries had no control. Indeed all these factors were combined by the 1980s to exert downward pressure on the demand for Arab oil and cause prices to fall drastically. The vulnerability of Arab economies, in other words, intensified as the relative importance of the oil sector increased. Second, the availability of foreign exchange induced the oil countries to expand their imports of consumer goods, services, capital goods, and arms at accelerated rates for both public and private sectors. This increase in imports created a whole range of dependency relations on the industrial countries, thus exposing Arab economies to yet another form of dependency. It would be no exaggeration to say that ultimately the viability of the economies and the political systems of Arab oil-exporting countries became increasingly dependent on the assured inflow of goods and services from industrial countries. Third, the placement of petrodollars in industrial country financial markets meant that the purchasing power of these funds was subject to currency fluctuations, inflation, and interest rate changes over which oil-producing countries have no control nor do they have any recourse for compensation in case of loss in purchasing power. According to Ali Tawfik Sadik the accumulated surplus of Arab oil-producing countries amounted to $355 billion for the period 1972–1981. But if one were to adjust the surplus to these countries' 1972 import price index, the real value of the surplus would decline to only $160 billion. Applying the same import price index to oil revenue for the period 1970 to 1982, Sadik's computations show that these countries' oil revenue, which amounted to $1.039 trillion, was worth $452 billion in 1972 prices.[29] It should be clear from this outline that far from attaining its political objectives or even enhancing political and economic independence, the oil price revolution seems to have increased the links between oil-producing countries and the industrialized countries with the consequent rise in their dependency on the West.

NOTES

1. See Ian Seymour, *OPEC: An Instrument of Change* (London: Macmillan Press, 1980), 110.

2. Ibid.

3. U.S. Senate Committee on Foreign Relations, Subcommittee on Multinational Corporations, *Multinational Corporations and United States Foreign Policy*, Pt. 7 (Washington, D.C.: Government Printing Office, 1974), 546–47. Henceforth, *MNC Hearings*.

4. See *Middle East Economic Survey (MEES)*, October 19, 1973, pp. iii–iv. According to Walid Khadduri this was the first time that Arab oil ministers agreed with the approval of Saudi Arabia to link oil exports to the Palestine question. See his "Arab Oil Decisions for the Years 1973–1974: A Study of Arab Decision Making" (in Arabic), in *How Decisions Are Made in the Arab Nation* (Beirut: Centre for Arab Unity Studies, 1985), 181–226, especially pp. 209–210.

5. Seymour, *OPEC*, 116–121.

6. See *MEES*, October 26, 1973, 4.

7. See F. Itayim, "Arab Oil—The Political Dimension," *Journal of Palestine Studies* 3, no. 2 (Winter 1974): 84–97.

8. Ibid.

9. See *MEES*, November 23, 1973, 10.

10. See *MEES*, January 25, 1974, p. x.

11. Ibid, 2.

12. Ibid.

13. See *MEES*, March 15, 1974, 10–11.

14. *MEES*, March 15, 1974 (Supplement), 2–3.

15. *MEES*, March 22, 1974, 1–5.

16. *MEES*, February 22, 1974, 4.

17. "Ten Years After the Oil Embargo" (in Arabic), *OAPEC Bulletin*, October 1983, 1.

18. OPEC, as was mentioned earlier, was founded in 1960 by Iraq, Saudi Arabia, Kuwait, Iran, and Venezuela. In addition to these five founding members its membership at present includes Qatar, the United Arab Emirates, Libya, Algeria, Indonesia, Nigeria, Ecuador, and Gabon. It is to be noted that the Arab member countries produced 64 percent of OPEC's total crude oil output.

19. For a more comprehensive treatment of the 1973–1974 price increases, see Seymour, *OPEC*, chapter 5.

20. See Edward Shaheen, "Step-By-Step in the Middle East," *Journal of Palestine Studies* 5, no. 3 & 4 (Spring/Summer 1976): 5–53.

21. See *MEES*, February 15, 1974, pp. 1–2, and March 1, 1974, p. xii.

22. *U.S. Department of State, Selected Documents No. 4* (Washington, D.C.: Government Printing Office, 1976), 20.

23. *The New York Times*, February 13, 1975, 50.

24. *MEES*, January 31, 1975, 8.

25. See International Monetary Fund, *World Economic Outlook 1983* (Washington, D.C.). It is to be noted that the World Bank's inflated projections could not of course have foreseen the second oil price revolution of the early 1980s, which pushed the price of Arabian Light to $34 per barrel. Taking the balance-of-payments effects of the higher prices of the 1980s, it is interesting to note that according to estimates prepared by the Bank of England all of OPEC's accumulated surpluses amounted to $456 billion at the end of June 1988. See *MEES*, February 20, 1989, B3.

26. See Jahangir Amuzegar, *Oil Exporters' Economic Development in an Interdependent World* (Washington, D.C.: International Monetary Fund, 1983), 63. Nor did the pattern change in subsequent years. Thus by the end of 1987 all oil-exporting countries had accumulated $473 billion. Of this only $60 billion or 13 percent was placed in developing countries with the remaining balance placed in the traditional markets of the industrialized countries. See *MEES*, May 23, 1988, B4.

27. For a detailed analysis of Arab economic aid see Mohammed Imady, "Patterns of Arab Economic Aid to Third World Countries," *Arab Studies Quarterly* nos. 1 & 2 (Winter/Spring 1984): 75–123. See also Ali Tawfik Sadik, "Managing the Petrodollar Bonanza: Avenues and Implications of Recycling Arab Capital," Ibid, 13–38.

28. Abdulla A. Saudi, "Arab Banking and the Eurocurrency Market," *OAPEC Bulletin* (August/September 1982), 19.

29. See Sadik, "Managing The Petrodollar Bonanza," 28–34.

6

THE ROLE OF SAUDI ARABIA AND THE UNITED STATES IN THE FALL OF OPEC

The failure of the Arab oil weapon was inevitable, given the nature of the dependency of individual economies on the oil sector and the broader pattern of security, political, economic, and cultural dependence on the industrial countries especially the United States. The multiple dependency linkages in virtually every facet of interaction between the Arab countries and the United States mitigated any genuinely independent actions by Arab governments. Arab governments were not only incapable of acting against United States interests, but they were unwilling to do so, given the long history of close alliances between Arab ruling elites on the one hand and the United States government on the other. From the perspective of any Arab government, there were no compelling reasons to act against their own self-interests by antagonizing the United States or undermining its interests in the region. Even the decades-old Arab-Israeli conflict was construed to be neither a sufficient nor a necessary condition to change the nature of dependent relations with the United States. An analysis of the actions of the Saudi government in the post–1973 oil price revolution will shed some light on the degree of Arab government reliance on the United States.

THE REGIONAL CONTEXT OF SAUDI ARABIA

The kingdom of Saudi Arabia occupies a special position of influence in the Arab region because of its geographical location, its role in influencing inter-Arab affairs, its leadership role in the creation of the Gulf Cooperation Council, and its special position in the Islamic world. In addition, the unique manner in which its oil sector was developed by American multinational oil corporations; the extraordinary size of its oil reserve endowment; the relative importance of its oil output within the Arab world, the Middle East, OPEC, and world output;

and the size of its invested foreign assets gave it an especially powerful role within the councils of OPEC. On the other hand, the kingdom suffers from certain structural difficulties. These include heavy dependence on oil; the absence of an industrial base; a small population; the lack of economic, administrative, and technocratic infrastructures; and heavy reliance on foreign labor.

These special features made it necessary for the kingdom's ruling family to involve itself in the affairs of the Arab and the Muslim worlds as well as in the direction and policies of OPEC in order to protect the kingdom's economic and political institutions from regional and global forces of change. For a long time the Saudis were able to stay out of most regional politics and shifting Arab alliances. The Saudis also managed to stay away from the major Western power rivalry that shaped so much of the evolution of the Arab region. Yet the Saudis could not remain completely insulated from forces of change in the region and the world for too long.

One such important force of change was the decision by the major world powers, first Britain and then the United States, to help the Zionist movement to create the state of Israel in Palestine. Since the Saudis looked upon themselves as guardians on behalf of the world's Muslims of the holy places in Palestine, the Saudis had no choice but to view the creation of Israel as a direct challenge not only to their Arab credentials but also to their special position within the Muslim world.

Another factor that drew Saudi Arabia to the Arab region's affairs was its emergence as an important oil-producing country. When multinational oil companies decided in the 1940s to push for a major expansion in Saudi oil output, one major outlet for Saudi oil exports was the loading terminals on the Mediterranean. Another major route was through the Suez Canal. In order to bring Saudi oil to the Mediterranean, it was necessary to build pipelines across the territories of Jordan, Lebanon, and Syria. This meant that the flow of Saudi oil was exposed to political events and wars outside Saudi national territory and thus beyond Saudi control. Since such interruptions were directly related to the Arab-Israeli conflict, the Saudis became influential in affecting political decisions in the Arab region.

The most powerful contributing factor to the emergence of Saudi Arabia as an important force in the Arab region was the immense reserves of oil that happened to be located in that country. Equally important was the fact that Saudi oil deposits were discovered and developed by United States–based multinational oil corporations. Saudi Arabia was the only oil-producing country in the Middle East whose oil was under the exclusive control of American corporations (first Socal alone, then Socal and Texaco, and then Exxon and Mobil in addition to Socal and Texaco).

The importance of the Saudi concession derives from its duration, the size of its reserves, the territories it covers, and its uniquely American character. It also derives from the intimate association of the United States government with the concession itself and with the Saudi Arabian government when the latter, together with Aramco, appealed to the United States government in 1941 to provide the Saudis with financial help. As was seen in an earlier chapter, President Roosevelt found it in United States interests to authorize the use of Lend-Lease funds to provide economic assistance to the government of Saudi Arabia by declaring that the defense of Saudi Arabia was vital to the defense of the United States.

This triangular arrangement among the Saudi government, the United States government, and American oil interests set the stage for a strong pattern of dependency relationships for Saudi Arabia, which was to be enhanced by the impact of the oil price revolution. But this dependency status placed the Saudi regime in a position where it had to explain or justify or rationalize or even attempt to change the thrust of American foreign policy in the Arab region. The Saudis found themselves in the indefensible position of having to balance the contradictions between their special arrangements with the United States government and their special position in both the Arab and the Muslim worlds. No issue has tested the special relationship between the Americans and the Saudis more than the Palestine question. The Israeli policies of occupation and expansion, which continued to receive the support of the United States government, placed the Saudis in a very difficult position vis-à-vis the mainstream Arab nationalist movement. In performing their balancing act, the Saudis tended to concentrate on three major policy approaches in the Arab region. First, they maintained that oil and politics were separate and that oil should not be used as an instrument of political pressure. Second, the Saudis have always appealed to the United States government to modify and/or change its policy toward the Arab region. Third, the Saudis used their oil income to provide loans and grants to certain Arab governments in order to influence policy in a direction that would be compatible with Saudi interests and United States foreign policy in the Arab region.

THE 1974 UNITED STATES–SAUDI AGREEMENT ON SPECIAL RELATIONSHIP

The year 1974 witnessed significant changes in the relationship between Saudi Arabia and the United States. The Saudis believed that they needed the United States as a major political ally and protector against what they considered to be forces of radicalism and extremism. They were also committed to the proposition that United States–based corporations and American technology should play an active role in the process of economic development. Oil was looked at as an exhaustible natural resource to be used as an agent for economic diversification and development. The Saudis looked upon American technology, management, capital equipment, arms corporations, and so on as necessary requisites for change. The mutuality of interests, both political and economic, was clear and compelling. The Saudis would expand their oil output to meet the needs of the world and sell such oil at a reasonable price in exchange for American protection and assistance in accelerating the process of economic development diversification.

The main (and perhaps the only) problem between the two governments was the total endorsement by the United States of Israeli policies in the Arab region. This commitment and Saudi political interests in the Arab region gave rise to certain conflicts between the two governments. Those conflicts however were subordinated by the Saudis to their overall national interests. An example of this is the Saudis' decision to reverse themselves and raise oil output as early as December 1973 and to advocate lifting the embargo soon thereafter. It is significant to note that while the embargo measures were supposed to be in effect, the Saudi government was engaged in negotiations with the United States government over important bilateral arrangements. These negotiations led to the conclusion of the Saudi Arabian–American cooperation treaty of June 8, 1974, which was introduced by the following statement:

Following the joint announcement of April 5, 1974, in which Saudi Arabia and the United States expressed their readiness to expand cooperation in the fields of economics, technology, and industry and in the supply of the Kingdom's requirements for defensive purposes. The visit also provided an opportunity to review the current status of United States efforts currently underway to work towards a just and lasting solution in the Middle East in accordance with UN principles and resolutions. Both sides expressed satisfaction with the progress made and expressed their hope for continuing early progress in this regard.[1]

Once the Saudis disposed of the political issues facing them by expressing their satisfaction with United States efforts toward a solution of the Arab-Israeli conflict, the path was cleared for an intensification of the special relationship. Thus the United States was to play a major role in a wide variety of Saudi economic, military, and social affairs. These included but were not limited to:

1. The creation of a Joint Commission on Economic Cooperation whose purpose would be to promote programs on industrialization, trade, manpower training, agriculture, and science and technology.
2. The formation of a United States–Saudi Industrial Development Council.
3. Mutual cooperation in the field of finance.
4. The establishment of a joint commission to review programs already under way for modernizing Saudi Arabia's armed forces.
5. Entering into an agreement that would facilitate the transfer of technical and advisory services.[2]

The extent of American involvement in the very process of change in Saudi Arabia can be appreciated by looking at the following partial list of projects that were to be implemented by the U.S. government and United States–based corporations:[3]

- supply assistance to the national airline
- develop a nationwide data bank system
- supply and maintain hospital equipment
- build roads and harbors
- manage and construct the Riyadh airport
- manage the national bus system
- operate and maintain the national telex system
- supply refrigeration systems for supermarkets
- supply cable systems
- design and construct fertilizer plants
- design, construct, and manage petrochemical complexes
- supply water treatment plants
- build university campuses
- design and construct an export refinery
- computerize customs posts
- construct desalination plants
- construct sewage plants

OIL REVENUE AND MILITARY EXPENDITURES

The oil price revolution of the 1970s made it possible for Saudi Arabia and other oil-producing countries to avail themselves of their newly found wealth to build their infrastructures, expand social services, and attempt to develop their economies. In addition to spending on the civilian economy, the availability of funds and foreign exchange prompted the government of Saudi Arabia, as well as those of other oil-producing countries, to increase their military expenditures and their imports of arms and other weapon systems.

It is worth remembering that arms sales to the countries of the Third World are not simple or one-time commercial transactions. In addition to their being commercial transactions, arms sales to the countries of the Third World are undertaken for political and strategic considerations as well. An arms supplier, normally a major industrial country, seeks political and economic advantage over other suppliers. The long cycle of delivery, training, and maintenance puts the supplier in a privileged position. The dependency of the arms-receiving country is continued through the provision of training, supply of spare parts, and the supply of ever more sophisticated and complex arms. The numerous links between the military complexes of both countries give rise to other forms of dependency. And since the cost of these arms packages is high, Third World countries find themselves constantly diverting larger and larger shares of their export earnings to meet the cost of arms imports.

In the case of the government of Saudi Arabia these factors and more were at work when the oil revenue explosion occurred. The availability of foreign exchange and the expanded armed forces and military facilities made the presence of the United States in the life of Saudi Arabia a permanent condition. The United States government and United States–based multinational corporations were producing the Saudi Arabian oil, selling it in the world market, advising on every facet of the Saudi economy, selling consumer and capital goods, providing financial investment outlets for Saudi petrofunds, and equipping and training Saudi armed forces.

The magnitude of Saudi expenditure on arms and on the military may be appreciated from the following observations and data. In 1974, the first full year after the 1973 sharp rise in oil prices, Saudi Arabia's military expenditures amounted to $2.6 billion or 7.5 percent of the value of Saudi oil exports. By 1985 Saudi military expenditures amounted to nearly $23 billion and absorbed more than 88 percent of the value of petroleum exports. It may be useful to note that military expenditures in 1985 absorbed 3.8 percent of the combined GNP of NATO Europe and 10.7 percent of the GNP of the Warsaw Pact countries. On a per capita basis the kingdom's military spending increased from $371 in 1974 to $1,708 in 1985. Saudi Arabia alone accounted for less than 14 percent of the military expenditures in the Middle East in 1974. By 1985 it was responsible for 31 percent of the region's total military expenditure. Interestingly the sharp rise in military spending was not associated with a similar rise in the size of the kingdom's military forces. In 1974 the size of its armed forces was 75,000 compared to 96,000 in 1985. This means that military spending per soldier increased from close to $35,000 in 1974 to $238,000 in 1985.[4] The obvious disparity between the size of the armed forces on the one hand and military spending on the other indicates that the increase in the latter was allocated for the purchase of weapon systems, arms, and support programs.

The other side of this picture is the sales that these expenditures generated for arms suppliers. These supplies ranged from the obvious—hardware, weapons, aircraft, missiles, munitions, and so on—to military support programs. The support programs included airfields, naval and military schools, ranges and ports, family housing and schools, roads and utilities, and medical and industrial facilities.

The United States supplied 51 percent of Saudi arms imports during the period 1970–1974 when the Saudi arms imports averaged only $.3 billion. The United States share of the Saudi arms imports market increased to 79 percent during the period 1975–1979 when the imports averaged $2.8 billion per year. The increase in Saudi arms imports together with the increase in Iranian arms imports raised the U.S. share of the Middle East arms imports from 34 percent in the 1970–1974 period to 61 percent in the 1975–1979 period.[5] The significance of purchase of American arms is reflected in the fact that of the $53.1 billion of American arms sales abroad during the period 1977–1982, Saudi Arabia alone absorbed $19.2 billion or 36 percent of the total.[6]

One of the most significant aspects of military sales to countries like Saudi

Arabia is the importance of the highly skilled labor that is needed to operate and maintain the weapon systems. The F–15 fighter bomber, for instance, of which Saudi Arabia had purchased sixty, required some 4,800 personnel to keep them operative with 95 percent of this labor force falling in the highly skilled categories.[7] This means that the Saudis had either to divert manpower from the civilian sector or import foreign personnel. Since Saudi Arabia relies on foreign labor in practically every part of its public and private sectors, it follows that such sophisticated weapon systems had to be manned by imported skilled workers, in this case Americans, whose cost did not enter into the calculation of arms imports. It has been estimated there is in Saudi Arabia one American adviser for every six members of Saudi Arabia's armed forces.[8]

POLITICAL DIMENSIONS OF THE SALE OF SOPHISTICATED ARMS

The significance of the sale of fighter bombers to the Saudis by the United States goes beyond the importance of Saudi Arabia as a market for American military goods and services or the desire to accelerate the recycling of petrofunds to United States money and capital markets. The sale of sophisticated planes was decided upon by the United States government as part of a package involving Saudi Arabia, Egypt, and Israel. There were several political and strategic considerations that motivated the United States to do so. It should be observed that by early 1978, when the sale of the F–15 was being processed officially, Egypt had already decided to conclude a peace treaty with Israel following President Sadat's visit to that country in November 1977. It was important for United States policy in the region that Saudi Arabia be given American support in order to draw it into the Israeli-Egyptian negotiations. The Carter administration, which had sponsored and encouraged the Sadat initiative, believed that it was in the "interest of Israel and the U.S." that Egypt and Saudi Arabia receive those jet fighters. Such a sale, it was postulated, would promote peace in the Arab region, and the planes were regarded as rewards to these moderate Arab regimes considered to be pro-American and pro-West. It was also thought to be advantageous for the United States and Israel that the Saudis buy their planes from the United States rather than from France or England because the Saudis agreed to abide by certain conditions relative to the positioning and the operating of the fighters. These conditions involved a clear compromise of the sovereignty of the state of Saudi Arabia over its own territories. The United States government was therefore secure in the knowledge that it would always have the option of not providing spare parts for the Saudis, should they consider ignoring the American stipulations.[9]

The restrictions placed on the Saudis' freedom to use these planes were so severe as to render the Saudi ownership devoid of any military importance. As one observer put it: "The Saudis will have an F–15 in name only, not in actual operational capability. . . . For the Saudis, the F–15 is a prestige item."[10]

But from the United States perspective the importance of the sale of the fighters to the three countries was that the United States would be in a position to shape the future military balance in the Middle East. If there were any real or imagined fears that the sale might affect Israeli military superiority in the region, they were put to rest by Secretary of Defense Harold Brown when he said: "Israel's forces have grown to 150 percent of their 1973 strength and have been modernized. . . . It is the judgement of the Defense Department—myself, the Joint Chiefs of Staff—that Israel could defeat any combination of likely opposing forces."[11]

The sale of the F–15 fighters to the Saudis was followed in 1981 by another sale of major proportion. This was the sale of five Airborne Warning and Control System (AWACS), a sale that was described as the single most massive weapons deal in American history. These five planes were estimated to have cost the Saudis $6 billion or $1.2 billion apiece (compared with $220 million apiece for which the United States government was prepared to sell to the shah of Iran).[12] Again, the AWACS had to be operated by American personnel, and the freedom of the Saudis to operate these intelligence-gathering stations was restricted by the terms of the sale. They were also considered to represent a prestige symbol for the Saudis. In the words of one Pentagon official: "Like the Iranians they have gorgeous facilities, fully stocked. But let us face it, they will be run by contractors forever."[13]

The importance of Saudi Arabia as a market for American arms sales and American skills is matched by the conviction that American-built bases and American-supplied arms were designed to be used, should the need arise, by the United States. The decision to sell the AWACS was made "to build surrogate bases in Saudi Arabia, equipped and waiting for American forces to use."[14] The president and the national security adviser at the time argued in favor of the sale on the grounds that the sale would "assure the presence of the United States in Saudi Arabia's security future."[15] A former ambassador to Saudi Arabia also supported the sale, saying that the AWACS would give the United States a "flying base in the region and the Saudis would have the privilege of paying for it."[16]

The belief that these AWACS would bolster the American strategic position in the Arab region in the aftermath of the collapse of the Iranian monarchy was viewed by the administration as follows:

The tough-minded Reagan administration, however, wanted a permanent U.S. military presence in the region that could respond to any crisis almost immediately. Above all, they believed that an American presence would both deter domestic insurgents from striking and provide Arab "moderates" with the confidence to act to preserve internal stability. President Reagan, for example, when asked by reporters in October whether he would "side openly" with the ruling Saudi family in case of revolt "and help to suppress it," simply answered "it won't happen if we're evident there." The basic problem facing the Reagan White House team was how to obtain a U.S. Middle East

presence at a time when nationalist sensibilities prohibited Arab governments from granting foreign bases. The AWACS deal, in part, provided the solution.

The 24th August State Department background paper illuminated how AWACS would
bolster U.S. military capabilities in the region. First, the paper asserted, the AWACS
package would make the Saudis more forthcoming on reaching the "kinds of security
cooperation, joint planning, combined exercises, and advanced preparation needed if the
U.S. is to defend shared interest in the Gulf." Second, the AWACS would provide the
support needed for U.S. intervention forces. AWACS, wrote the state department, "will
provide the basis for a comprehensive military command, control, communications and
logistics infrastructure which could be compatible with U.S. tactical forces, capabilities
and requirements and could become the nucleus of support for U.S. forces if we are
asked by regional states to respond to a crisis." Third, it would necessitate the introduction
of at least 360 American personnel into Saudi Arabia who would "maintain key elements
of the System for its entire life."[17]

To summarize, the evolution of the oil sector in Saudi Arabia and by extension
the Saudi economy has always been closely linked to the American economy,
American-based multinational oil corporations, and United States government
policy objectives in the Arab region. Indeed, at an earlier stage in the evolution
of the kingdom, the United States took over from the oil companies the task of
providing the Saudi budget with direct subsidy under the Lend-Lease program.

The oil revenue explosion created an opportunity for the deepening and broadening of economic, military, technological, and cultural links between the United
States and Saudi Arabia. The Saudi economy and the Saudi military forces
became highly dependent on the United States government and American-based
firms to meet their necessary and/or deemed needs. This dependency had the
effect of insuring a special role for the United States in the Arab region and for
Saudi Arabia a role in United States regional and even global strategic designs.
The usefulness of the Saudi government to United States foreign policy objectives
was underlined when it was revealed that as part of the arrangements to buy
AWACS, in 1981 the monarch of Saudi Arabia agreed to a request by the United
States government to channel funds to the Contras in Nicaragua and similar
groups in other parts of the world such as the United States–supported antigov-
ernment forces in Afghanistan.[18]

Not only did Saudi Arabia provide lucrative markets for American goods,
services, and arms, but it also joined the United States government in some of
its covert actions in the Third World. Moreover, the Saudi government succeeded
in serving United States energy policy objectives by the virtue of its predominant
position within OPEC.

SAUDI ARABIA, OPEC, AND UNITED STATES ENERGY AND
POLITICAL OBJECTIVES

The Organization of Petroleum Exporting Countries (OPEC), as was stated
in earlier chapters, was created in 1960. Saudi Arabia was one of its five founding

members; the others were Iraq, Iran, Kuwait, and Venezuela. The immediate reason for the creation of OPEC was a decision by the oil companies to lower oil prices, thus reducing government revenue from oil. The moving forces behind the creation of OPEC were the Venezuelan oil minister Perez Alfonzo and the Saudi oil minister Abdullah Tariki. Perez Alfonzo grasped, as early as 1940, the importance of countervailing power that an association of oil producers could have in their dealings with multinational oil companies. Not until the late 1950s, however, did a Saudi technocrat, Tariki, embrace the ideas of the Venezuelans. Then it became just a matter of time before an organization of oil producers would be created. The unilateral price reductions in 1959 and 1960 by the multinational oil corporations provided the immediate pretext for the formal establishment of OPEC in September 1960. Tariki, who had thought of OPEC as an instrument for economic emancipation, was replaced by Yamani in March 1962 to carry out the oil policy of King Faisal.

The new king's policies stressed close cooperation with Aramco. Prices and output levels were to be determined by the oil companies. Notions such as the "Arabization" of Aramco or production prorationing or changing the terms of the concession agreements, which Tariki had advocated, were no longer part of the new king's oil agenda.[19] While Tariki was Pan-Arabist in his outlook, Yamani was concerned with the immediate fiscal interests of the kingdom. While Tariki was willing to see differences between the interests of his country and those of the oil companies, Yamani was inclined to see more compatibility of interests between his country and the companies. And while Tariki was able and willing to recognize conflicts between the interests of his country and those of industrial market economies, Yamani was unable or unwilling to recognize such conflicts. In short, the views of Yamani were more reflective of the ideological and political orientation of the Saudi ruling family than those of Tariki. These views came to exert powerful influence on the behavior of Saudi Arabia within OPEC and by extension on the role that OPEC played in the international oil industry and the international economy.

While the Saudis were more concerned with their narrow national interests, they were by no means isolationists. As stated earlier, they could not afford to be in the Arab world. On the contrary, the Saudis were very active in regional Arab affairs especially after the 1967 June war. Their involvement did not have a Pan-Arab context or objective. It had and continues to have as its primary objective the attempt to manage and control events in such a manner as to minimize threats to established Saudi political and economic interests. The necessity for the Saudis to exert their influence in the Arab region to further their own interests was captured by Henry Kissinger in the context of the oil embargo when he said:

The immediate aftermath of the embargo found Saudi Arabia in a most uncomfortable position. It prized its friendship with the United States for emotional and practical reasons. It feared the tide of radicalism. Yet Arab solidarity corresponded to its moral convictions and to the security needs of the Kingdom. It could not afford isolation in the Arab world; it dreaded being an outcast, stigmatized as reactionary or accused of insufficient dedication to the Arab cause. The oil weapon had sharpened its dilemmas.[20]

While the Arab context of Saudi interests imposed at times certain modes of behavior and restraints, the framework of OPEC within which the Saudis functioned did not have similar limitations. On the contrary, Saudi Arabia by virtue of its position within OPEC and the oil industry, played a pivotal role in shaping the outcome of most decisions, not hesitating at various times to resort to pressures, threats and the actual inflicting of damage upon other member countries.

It may be useful at this point to make a few observations about the energy objectives of the United States and the role that the Saudis played in helping these objectives by the virtue of their position within OPEC. The oil price changes of 1973–1974 disrupted, as might be expected, the pattern of international payments of the industrial countries, the main importers of OPEC oil. The rise in the cost of imported oil prompted many countries to enter bilateral trade arrangements in order to minimize balance-of-payments effects of the price changes. Entering such arrangements, however, meant at least two things from the American perspective. First, the international economic system that had been constructed by the United States and other industrial countries would be subjected to added stresses and strains. Second, American political influence over its allies and in the Third World would be weakened if a small group of Third World countries were to succeed in influencing international policy-making and transactions. In other words, the United States was opposed to seeing the emergence of several centers of economic power that would jeopardize its global interests and leadership.

In order to retain such a position of leadership in the world economy, the United States took the initiative in February 1974 in sponsoring a meeting of the industrial countries to deal with the ramifications of the new oil changes. The efforts of the United States government were centered on having the governments of industrial countries enter an agreement to establish a mechanism to deal with energy issues in such a manner as to reduce dependence on OPEC oil, to minimize the effects of any future disruption to the flow of oil imports, and to make such disruptions costly in political and financial terms to oil-exporting countries. The thrust of the United States position was that the industrial countries should develop policies to deal with conservation, alternative energy sources, emergency sharing of oil supplies, international financial cooperation, research and development, and consumer-producer relations.[21]

The February 1974 energy conference led to the creation of the International Energy Agency (IEA) in November of that year. The main objectives of the IEA were:

- To promote secure oil supplies on reasonable and equitable terms.
- To take common, effective measures to meet oil supply emergencies by developing an emergency self-sufficiency in oil supplies, restraining demand, and allocating supplies among member countries on an equitable basis.

- To promote cooperative relations with oil-producing countries and with other consuming countries including those of the developing world.
- To play an active role in relation to the oil industry by establishing a comprehensive international information system and a permanent framework for consultation with oil companies.
- To reduce dependence on imported oil by undertaking long-term cooperative efforts on conservation of energy, on accelerated development of alternative sources of energy, and on research and development in the energy field.[22]

The United States political objectives in establishing the IEA were viewed as follows:

> Creation of the IEA was very much an American initiative. The Agency was regarded in large part as a reflection of Secretary of State Kissinger's desire to reassert U.S. leadership in the industrial world; to prevent debilitating competition among the industrial countries which could result in even higher prices for oil supplies and also in preferential arrangements between particular consumers and producers which might exclude the United States; and to confront OPEC with a counterweight of consuming states. Henceforth, it would cost the oil producers considerably more financially and politically to use the oil weapon.[23]

It is significant to note that while the United States government was busy attempting to put together an energy alliance under its leadership, it was also busy developing its own special relationship with Saudi Arabia, a fact that did not go unnoticed on the part of IEA negotiation participants:

> The other participating countries were understandably surprised when, in the very midst of the negotiations for the creation of the IEA, Washington announced the establishment of its own special relationship with Saudi Arabia. While the United States attempted to explain that it covered only economic and military matters, no one around the IEA table thought for one minute that oil was not involved.[24]

SAUDI ARABIA AGAINST OPEC

Having brought other industrial countries under its energy leadership, the next United States policy objective was to promote investment in new energy sources in order to lessen dependence on OPEC oil. This meant that oil prices should remain high enough to encourage such investment but not so high as to cause further balance-of-payment difficulties.

The position of the United States on the issue of prices, costs, and non-OPEC sources of supply was articulated as follows:

> We must insure that our energy investments are protected against disruptive competition. For much of the Persian Gulf, production costs are only about 25 cents a barrel. Most of the major continental energy sources—new Alaskan North Slope oil, the U.S.

outer continental shelf, North Sea oil, nuclear power everywhere—will be many times more costly to produce. If the cartel decides to undercut alternative sources by temporary, predatory price-cutting, investment in alternative sources may be inhibited or abandoned. The producers' pricing policies could thus keep us in a permanent state of dependence, and we would hardly have assurance that the price would not be raised again once our dependence was confirmed.

This is why we in the IEA have agreed in principle on the safeguard price mechanism. Only if consumers develop massive new energy sources will the oil producers lose their ability to set prices at high, artificial levels. But these sources will not be developed if producers retain the ability to thwart our energy programs by temporary, predatory price cuts. A minimum safeguard price—well below the current world price level—can help insure that these alternative sources will be developed.

We are obviously not proposing a guaranteed price for OPEC. On the contrary, if our policy succeeds, and as large quantities of new energy become available, OPEC's selling price could fall below the protected level. The minimum safeguard price can be implemented in a variety of ways—through tariffs, quotas, or variable levies. The difference between the world price and the higher domestic price would thus accrue to our governments in the form of import taxes and levies.[25]

The United States position as articulated in this policy statement called for a two-tier pricing system. On the one hand, the United States government was interested in seeing lower prices for OPEC oil while at the same time it was interested in keeping energy prices in oil-importing countries high enough to stimulate and protect capital investment in oil and other forms of energy in order to lessen dependence on OPEC and to weaken it as a force in international oil. That aspect of the United States policy that aimed at lower prices for OPEC oil was taken up with vigor by the Saudis soon at the March 1974 OPEC price conference. Although OPEC's own economic commission had recommended that prices be raised for the second quarter of 1974 (a position that was supported by the majority of member countries), the Saudis insisted that no such action should be taken. The Saudis went so far as to threaten to lower their prices should OPEC decide to raise oil prices. These threats had the effect of convincing most member countries not to raise prices and a decision was reached to freeze crude oil prices for the second quarter of 1974.[26] The Saudis also insisted that a special OPEC conference could be called by any member country with a view to revising posted prices. Behind the Saudi insistence on another OPEC meeting was the expectation that with the lifting of the embargo and the output reduction measures, market prices would decline, thus providing them with a stronger rationale to push for a downward revision of crude oil prices.

Although the Saudis failed to force other OPEC member countries to lower prices, they succeeded in establishing a precedent and a policy instrument that governed their actions within OPEC for most of the decade. The precedent was that it was difficult for the views of an OPEC majority to prevail without the explicit or tacit approval of the Saudis. The instrument was simple enough. The Saudis discovered at that meeting that the threat of pursuing their own pricing policies would force most OPEC member countries into following their leadership. And behind the ability of the Saudis to force other member countries to accept their views was their massive leverage of crude oil output.

In June 1974 another OPEC conference was convened to deal with the price issue. Again, although the Economic Commission of OPEC recommended an increase in the price of crude oil of $1 per barrel (or less than 10 percent of the price of $11.62 per barrel) to offset the effects of world inflation, the Saudis countered by advocating a reduction in the price by $2 per barrel.

In opposing the commission's recommendation, the Saudis took the position that higher oil prices were undermining the economies of the industrial countries as well as the economies of developing countries. They threatened once again that should the majority insist on a price increase, they would retaliate by increasing their output by 3 million barrels per day (MBD), or by 35 percent. Under these conditions the majority of OPEC member countries decided to succumb to Saudi demands. Prices were frozen again for another quarter in 1974.[27]

The serious implications of the Saudi position vis-à-vis the rest of the OPEC member countries may be appreciated in the following statement made by the Algerian oil minister.

The determination of the OPEC countries to resist any pressure showed clearly in the two decisions taken by the conference. This is due to the fact that all the member countries are agreed in principle that the value of their oil must be protected, and that if the price is affected by outside factors such as inflation or monetary fluctuations it must be correspondingly corrected.

In any case, Saudi Arabia—whose position on the question is well known—presented arguments . . . which appeared all the less convincing . . . for arriving at conclusions which flagrantly contradict market conditions and the inflationary situation in the world. This is why, despite its considerable potential for production . . . Saudi Arabia found itself isolated.[28]

The failure of the Saudis to effect a price reduction prompted the United States government to embark upon a campaign of threats and intimidation aimed at producing countries. The campaign was inaugurated by President Gerald Ford when he warned that:

Sovereign nations cannot allow their policies to be dictated or their fate decided by artificial rigging and distortion of world commodity market. No one can foresee the extent of the damage nor the end of the disastrous consequences if nations refuse to share nature's gifts for the benefit of all mankind.[29]

President Ford's theme was underlined by Secretary Kissinger before the United Nations General Assembly when he said:

Unlike the food prices, the high cost of oil is not the result of economic factors, of an actual shortage of capacity or of the free play of supply and demand. Rather it is caused by deliberate decisions to restrict production and maintain an artificial price level. We recognize that the producers should have a fair share; the fact remains that present prices even threaten the economic well-being of producers.[30]

Secretary of Treasury William Simon warned oil-producing countries that the United States might be compelled to change certain of its policies toward the producers in order to force price reduction.[31]

It is significant to observe that this campaign of intimidation failed to receive the endorsement or the support of other major oil-importing industrial countries such as Japan, Germany, France, and Britain. All oil-producing countries reacted to the United States threats with incredulity. But the reaction of the government of Venezuela seems to have captured the essence of the American strategy:

The U.S. strategy is clear, namely to pin the blame for the current world-wide inflation on oil producers—which is simply not the case. The root cause of this inflation, in our view lies in the expansion of U.S. economic interests throughout the world together with the spiralling increases in the prices of manufactured goods and other commodities—not just oil alone. The rise in energy costs has been responsible for only a very modest contribution to the rise in prices of manufactures in the U.S. We blame the U.S. for the current chaotic financial situation in the world, which they have aggravated by, among other things, several times devaluing the dollar and thereby reducing the value of the dollar holdings of the oil producing countries.

We do not consider the present level of oil prices as exorbitant. "Rigging" prices— which was the term those U.S. leaders used—is synonymous with economic exploitation, which is characteristic of the U.S. and not of OPEC.

Before the energy crisis and before oil prices reached the levels they now stand at, the raw materials our countries produce were acquired year after year at prices which at no time bore any relation nor where in any equilibrium with those of manufactured products which our countries need for their development.

These manufactures were in great part bought in the U.S. not only for geographic reasons but also because of credits tied to the U.S. economy which traditionally supplied them to us.

Year by year we producers of coffee, meat, tin, copper, iron or oil have been providing a greater amount of our products to obtain machinery or other manufactured goods which we import, thus producing a continuing and growing outflow of capital and impoverishment of our countries.[32]

The campaign of threats against oil-producing countries to lower oil prices was viewed also as another illustration of the overall policy of segmenting the Middle East question into what Kissinger had called manageable components. As the Egyptian foreign minister Ismail Fahmy told the United Nations, the Arabs had used their oil only to secure their legitimate rights and only after warning the countries that support Israel in its policy of occupying Arab territories and that Kissinger had sought to break the link between the issues of supply and prices of oil on the one hand, and the Middle East controversy on the other. He went on to say that this question could not be tackled on the basis of isolating political factors from economic considerations.[33]

The September 1974 OPEC decision to freeze oil prices for the balance of 1974 was followed by another decision in December approving another freeze of posted prices for the first nine months of 1975. The decision to freeze posted prices for almost two years (January 1, 1974, to September 30, 1975) meant a substantial decline in the real price of oil, given the high inflation rates that prevailed in the world economy at the time. This decline in oil revenue purchasing power was not sufficient to meet United States government policy objectives. What the United States government wanted and what the OPEC countries appeared to have been unwilling to concede was an announced reduction in the official selling prices of crude oil. The motive for the respective positions of the United States government and OPEC member countries was the same—the symbolic act of forcing a group of Third World countries to lower the price of a commodity necessary to the economies of industrial countries. And it was this same pressure that OPEC member countries refused to accept so soon after they had acquired controlling power over their oil.

Although the Saudis tried to exert their power within the councils of OPEC to see to it that American demands were met, such attempts were bound to fail for at least three reasons. First, political considerations within each member country (especially in the aftermath of the October war for the Arab members of OPEC) made it almost impossible to engage in acts that might cause political instability. Second, the Saudis had concluded that the Americans were not serious about lowering oil prices. The third consideration was that there was no agreement among the industrial countries to reduce prices through threats and intimidation. Most industrial countries had already acknowledged the new realities of higher oil prices and were willing to make their adjustments either collectively or on a bilateral basis.

THE UNITED STATES AGAINST OPEC

The failure of the Saudis to force a price cut formally led the Americans to the conclusion that a different approach must be relied upon to bring about a reduction in the price of crude oil. This assessment was explained by Secretary Kissinger in an interview with *Business Week*:

Q: Businessmen ask why we haven't been about to exploit King Faisal's fear of communism to help lower prices?

A: We have a delicate problem there. It is to maintain the relationship of friendship that they have felt for us, yet make clear the consequences of these prices on the structure of the West and of the non-Communist world.

I think we will find that Saudi Arabia will not be the leader in the reduction of prices, but that it will not be an impediment to a reduction if enough momentum can be created in the Arab world—indeed it will be discretely encouraging.

The Saudi government has performed the enormously skillful act of surviving in a leadership position in an increasingly radical Arab world. It is doing that by carefully balancing itself among the various factions and acting as a resultant of a relation of forces, and never getting too far out ahead. Therefore, I never for a moment believed, nor do I believe today, that the lead in cutting prices will be taken by Saudi Arabia. On the other hand, the Saudis will happily support a cut in prices proposed by others. The Saudis have no interest in keeping up prices. They don't know what to do with their income today.[34]

Having reached this conclusion, the American secretary of state decided to give the Saudis a helping hand once again by initiating a new campaign of threats and intimidation that was more menacing than the earlier one:

Q: One of the things we also hear from businessmen is that in the long run the only answer to the oil cartel is some sort of military action. Have you considered military action on oil?

A: Military action on oil prices?

Q: Yes.

A: A very dangerous course. We should have learned from Vietnam that it is easier to get into a war than to get out of it. I am not saying that there's no circumstance where we would not use force. But it is one thing to use it in the case of a dispute over price, it's another where there's some actual strangulation of the industrialized world.[35]

This threat of military intervention was discussed, elaborated on, refined, contradicted, and modified by other members of the United States government such as the secretary of defense and the secretary of the treasury.[36]

A legitimate question may be asked: Since OPEC member countries made it abundantly clear that they were not going to reduce prices, especially in response to public threats, why did the United States government persist in its posture? There are several answers to this question. One explanation may be found in the response of President Boumedienne of Algeria:

The world is at present going through the stage of eliminating direct occupation and ridding itself of imperialism. I don't know how the Americans can go against the tide of history, because intervention, if it is carried out can only be considered as imperialism.

The struggle of the oil producing countries is part of the fierce struggle of the Third World to revalue its raw materials and establish a new world economic system, and therefore this issue must be put in this context, which requires farsightedness.[37]

Another explanation was provided by the reaction of Iraq to Kissinger's threats as merely intending:

to provide an excuse for those oil producers which have close relations with the U.S. and the oil cartels to withdraw oil from the battle, on the one hand, and to respond to

Washington's oil demands under the pretext of avoiding confrontation and danger on the other hand.[38]

A third answer may be found in the failure of economic policy in industrialized countries to solve the twin problems of inflation and stagnation. According to Paul A. Samuelson:

On analysis, I find no merit in the common view that our economic troubles were appreciably due to the fact that Richard Nixon was so busy fighting for his political life that he was unable to devote the time needed to devise government policies to cure inflation. If he had all the time in the world, we'd still face our present problem of stagflation.

There are no feasible policies that President Ford can now be expected to formulate with the help of a cooperative Congress that will succeed in doing much about such inflation.

No mixed economy—not the U.S. or UK, Sweden or Switzerland, Germany or Japan, France or Italy—knows how to have sustained full employment with price stability.[39]

Another reason for such American persistence could very well have stemmed from the need to divert attention from domestic economic failure by attributing economic problems to the oil price increases. The perpetuation of the myth of an energy crisis as late as early 1975, when demand conditions were depressed and when there was actually an oil glut in the world oil market, drew the following observation from Samuelson:

Bluntly, there is no need for us to do anything to mitigate the long-run energy problem in this recession year of 1975. Although I have no tapes to prove it, the entrails I examine suggest that it is a holy alliance between Henry Kissinger and Alan Greenspan [chairman of the President's Council of Economic Advisers] that has cooked up the Ford energy proposals. The former thinks we are in a crisis that threatens our national prestige and basic foreign-policy interest. The latter, by his own account, has gone to Washington to defend the encroachments upon market freedoms of today's populist electorates: to this end, he espouses an increase in the price of energy as the only proper way to ration its use and to coax out new sources of domestic supply.

The whole problem can disappear for the immediate time horizon if President Ford will open his eyes and repeat firmly: "There is no energy crisis. Repeat: no energy crisis."

Dr. Kissinger's Ph.D. was earned in the field of political science, not economics. His notion that we must guarantee for years to come a high price of oil has no sanctions from the vast majority of economists who have been addressing themselves to energy problems.[40]

Yet Samuelson missed an important explanation for the Ford administration's energy proposals. The Ford administration, in introducing its energy plan, had other things besides the price of oil on its mind. In the words of Edward Cowan:

According to several confidential sources, the Secretary of State exerted a dominant influence on the over-all shape of the program as well as some of the specifics. The officials say that Mr. Kissinger's influence explains largely why Mr. Ford asserted that there was an urgent vital national need to raise oil prices quickly, by April 1, through a combination of new taxes and termination of price controls for crude oil.

Mr. Ford's long-term goal to make the United States invulnerable by 1985 to another cutoff of foreign oil, is rejected by no official.

In this view, development of new supplies around the world is more critical to breaking the cartel price than the limited conservation that can be induced by higher prices. Some officials would encourage, through a selective tariff, production by countries believed to be relatively secure sources of future oil supplies—Nigeria, Indonesia, Venezuela and perhaps Mexico.

The grand design of the Ford energy program was stated, but understated, in the President's State of the Union message. In a passage that is reliably reported to show the hand of Alan Greenspan, chairman of the Council of Economic Advisers, Mr. Ford held out the prospect that by the turn of the century the United States could supply a significant share of the energy needs of the Free World.

Like Secretary Kissinger's persistent bid for energy leadership among the consuming countries, the goal of exporting fuel and energy technology plainly is a bid for international power.[41]

However, in order to attain its global objectives, the United States government had to be secure in the knowledge that OPEC would not act in a disruptive manner. Threats of political, economic, and military intervention in the affairs of the OPEC countries combined with Saudi threats to flood the world market with their oil were remarkably successful in restraining OPEC.

The Saudis once again threatened economic damage to their partners in September 1975 when OPEC countries were attempting to raise prices. Although they admitted the price of crude oil was lower than what it should have been, they again were opposed to a price increase. When an OPEC majority voted a price increase that was not acceptable to them, the Saudis made "an unequivocal threat to counter such a move by leaving their own prices frozen at current levels and letting . . . production rise to the limit of the Kingdom's formidable surplus capacity."[42]

The certainty that they would lose market shares to the Saudis caused OPEC member countries to go along with the Saudis for a mere 10 percent price increase. Even when OPEC member countries found it necessary not to succumb to Saudi threats, they found out to their detriment that the Saudis actually meant what they said. This situation may be illustrated by what happened to oil prices and output in the first half of 1977.[43]

At the December 1976 meeting of OPEC the majority failed to convince the Saudis of the need for a uniform price change. Saudi Arabia and the United Arab Emirates decided to raise the price of crude oil by 5 percent while the other countries voted for a 10 percent increase effective January 1977, to be followed by another 5 percent price increase in July 1977.

The political significance of the Saudi insistence that prices not be raised by more than 5 percent may be judged by the diverse reactions to the decision. In the United States, President Ford praised the 5 percenters (Saudi Arabia and the United Arab Emirates) for exercising international responsibility and criticized the 10 percenters for the irresponsibility of their actions and for ignoring the destructive consequences of such actions.

While the United States was praising the Saudis, other countries had entirely different reactions. The Algerian oil minister, for instance, described an increase in oil output by Saudi Arabia that would support the smaller price rise as an act of direct aggression against OPEC. The Iraqi oil minister accused the Saudis of acting "in the service of imperialism and Zionism" and stated that Saudi Arabia was seeking to make OPEC "succumb to pressure from oil monopolies and imperialist forces by perpetuating a price freeze."[44]

No sooner did the Saudis break ranks with OPEC than they decided to lift the 8.5 MBD ceiling on output as a punitive measure to force other OPEC member countries to accept Saudi leadership of OPEC. The significance of the Saudi decision to increase output may be appreciated when it is realized that Saudi oil output reached 10.2 MBD in April 1977 compared to an output level of 8.5 MBD in January 1977, or an increase of 20 percent.

By May 1977 it became evident to OPEC member countries that they could not go ahead with their earlier decision to raise prices by 5 percent effective July 1, 1977. Instead, a compromise was reached whereby the Saudis agreed to increase their price by 5 percent, bringing the total increase to 10 percent while other member countries decided to reverse their position and forfeit the scheduled 5 percent price increase. These decisions put an end, at least temporarily, to the two-tier price system that prevailed in the first half of 1977.

The ability once again of Saudi Arabia to use its considerable surplus productive capacity to discipline other member countries prompted President Carter to say that he and Prince Fahd (now king of Saudi Arabia) had discussed the question of oil prices and suggested that both countries use their combined economic and political weight to persuade the OPEC countries to freeze oil prices for as long as possible.[45]

This Saudi-American alliance succeeded once again in keeping OPEC prices frozen in 1978. The shift in the Iranian position from constant advocacy of price increases to that of a price freeze left no doubt about the prospects for a price freeze in 1978. As the Indonesian oil minister observed, "Indonesia cannot afford a price freeze—it needs the money. . . . If the two major producers, Iran and Saudi Arabia, favor a freeze, the arithmetic is then clear, you cannot really do anything about it."[46]

In order to insure that oil-producing countries would not raise prices in 1978, the United States found it necessary to pressure other OPEC member countries to continue the price freeze in 1978. The pressure exerted on these countries was exposed by President Carlos Andres Perez of Venezuela in his speech to the OPEC conference held in Caracas in December 1977:

We, producers of raw materials, cannot be asked to continue subsidizing the world's economy as is being proposed. It is not only oil, a fundamental and basic product, which is being depleted with alarming speed.

A strong pressure has been exerted upon the 13 member nations of OPEC, from the highest summits of world economic power, to make us see that the economy of the world could not sustain new increases in the price of oil at least until their present depressive state is redressed. In the meantime, all of the manufactured and capital goods that we import have increased in price. And the dollar, the currency in which we market our oil, has also lost position vis-à-vis other currencies in the industrialized world. The deterioration in the price of our oil is evident. The same thing has happened to the rest of the raw materials produced by the Third World countries. The terms of trade have suffered new and serious setbacks.[47]

The 1978 price freeze, which both the United States and Saudi Arabia were hoping to extend into 1979 and 1980, came to a sudden end under the impact of the Iranian Revolution. The reaction of the consuming countries to the unfolding events of the Iranian Revolution gave rise to what came to be known as the second oil price shock. These events and the implications of the second oil price shock will be explored in a subsequent chapter.

THE AMERICAN-SAUDI ASSAULT ON OPEC, 1973–1978: A SUMMARY

A careful reading of the record of economic/political/oil developments for the period 1973 to 1978 shows the United States government and the government of Saudi Arabia were engaged in collusive behavior to render OPEC ineffective in determining crude oil price structures. The much-discussed oil price revolution, which changed the terms of trade of the oil producing countries dramatically as a result of the quadrupling of oil prices in 1973–1974, proved to be short-lived. First, the Saudis and the Americans initiated negotiations early in 1974 to restructure their economic and military relationships. The United States was made the single most important influence in shaping the development of the Saudi economy, military, infrastructure, and government agencies. In exchange for being the principal arms supplier and the main counselor on economic change, the Saudis agreed to serve American policy objectives in the Arab region, in the Middle East, and vis-à-vis other oil-producing countries.

As far as oil was concerned, the American objective best served by the Saudis was for the Saudis to force OPEC member countries not to raise prices. Although it was beyond the ability of the Saudis to induce an absolute reduction in prices, they were successful in forcing a freeze for a five-year period, 1974–1978 (except for the 10 percent increase effected in September 1975 and the 1977 price increase of another 10 percent).

The price freeze that the Saudis were so successful in enforcing led by 1978 to the vitiation of all the gains that the oil-producing countries were able to achieve in 1973. In other words, the real price of crude oil has eroded so much during the five years of Saudi domination of OPEC that the purchasing power of a barrel of oil revenue in 1978 was no more than it was in 1973. On this loss of oil revenue purchasing power the Saudis and their adversaries in OPEC have no disagreement.

In commenting on the role of Saudi Arabia, a former American ambassador to Saudi Arabia had this to say: "The most important reason for the Saudi position is a political one: that is the United States had asked Saudi Arabia to produce more oil, to hold down prices, and to defend the dollar. The Saudi response has been consistently and dramatically positive in all fields."[48]

NOTES

1. Department of State, *U.S. Policy in the Middle East: December 1973–November 1974* (Washington, D.C.: Government Printing Office, 1975), 23–24. Henceforth *Special Report*.

2. Ibid.

3. *Middle East Economic Digest* (MEED), various issues.

4. For military expenditures see United States Arms Control and Disarmament Agency, *World Military Expenditures and Arms Transfers* (Washington, D.C., Annual). For value of petroleum exports see Organization of Petroleum Exporting Countries, *Annual Statistical Bulletin* (Vienna).

5. See Joe Stork and Jim Paul, "Arms Sales and the Militarization of the Middle East," *MERIP (Middle East Research & Information Project) Reports* (February 1983), 6.

6. Ibid.

7. John T. Cummings, Hossein G. Askari, and Michael Akinner, "Military Expenditures and Manpower Requirements in the Arabian Peninsula," *Arab Studies Quarterly* 2, no. 1 (Winter 1980): 38–49.

8. Ibid., 42.

9. Ghassan Bishara, "The Middle East Arms Package: A Survey of the Congressional Debate," *Journal of Palestine Studies* 7, no. 4 (Summer 1978): 67–78.

10. See "Interview: Military Options in the Middle East," Ibid., 100–102.

11. Bishara, "*The Middle East*," 10.

12. See James E. Akins, "Politics and Saudi Oil Policy," *MEES*, October 12, 1981, ii.

13. Stork and Paul, "Arms Sales," 10.

14. Ibid., 8.

15. Ibid.

16. See Altaf Gauhar, "The Hidden Cost of the Arms Race," *South*, July 1982, 7.

17. See Rex B. Wingerter, "AWACS and U.S. Strategy," *Journal of Palestine Studies* 11, no. 2 (Winter 1982): 189–191.

18. See *The New York Times*, February 4, 1987, p. 1. See also Bob Woodward, *Veil: The Secret Wars of the CIA, 1981–1987* (New York: Simon and Schuster, 1987), 502.

19. For an outline of the main initiatives which led to the creation of OPEC see Fuad Rouhani, *A History of OPEC* (New York: Praeger Publishers, 1971), chapter 4. See also Pierre Terzian, *OPEC: The Inside Story* (London: Zed Books, 1985), chapter 4.

20. Henry Kissinger, *Years of Upheaval* (Boston: Little, Brown, 1982), 878.

21. U.S. Department of State, *U.S. International Energy Policy October 1973–November 1975* (Washington, D.C.: Government Printing Office, 1975), 6. Henceforth *U.S. Energy Policy*.

22. Mason Willrich and Melvin A. Conant, "The International Energy Agency: An

Interpretation and Assessment," *Journal of American Society of International Law*, April 1977, 201.

23. Ibid.

24. Ibid.

25. *U.S. Energy Policy*, 19–20.

26. See *Middle East Economic Survey* (*MEES*), March 22, 1974, 5A.

27. *MEES*, June 21, 1974, 1–4.

28. *MEES*, July 5, 1974, i–ii.

29. *MEES*, September 27, 1974, 1.

30. *MEES*, September 27, 1974, 3.

31. *MEES*, September 27, 1974, 8.

32. *MEES*, September 27, 1974, 5.

33. *MEES*, October 4, 1974, 8.

34. *Business Week*, January 13, 1975, 67–68.

35. Ibid, 69.

36. *MEES*, January 17, 1975, i, and January 24, 1975, iii.

37. *MEES*, January 10, 1975, viii.

38. Ibid, ix–x.

39. See Paul A. Samuelson, "Coping with Inflation," *Newsweek*, August 19, 1974, 69.

40. Paul A. Samuelson, "Energy Policy," *Newsweek*, March 24, 1975, 76.

41. Edward Cowan, "Ford's Energy Plan: Foreign Policy vs. Economics," *The New York Times*, January 26, 1975. *The Wall Street Journal*, February 4, 1975, in discussing the Ford energy plan gave its report this title: "Kissinger Discloses Strategy on Energy Aimed to Break OPEC's Economic Power."

42. *MEES*, September 19 & 26, 1975, 1.

43. Ibid, 5–6.

44. *MEES*, December 27, 1976, i–v.

45. *MEES*, July 11, 1977, p. 2. A few months after President Carter made this statement, Prince Fahd said that oil prices would remain frozen in 1978 and hoped to see them remain frozen in 1979 and 1980 as well. See *MEES*, January 16, 1978, 2.

46. *MEES*, November 28, 1977, p. 3. It was suggested in this connection that Iran's support of price freeze was in exchange for the American readiness to meet Iran's defense needs. See *MEES*, November 21, 1977, 1–2.

47. *MEES*, January 2, 1978, i–iv.

48. See James E. Akins, "Politics and Saudi Oil Policy," *MEES*, October 12, 1981, ii.

7

THE 1980s, THE IRAN-IRAQ WAR, AND THE MYTH OF ARAB OIL POWER

The decade of the 1980s witnessed some major developments in the Middle East and in the international oil industry and the world economy that exploded what was left of the lingering myth of Arab and/or OPEC oil power. In order to appreciate the working of some of the forces that led to this outcome and to the decline of the so-called Arab or OPEC oil power, it is necessary to highlight the crucial role that Saudi oil policy played in determining the scope and the effectiveness of Arab and OPEC oil in the world economy.

DETERMINANTS OF SAUDI OIL POLICY

There are two general principles that shape Saudi economic thinking. The first is the belief in the major tenets of the Western economic system. Capitalism, private property, private enterprise, and market forces are governing determinants of Saudi thought and policy as witnessed by statements like those by Saudi policymakers: "the market is king," "the law of supply and demand is a king," or "the law of supply and demand is more powerful than any state or combination of states." Second, the Saudis somehow perceived themselves to be responsible for the viability of the international economic system. They believed it was their obligation to defend, support, and protect the system even at the expense of their own national interest, not to mention the interests of other oil-producing countries. In explaining why his country rejected the OPEC majority position in 1976 to raise the price of crude oil by 10 percent, Prince Fahd said:

Saudi Arabia has a clear and unequivocal oil policy based on the convictions of its leaders. The main pillar of this policy is that oil should not be a cause of world economic instability or of increasing inflation, but rather that it should be an effective instrument for the promotion of stability and economic development throughout the world and for the fight against inflation which is a world-wide problem. . . . The Kingdom shouldered its responsibilities and acted to stop the snowball of inflation from continuing on its course.[1]

The same point of view was reiterated by the Saudi minister of finance, Muhammad Aba al-Khail when he pointed out that his country's insistence on an oil price freeze was in part dictated by an attempt to control international inflation.[2] Yamani articulated the Saudi responsibility toward the world economy in these terms:

We cannot give free reign to our nationalistic point of view and ignore the world economic situation by producing enough oil to meet our own needs. In the first place this would lead to a deterioration in the world economic situation, undermine the various economic systems of the world and spread unemployment. This would certainly lead to war, and in such a war we would be both a participant and a target.[3]

In an interview with the British Broadcasting Corporation in May 1978 Yamani was almost cheerful in admitting that Saudi Arabia was acting against its own interest:

Because we are producing much more than what we need for our financial requirements, we are depleting our oil resources. Then we are accumulating a surplus and losing on that surplus. If I compare the appreciation of a barrel of crude in the ground in Saudi Arabia with the rate of return I get from my dollar invested in the world market there is no comparison. It is a net loss. So I think in this area we are not really serving the real interest of Saudi Arabia. But we also look at the world economy and what you need, and if we don't produce that much—for instance if we reduce our production to something like 4 or 5 million b/d—we immediately create a shortage.[4]

The Saudis' notion of the special importance of their pricing decision to the state of the world economy was serious, exceedingly exaggerated, and hopelessly naive. Nothing illustrates the overinflated belief in the importance of the Saudi pricing decision to the world economy better than Yamani's own assessment: "I do not want to be overmodest. It is quite true that my office has become one of the most, if not the most important center of decision making in the world."[5]

One cannot help but think that the Saudis were led to or they chose to believe, mistakenly of course, that their price actions had serious implications for the economic stability of the world. In actuality, Saudi oil exports peaked at 6.1 percent of total world exports in 1981 and world expenditure on Saudi oil was a minuscule fraction of the world total expenditures on goods and services. Moreover, the mechanisms of inflation creation (whether it was of the demand-pull or the cost-push variety) and its perpetuation were rooted in the monopoly power of large economic entities and institutions—governments, big business, and labor unions—in the major industrial countries and not in whether the Saudis raised the price of their oil by 5 percent or 10 percent.

This frame of mind seems to have led the Saudis to project the importance of oil for their economy and political system on the economies and political systems of the industrial countries. They thought, for instance, that by freezing prices they would preserve political stability in certain European countries and prevent takeover by Communist parties. Yamani in an interview with *Der Spiegel* in January 1977 said:

Q: Why did you not go along with the price increase?

A: There were important economic and political reasons. . . . We are extremely worried about the economic situation in the West, worried about the possibility of a new recession, worried about the situation in Great Britain, Italy, even in France and some other countries. And we do not want another regime to come to power in France or Italy.

Q: You mean a communist regime?

A: Yes. The situation in Spain is also not so healthy, and the same is true in Portugal.[6]

It should be stressed in this context Saudi Arabia's GNP in 1976 was 4 percent of the combined GNP of the five countries whose political systems Yamani sought to protect by raising the price of crude oil by 5 percent instead of 10 percent.

The Saudis also pursued a number of other policies that ran counter to the interests of other oil-producing countries. Their position on the issue of oil price indexation is a good case in point. The OPEC Economic Commission and almost all OPEC member countries argued throughout the 1970s that the purchasing power of oil revenue was eroding under the impact of inflation and dollar depreciation and that oil prices should be adjusted according to an index to compensate for such erosion. The Saudis on the other hand maintained that the welfare of the West argued against indexation. The Saudis have always acknowledged the erosion problem, but their commitment to keeping prices frozen led them to adopt a policy posture that frustrated all attempts at indexation.

The opposition of the Saudis to output regulation by OPEC was another policy that ran counter to the interests of other member countries. The Saudi policy position on oil output was a multifaceted one. It stemmed from the belief that their national interest could not permit oil output to be determined jointly with other countries. They maintained that oil output regulation was contradictory to their professed position that the West should be supplied with all the oil it needed and that any control of output of oil-producing countries would undermine Saudi control over the behavior of OPEC. Their instrument of pressure was the volume of their own oil output, which they used to accomplish their objectives. As Yamani put it: "In fact the level of the Kingdom's oil production is a matter of serious political and economic concern not only for the Kingdom but for the whole world as well."[7]

While the Saudis were opposed to any interference by OPEC, they never hesitated to determine what other OPEC member countries could produce by raising their own output to influence prices. And while the Saudis always maintained that the forces of supply and demand should be allowed to determine output and prices, this pretentious belief in the free play of market forces was nonsensical, since it was constantly contradicted by Saudi oil output policy as it was actually practiced. The Saudis time and again deliberately and blatantly increased their output and their share of the market in order to impose their will on other OPEC member countries.

The dedication of the Saudis to the Western economy was reinforced in the 1970s as a result of their vast accumulation of financial assets in Western money and capital markets. When asked whether he was prepared to accept an OPEC proposal to replace the dollar by a basket of currencies, Prince Fahd's response was categorical: "We have rejected the proposal for substituting a basket of currencies for the U.S. dollar and we shall not accept it. . . . Furthermore, if we were to accept the basket of currencies, our dollar income and investments would be affected, and this is what we are trying to avoid as the biggest producer."[8]

THE SAUDI-LED LONG-TERM STRATEGY FOR OPEC

The attempt by the Saudis to impose on OPEC member countries another price freeze for 1978 became untenable in the face of the serious depreciation in the value of the dollar, continued inflation in industrial countries, and the consequent loss in the real value of oil revenues and accumulated financial assets. It will be recalled that during the decade of the 1970s OPEC was intimidated by internal and external forces—the combined effect of the collusive behavior of the United States and Saudi governments—into freezing crude oil prices in the face of rampant world inflation. This in turn meant a considerable loss in the purchasing power of oil revenue and accumulated financial assets. Using 1972 as the base year, Ali Tawfik Sadik calculated that between 1972 and 1982 the OPEC import price index rose from 100 to 323. Applying this change to oil revenues of the Arab members of OPEC he concluded that while these countries received more than $1 trillion, the real oil revenues amounted to only $452 billion. By the same token the real value of the $355 billion balance-of-payments surplus that the same countries accumulated between 1972 and 1981 had declined to $161 billion using the same import price index.[9]

By 1978 it became clear that the Saudis could not continue to use their oil power against their fellow OPEC member countries without endangering the cohesion of OPEC itself. The interests of the Saudis argued in favor of the continued existence of the organization. OPEC performed a very useful function for the Saudis by providing a framework for the legitimization of their national output and pricing policies. It also ensured that member countries would not engage in any disruptive price and output tactics. The role of Saudi Arabia in OPEC was similar to that of the largest producer in a market dominated by few sellers where independent behavior of some producers could lead to ruinous consequences to all sellers. In order to ensure compliance with its desired objectives, Saudi Arabia had to ensure that conditions of compliance were at least tolerable to other producers.

This Saudi interest in preserving OPEC led them to propose in 1978 that an OPEC Long Term Strategy Committee (LTSC) be created. The LTSC, which was created at an informal OPEC meeting, was composed of six ministers with Yamani as chairman. The main thrust of the committee's focus was to play the role of a "think tank" regarding the future behavior of oil market conditions and make certain policy recommendations to OPEC.

According to the committee's chairman, oil was likely to go through three phases: a phase of excess capacity, which he estimated to last until about the end of 1979; a phase of supply-and-demand balance; and finally some time in the 1980s a phase of shortage. During the third phase the price of oil would inevitably rise in accordance with the law of supply and demand. Member countries, according to this view, need not do much, since market forces would see to it that prices went up.[10]

The formation of the LTSC, which was intended to shift the focus of attention from OPEC problems of oil glut, inflation, dollar depreciation, frozen prices, and the absence of any output programming, elicited a highly critical response from Algeria. The official Algerian statement said in part:

Certainly, the energy question is a big international problem. But at the same time there exists a whole series of important questions of interest primarily to the oil producing countries—namely, oil prices, the availability of energy, the relative balance between consumption and production, and the relationship between the economic problems of the industrialized countries and those of the Third World. And, finally, there is the question of the responsibility of OPEC governments vis-à-vis their own peoples. . . . In fact, the essential objective—namely, the protection of the purchasing power of the oil barrel—has not been achieved and oil prices have fallen. . . . Furthermore, what is euphemistically called the "dollar crisis" masks in fact a conspiracy of monetary manipulations which aggravates the erosion of oil price. Thus the oil price freeze which is actually a reduction, the price discrimination as regards capital goods sold to the OPEC countries, and inflation together with monetary manipulations of the dollar—these have been the main means used by the industrialized countries in order to wipe out completely the oil price increases of 1973.[11]

The Algerian reaction reflected their view of the working of the international economic system, their own economic conditions, and their future expectations. With a small oil reserve endowment (less than 4 percent of that of Saudi Arabia) and a relatively large population (more than twice the size of Saudi Arabia), the Algerians could not afford to suffer oil revenue losses. The problem for them was immediate. They needed money to carry out their development plans. The Algerians also had a more realistic assessment of the international economic system. To the Algerians talk of the law of supply and demand, market forces, and so on was no more than claptrap.

The report of the LTSC, which was supposed to be presented at the OPEC summit of 1980, never saw the light of day. The summit was canceled because of the Iran-Iraq War. However, enough materials from the report were made public to justify comment.

The thrust and recommendations of the report were built upon two key assumptions: (1) the belief that the demand for OPEC oil would some time in the 1980s exceed the oil productive capacity of member countries, and (2) that a minimum floor price had to be adopted, which would be adjusted to reflect inflation in industrial countries and exchange rate fluctuations. These two adjustments would maintain the price of oil in real terms while a third element, based on real GNP growth rate, would be added to provide a gradual movement toward the equalization of oil prices with the cost of alternatives.[12]

There were certain flaws in the proposed price strategy. The most important was the belief, contrary to overwhelming evidence, that an oil shortage was going to develop in the 1980s. In fact OPEC crude oil exports declined in the 1970s considerably, from 27.5 MBD in 1973 to 22.9 in 1980.

Not only did the LTSC base its plan for future pricing on some dubious assumptions, but it failed to link prices to output regulation in any serious manner. The responsibility for this failure can be attributed to the Saudis, since any serious discussion of output regulation and programming was not acceptable to them. Yamani was very clear on this issue: "As far as production programming is concerned so far there had been no change in Saudi policy—we are not prepared to discuss it."[13]

While the LTSC was considering some form of long-term policy rationalization, there were other forces at work that proved too powerful for OPEC to overcome and that ultimately led to its collapse. These forces include the policies of industrial countries with respect to oil stockpiling, conservation, substitution, and the Saudi-engineered oil glut.

THE ROLE OF STOCKPILES

One of the most significant changes in international oil during the period since 1979 was the buildup by the industrial countries of substantial stockpiles at a time when oil prices were fast rising. This was not done to meet the needs of seasonal fluctuations in demand nor because of a pending oil shortage. (OPEC output in the first quarter of 1979, the height of the Iranian oil shortage, was actually higher than its output in the comparable quarter of 1978.) According to OPEC, "accelerated purchase of crudes characterized by the psychotic atmosphere of supply uncertainty, brought about rapid stock build-up at any cost and almost any price."[14]

The buildup continued for the years 1980 and 1981 in spite of the evident decline in demand for energy and oil and the conditions of recession in the industrial economies. While inventories are considered a normal operational tool designed to meet the usual seasonal gaps and unexpected supply interruptions, the continued buildup well after the events of the Iranian Revolution and the temporary decline in oil output associated with the Iran-Iraq War gave OPEC staff a pause.

OPEC apprehension can be seen in the way changes in inventories were reported in its Annual Reports. The following is from the 1979 Annual Report:

This rapid build-up in stock was implemented at such high speed that, by December 31, 1979, IEA oil stock had reached a record level of 426 million tons, representing about 129 days of net imports and being 7.85 percent higher than at the start of 1979.[15]

The 1980 Report found the buildup to be more disconcerting:

although real demand had already started to decline: due, however, to many factors, including the fear of supply interruptions after the Iranian Revolution, there was a rush to stockpile large quantities of crude oil to a level much higher than that either envisaged or suggested by the International Energy Agency (IEA).[16]

The report went on to describe the consequences of the buildup:

However, as the level of stocks reached intolerable heights during the last quarter of 1980, and as oil consumption in most industrialized countries continued to decline, both oil companies and oil stockholders were in a dilemma as to how to trim this unjustified level of stocks.[17]

By 1981 OPEC had this to say about the stock buildup:

As these oil inventories became commercially unattractive, the idea of a "flexible stocking policy" was adopted by both the major oil companies and the IEA member countries, and the accumulated stocks became an instrument for "sub-crises" management or just simply to be used as "political tool."[18]

While oil stocks were increasing, so were the costs of holding and maintaining them. This meant that prices had to continue to increase to justify the cost of holding these oil stockpiles. As soon as the conditions that gave rise to such hoarding ceased to exist, so did the incentive to hoard.

The realization that the Iran-Iraq War was of no consequence to oil supplies, the emergence of glut conditions in the world oil market, the decline in demand for oil and the continued rise in interest rates in 1981, and the stability of official and spot prices induced industrial countries to dip into their accumulated oil stockpiles to meet part of their consumption requirements instead of importing oil from OPEC member countries. It was the manipulation of oil inventories, which together with conservation and substitution, led eventually to the 1983 oil price reduction.

SUBSTITUTION AND CONSERVATION

The increase in the price of imported oil led industrial countries to adopt measures that were specifically designed to slow down the rate of increase in the consumption of energy and oil. Oil, which fueled the economic growth in industrial countries in the 1950s and the 1960s, ceased in the 1970s to be the low-cost source of energy to which the industrial countries were accustomed. The higher cost of imported oil became a source of concern to many industrial countries, but the shift of control over oil decisions to oil-producing countries gave rise to another source of concern.

In response to these changes, industrial countries, individually and collectively through IEA, decided to reduce the rate of increase in the consumption of energy and oil and to reduce also their degree of dependence on imported oil. In order to achieve these objectives several policy measures were adopted to increase the efficiency of energy use and to increase the supply of alternative sources of energy—both oil and nonoil.

In the area of substitution there was increased reliance on coal and nuclear energy. Additionally, non-OPEC sources of oil such as Mexico, the North Sea, Alaska, and Egypt made their contribution to the world supply of oil. More important was the achievement in the area of conservation through reduction in demand in response to the price increase through the increased efficiency in the use of energy. Both factors—substitution and conservation—plus the condition of stagnation in industrial countries led to significant savings in energy consumption in all sectors of the energy market.[19]

In the OECD countries as a group there was such a reduction in energy requirements per unit of output that OPEC concluded that there was "for the first time since the 1960s, an uncoupling of energy requirements from the pace of aggregate economic performance."[20]

These changes in the pattern of energy consumption led the IEA to make the following conclusions with respect to the period 1973–1980 in the OECD group of countries: (1) real GNP increased by 10 percent, but energy consumption increased by only 4 percent, reflecting a 13 percent decline in the energy used to produce one unit of GDP; (2) the successful energy policies of industrial countries led to a decline by 14 percent in oil imports; and (3) oil requirements to produce one unit of GDP declined by 20 percent.[21] It is clear from these observations that there was a major transformation in the structure of the demand for oil, which resulted from the deliberate and coordinated policies of the major oil-consuming countries.

The underlying dangers for oil-producing countries of OECD conservation policies were recognized as early as 1977 by Fadhel al-Chalabi when he warned of the negative implications for OPEC of the IEA conservation strategies:

Such strategies run contrary to the short and medium term interests of oil producing countries and could well adversely affect those countries' economic development as well as apply pressure upon the OPEC price structure in the international market. What is so far known of the "conservationist" approach to energy policies suggests that priority is being given to creating such conditions in the international oil market as will prevent the OPEC price from rising substantially, if not actually reducing it in real terms. Meanwhile, the cost structure of energy deemed to be the right price to be paid by end-users in the industrialized countries is to be isolated and made attainable through internal taxation and not through payment of the right price of oil to its owners.[22]

He went on to say that these policies, if successful, would mean the continuation of OPEC's present oversupply beyond 1985. He also likened the danger of the conservation policies to those of other confrontational tactics:

The above analysis, if correct, would suggest that the "conservationist" approach of the IEA is no different from the previous "confrontational" attitude adopted by the architects of this "grouping of consumers" whose declared objective was the breaking of OPEC by economic means, or even by military action. Whether the new approach will have greater chances of success, only the future can reveal; however, serious doubts have already been cast on its feasibility. Nevertheless it indicates how the West looks at the problem of energy and growth distribution, namely, by trying to repeat the same historical pattern of growth at the expense of the oil producing/exporting countries.[23]

Another factor that contributed to the price spiral was the United States government decision to pay a subsidy of $5 a barrel to importers of petroleum products in order to build up American inventories of these products. The effect of the subsidy was that more American refiners entered the world oil market to buy up products and therefore push prices upward. The seriousness of the U.S. decision was underscored by the reaction of America's European partners in the IEA, who saw the decision as a callous attempt by the United States to hog limited supplies.[24] In addition, major oil-consuming countries decided in the aftermath of the Iranian Revolution to accelerate the buildup of their stocks or inventories of crude oil and products.

THE SAUDI-ENGINEERED OIL GLUT

Although it became clear in early 1979 that there was no basis for fear of an oil shortage, the demand for oil, however, was not justified by consumption needs in the industrial countries. Instead it reflected policy considerations that oil inventories should be increased.

Stock accumulation, successful conservation policies, worldwide recession conditions, increased output of oil outside OPEC, and the increase in the supply of nonoil sources of energy combined to set the stage for a sharp decline in demand for OPEC oil. A rational policy under these conditions on the part of OPEC required a concerted effort to reduce output. But this was not to be. The Saudis, who were always opposed to such coordinated policy, found no reason to change now. On the contrary, they persisted in keeping their output at high levels even in the face of an oil glut.

The Iranian Revolution, which gave the Saudis the pretext to raise output, also deprived them of their leadership role in OPEC, since they increased output to capacity. With the rise in spot market prices and OPEC prices, the Saudis found it to their advantage to keep their prices lower than those of other OPEC member countries. This price differential helped the Saudis and the Aramco owners to increase Saudi oil exports from 8.1 MBD in 1978 to 9.6 MBD in 1980 and close to the same level, 9.5 MBD, in 1981. The rise in Saudi exports took place in the face of a drastic decline in oil exports by other OPEC member countries from 19.9 MBD in 1978 to 10.9 MBD in 1981, a decline of 45 percent.[25]

The expansion in the Saudi market share was a direct result of deliberate policy to create a glut in order to force other OPEC member countries once again to follow the leadership of Saudi Arabia. The policy of creating an oil glut was acknowledged by Yamani in this exchange:

Q: As a result of conservation, a stagnant economy and other factors, there is now an oil glut on the international market. Some nations and some American companies have been lowering prices. Would your country have any plans to lower production or lower prices?

A: Well, as a matter of fact, this glut was anticipated by Saudi Arabia and almost done by Saudi Arabia. If we were to reduce our production to the level it was at before we started raising it, there would be no glut at all. We engineered the glut and want to see it in order to stabilize the price of oil.[26]

While Yamani was correct in assuming responsibility for the glut, he was totally wrong in believing that a reduction in his country's output would have removed it. He was wrong because output data for OPEC indicate that between April 1980 and April 1981, when Yamani had his interview, OPEC output (excluding Saudi Arabia) had declined by 4.4 MBD, from 18.1 MBD to 13.7 MBD. Since Saudi output in April 1981 was only 1.7 MBD above the traditional Saudi ceiling of 8.5 MBD, it is clear that in order to be willing to remove the glut, the Saudis would have had to reduce the output considerably below the ceiling. The Saudis were not prepared to take such a course of action.

But the persistence of the Saudis in their policy of creating an artificial glut coincided with other forces that led to a drastic reduction in the demand for OPEC oil. The decline in the demand for OPEC oil was accentuated by oil price cuts by non-OPEC oil producers. This made clear to OPEC member countries that official prices could not be supported under conditions of glut, destocking, substitution and conservation, and price reduction by other oil producers. In order to protect their shares of the market from further erosion, member countries resorted to discounts of official prices. Although OPEC succeeded in November 1981 in its efforts to reunify prices (at $34 a barrel), the pressure of declining demand forced many countries to resort again to the practice of open or hidden discounts or outright reduction in the official price. Ironically this time it was Saudi oil that became overpriced relative to oil from other member countries as the Saudis adhered to the official price.

The move by OPEC member countries to cut prices was made in response to price reductions effected by oil-producing countries outside OPEC such as Britain, the Soviet Union, Mexico, and Egypt. With non-OPEC oil output reaching the level of that of OPEC and with increasing exports from non-OPEC countries, it became clear that OPEC was not determining prices. Thus, the Saudis found themselves pressured by OPEC as well as non-OPEC countries to lower output and lose a share of their market to their competitors. In January 1982 Saudi crude oil output was 8.7 MBD. By the end of the year it plummeted to 5.3 MBD, a decline of 39 percent. Other OPEC producers by contrast increased their output from 12.2 MBD to 13.7 MBD. And so at long last the so-called market-determined price had caught up with the Saudis.

In order to stabilize their share of world oil market, OPEC member countries agreed in 1982 on a kind of quota system. Most member countries, however, failed to observe their allotted shares and produced above their quotas. This situation was clearly untenable especially when prices were being reduced.

Although observers throughout the world insisted that OPEC had to reduce its official prices if it were to retain its market share, attempts were made by its members throughout 1982 to stabilize the official price of $34 per barrel. The efforts to support the official price of $34 per barrel were strongly supported by the Saudis and led by them. The Saudis were so convinced that the official price could be maintained that one keen observer of OPEC, Robert Mabro had this to say:

Everybody expected Saudi Arabia to lower the market price of Arabian Light. Self-appointed experts went so far as affirming that the new market price would be $28–30. The news media were so taken by these predictions as to give them priority for the headlines over an official statement made . . . by Shaikh Yamani who solemnly declared that Saudi Arabia would hold the price line. One would have thought that Shaikh Yamani is a more authoritative source on Saudi Arabia's and OPEC's intentions than some third-rate analysts of New York stock-brokering firms.[27]

The view that prices should not be reduced was based on the belief that the oil glut was temporary. Based on estimates by Saudi experts, Prince Fahd declared in April 1982 that "the crisis caused by the surplus will end in two or three months."[28]

Thus, the self-deception that the Saudis practiced for so long and with such confidence had to give way ultimately to the realities of changing conditions. Saudi Arabia led OPEC in March 1983 to reduce prices for the first time in its twenty-three-year history. The reduction was massive, from $34 to $29 per barrel of Arabian oil. Ironically, the "third-rate oil analysts of New York brokering firms" whom Mabro ridiculed were proven to be far more correct in their assessment of the changing conditions in the oil market than Yamani, the oil minister of the kingdom of Saudi Arabia.

THE 1980s: FROM PRICE REVOLUTION TO PRICE COLLAPSE

In the decade of the 1970s, before the Iranian Revolution, OPEC's oil output, exports, and revenue peaked in 1977. In 1978 OPEC experienced the first decline in the three indices in the decade of the 1970s. The 1973–1974 price increases, the successful effort to reduce reliance on oil through conservation and substitution, the rise in non-OPEC oil output, and the extended economic stagnation of the 1970s were factors that contributed to the decline in OPEC's economic fortunes. The events of the Iranian Revolution, which began toward the end of 1978 and which succeeded in the overthrowing of the Iranian monarchy in 1979, arrested and temporarily reversed for the time being the impact of the underlying forces of demand for oil. This in turn created an atmosphere of panic buying which, as was noted earlier, pushed oil prices to unprecedented high levels. And when the Iran-Iraq War broke out in September 1980, the panic buying was heightened, causing prices to reach still higher levels of $34 per barrel in 1981 for Saudi Light crude, the marker crude for OPEC.

Saudi Arabia proved to be the primary beneficiary of the revolution and the Iran-Iraq War, as they provided it with an unparalleled opportunity to boost output and increase revenue. Saudi oil output was increased from 7.1 MBD in September 1978 to 10.4 MBD by December of that year, or by 46 percent. Although the market had been suffering from an oil glut, the Saudis persisted in keeping their output at high levels. Thus by 1981 the Saudis managed to produce 44 percent of OPEC's total output compared with 28 percent in 1978. This in turn increased their share in OPEC revenue from 30 percent to 45 percent between 1978 and 1981.

Saudi policy of high output was criticized by Iraq and other producing countries as harmful to their interests and intended to prolong the Iran-Iraq War.[29] In order to counteract the Saudi policy of high output and regain some of the market shares, oil-producing countries started to offer buyers discounts from the official prices. Since the Saudis continued to adhere to the official price, they found themselves losing market share as well as influence over OPEC oil policies to the point that Saudi Arabia together with other members of the Gulf Cooperation Council (Kuwait, the United Arab Emirates, Qatar, Oman, and Bahrain) issued a statement attacking other OPEC members for their "misguided action" and "irresponsible behavior" and saying that they will have "to shoulder the blame tomorrow."[30]

The Saudi-sponsored GCC statement, which implied the use of Saudi oil against other OPEC members, meant that the use of the so-called "oil weapon" had come full circle in that it was being deployed now to undermine Arab economic interests. Yet the Saudi-led coalition had long been overtaken by market conditions. The persistent decline in demand for oil, continued efficient use of energy in industrial economies, the effective use of stockpiles by industrial countries to increase available supplies, and the rising importance of non-OPEC exporters forced OPEC in March 1983 to lower its official price from $34 to $29 for the first time in its history.

But market conditions that led OPEC to reduce prices remained at work, forcing OPEC to accept smaller shares of the world oil market as it continued to defend its own official price while non-OPEC exporters were free to lower prices and expand their market share. This untenable situation finally forced Saudi Arabia and other OPEC members toward the end of 1985 to abandon its and OPEC's role as the crude oil price administrator and residual supplier and switch instead to a strategy that would maximize market shares.

In order to expand their share of the market and sell more oil, the policy of setting official selling prices for crude oil was discarded and a new market-determined price formula was adopted. According to this formula or "netback pricing," an oil exporter price is determined by the price the refiner in a con-suming country receives for petroleum products. This new pricing policy in combination with the new market share strategy led ultimately to the collapse of 1986 when crude oil prices plummeted to as low as $7 per barrel.[31]

The adoption of the new pricing formula was an act of retrogression for the oil-producing countries, since their national revenue and national income had become once again a function of the policies of governments and corporations in the industrial countries. Indeed President Ronald Reagan went as far as saying that it was his administration's policies that were responsible for OPEC being "dramatically undercut" and for the collapse in oil prices.[32]

The 1986 price collapse had a dramatic impact on OPEC's oil income. For example, in 1985 OPEC's petroleum exports amounted to 13.3 MBD and generated $131 billion in income. In 1986 by contrast OPEC increased its exports to 15.5 MBD or by 17 percent only to see its income plummet by nearly 40 percent to $79 billion.[33] In spite of many attempts to restore its position of leadership in the world oil market through price administration and various production quota systems OPEC continued to have a declining share of world oil output. By 1988 its share of the world oil output declined to 32 percent, compared with 51 percent in 1977.

THE MYTH OF ARAB OIL POWER

The 1973–1974 sharp rise in the price of oil, Arab oil output and embargo measures, and the inevitable slow process of adjustment to the new oil conditions gave rise to the belief that Arab oil-producing countries (and especially Saudi Arabia) were in a position to play a decisive role in shaping events both in the Arab region and throughout the world. This belief was strengthened by three important considerations. First was the success of the Saudis in shaping the pricing behavior of OPEC member countries by threatening to raise their oil output. Second, the generally held notion that there was a special relationship between the Saudis and the Americans served to endow the Saudis with some leverage of influence regarding American policy toward the Arab region. Third, the accumulation of Saudi financial assets in American and other Western financial institutions was thought to have given the Saudis and other balance-of-payments-surplus states a potential influence over foreign policy considerations of the United States and other industrial countries.

The belief that the Saudis have a special relationship with the United States and that they could or would use this special relationship to influence foreign policy outcomes was so prevalent that some writers referred to it as the "Saudi era." An examination of the assumptions, the facts, and the record will show, however, that the Saudis had neither this perceived kind of special relationship with the United States nor did they have the levers of power that could influence policies toward the Arab region and the Palestine question.

In an article that appeared shortly after the 1973 October war, Ghassan Tueni, a noted Arab journalist and diplomat, concluded that the anti-Saudi alliance of the radical regimes in the Arab world led to the Arab defeat of 1967. By contrast the triple alliance of the moderate regimes of Syria and Egypt plus Saudi Arabia, which conducted the operations of 1973, paved the way for a settlement of the conflict. Tueni went on to say that radicalism had its day as revolutionary war had been found wanting, that the era of ideologies and mythology was past, and the age of oil and reason was starting. Tueni noted that while the Arabs make war with Russian armaments, they make peace through American diplomacy. As to the role of Israel in defending American interests in the region, the October war made clear according to him that the dependent state left much to be desired and that the new intensity of Arab-American relations would no doubt give diplomacy its opportunity to work its miracle in solving the Middle East conflicts. Even the Palestinian resistance was behaving like a government, since the resistance supported the moderate political alliance of King Faisal and President Sadat. This phenomenon, he said, had given birth to a new idea: diplomacy in revolution. In addition, the October war caused Israel to become completely subordinate to the United States. This greater Israeli subordination, he believed, opened up opportunities for the Arabs in that they could demand stronger American pressures. In the long run the United States could not endure Arab hostilities especially if one recognized the fact that a stable Middle East was an essential condition for the industrial and postindustrial societies. The coincidence of the interests of the Arabs and the Americans in peace in the region stood in sharp contrast to the coincidence of the interests of the Arabs and the Soviets in war. The American policy of total support of Israel propelled the Arabs to seek Soviet help and arms. He concluded that the Americans were going to distance themselves from the Israelis and begin to look at their interests more realistically with the prospects of both peace and the removal of the Soviet influence in the region enhanced.[34]

Beneath all these assertions there ran a simple theme, the essence of which was that the Arabs should rely on the United States exclusively to seek relief from Israeli occupation and that the use of oil in this context was necessary. Since Saudi Arabia was the superpower of oil, it followed that peace in the Middle East would of necessity have to be sponsored and conducted by the Saudis. With peace would also come the removal of Soviet influence in the Middle East.

The importance of the Saudis in this scenario was expanded and elaborated upon to a relatively high degree of sophistication by another writer, Muhammad Hassanein Heykal. Writing in May 1977, he asserted that Saudi Arabia was in a position to play a decisive role in the Arab world especially in terms of its capacity to bring pressure to bear on the United States for a peace settlement. Heykal had the notion that Saudi Arabia would be courted by Washington, not the other way around. The reason for this interesting turn of events was that Saudi Arabia was in the stronger position vis-à-vis the United States. Heykal's explanation was, ''The heart of the matter is that Saudi Arabia with its immense revenues and the major role it performs at the present stage—the Saudi era in contemporary Arab history—and with the values it represents and advocates, is not an ordinary state.''[35] As to the source and basis of Saudi power Heykal stated, ''There is a small country—Saudi Arabia; and a big country—the U.S. To live, the big country needs the resources of the small country.''[36] Thus, once again the whole matter hinged upon one thing and one thing only, oil. In presenting his argument Heykal quoted extensively from United States government sources to show that the United States would be more dependent on Saudi oil as time went on. But once the oil factor was removed from the analysis, the importance of Saudi Arabia and its role in the region and the world disappear. More important, Heykal and other writers who shared these views engaged in self-delusion when they projected the degree of American dependence on Saudi oil. In no year did the United States find itself importing more than 7.7 percent of its oil or about 3.5 percent of its total energy consumption from Saudi Arabia. Therefore, uninformed and groundless assertions had to give rise to dangerously false and unwarranted high expectations as to what could be done for the Palestinian and Arab cause and aspirations. This is precisely what Heykal found himself doing: ''For the Saudi era in contemporary Arab history can greatly increase the credit balance of the Arab nation and it comes at an extremely important and dangerous time.''[37] Moreover, given the special position of the state of Saudi Arabia in the Arab order, Heykal concluded that the Saudis could not accept just any solution of the Middle East crisis, but rather one that accepted the Arab character of Jerusalem.[38]

Ironically, while Heykal was busy exaggerating the role of Saudi oil in American life and in the Arab world the Saudis had no similar illusion about their position vis-à-vis the United States. Only a few months after Heykal wrote his analysis, an Algerian delegation led by President Houari Boumedienne came back from Saudi Arabia with the following appraisal:

The Algerians say that their visit to Saudi Arabia was useful and that while they were there they became aware of the extreme perplexity and disappointment felt by the Royal family. . . . The Saudis now feel that their role in the area (and to a great extent in the whole world) has been eliminated or so reduced that it is circumscribed and no longer influential or effective.[39]

To speak of the Saudi era, if there ever was one, one should confine the influence of the Saudis to the Arab region, more precisely to certain regimes at certain times. One can say that the Saudi era started in 1967 when the Saudi views of the Arab-Israeli conflict were accepted at the Arab summit in that year. The Saudis, as noted in an earlier chapter, were able in the aftermath of the 1967 Arab defeat to bring President Nasser of Egypt around to their views. The first year that the Saudis started to use their oil money on a massive scale to influence Arab government policies was also 1967. In that year the governments of Saudi Arabia, Kuwait, and prerevolutionary Libya agreed to provide the governments of Egypt, Syria, and Jordan with considerable fiscal aid on an annual basis. Like all foreign aid the Saudi subsidy was not without conditions. The conditions were that the aid-receiving regimes would coordinate their policies toward the United States and toward a settlement to the Arab-Israeli conflict with those of the Saudis.

As Sadiq al-Azm observed, the Saudi era meant that policy initiative had passed from Nasser's Cairo to the conservative Saudi establishment.[40] This in turn boiled down to the capacity of the Saudi regime to manipulate other regimes and groups in the region through fiscal means. It is difficult, however, to see how one can project the influence of the Saudis from regional to the global level and say that the Saudis were in a position to influence United States foreign policy. For over six years between 1967 and 1973 the Saudis did attempt to convince the United States that an American-led settlement of the Middle East conflict would be beneficial to all. Yet the Saudis failed consistently to budge American policymakers from their total support and endorsement of Israeli policies of occupation. Even when the Saudis were finally driven to join other Arab countries to impose their oil measures, they were far from serious in that endeavor. No sooner did they impose restrictive oil measures than they started to destroy the credibility of the measures by advocating their relaxation and removal.

It can be safely said that whatever influence the Saudis may have wielded in world affairs, such influence lasted for no more than a few weeks when they and the other Arab oil-producing countries seemed to be serious in using oil as an instrument of political pressure. Once they abandoned the political dimension of oil, the Saudis and other oil-producing countries returned to their earlier political station and to impotence and dependency. Thus to speak of a Saudi era in the sense that the Saudis wielded some influence over American foreign policy decisions is no more than an exercise in self-deception at best. It is significant to note in this context that on more than one occasion Yamani himself accused the United States and the West of following policies aimed at the destruction of the effectiveness of the oil power of Saudi Arabia, other Arab countries, and

OPEC as may be seen in the following interview that took place in 1977 at the height of Saudi oil power:

Q: Do you feel that this oil weapon you possess is, or has been, exposed to danger?

A: Undoubtedly, most certainly—the danger is there. Conspiracies are being hatched, and by big powers. Their sole concern is to render this weapon impotent. Not only that, but to deprive us of it altogether.

Q: Which countries are interested in destroying this weapon or taking it over from us?

A: The industrialized countries in general. More specifically, the United States. It is the country that is promoting the campaign against this Arab weapon.[41]

Almost a decade later Yamani accused the West of having caused the price collapse when he stated, "the actual collapse was the result of a Western plan" that was intended "to destroy OPEC and remove it from the scene."[42]

The impotence of the Saudis vis-à-vis American foreign policy in the region can best be illustrated by the decisions of the Egyptian government to sign a separate peace treaty with Israel in 1979 only two years after Muhammad H. Heykal was speaking of the Saudi era.

The 1979 peace treaty between Egypt and Israel, which resulted in the expulsion of Egypt from the Arab League and its specialized agencies, constituted a major defeat to the policies of Arab states and Arab summit resolutions. The Egyptian-Israeli treaty was an especially severe blow to the Saudis. The Saudis since the October war thought, as many other people did, that the way to Washington was through Riyadh. It was thought that Saudi Arabia was too important for the United States not to be included in major regional negotiations, especially those with such far-reaching implications as the Arab-Israeli conflict. The fact that Sadat was willing to ignore the Saudis and their finances and was able to replace them with American money revealed the hollowness of the presumed importance of the Saudis as an independent force in Arab-American affairs. Not only did the Sadat defection from Saudi control prove to be feasible, but it also exposed as inconsequential the position of Saudi Arabia in American Middle East policy designs.

In order to force the Saudis behind the American-led Egyptian-Israeli peace negotiations, the United States engaged in a series of threats regarding the use of force to secure oil supplies if necessary.[43] While threats of intervention were general in that they were directed at all oil countries, there were, however, more specific and more ominous threats directed against the very political and territorial integrity of the kingdom of Saudi Arabia. This can be seen from the following assessment of the Saudi predicament.

According to high-level Arab sources the Saudis' public announcement of their disagreement (limited though it is) with Carter, following his visit to the country, was an implicit answer to various American threats that reached them before the visit, the most significant being that to the unity of the kingdom. For the Americans told the Saudis in a round-about manner that the kingdom was too young for people to have forgotten the tribal disputes that used to rage there. . . .

Also, of course, most of the oil is in the eastern area—which faces Iran across the Gulf. Therefore, the American threat, in the form of direct encouragement to Iran to play a greater role in the Arabian Peninsula and the Gulf, accompanied by the establishment of an Egyptian-Israeli alliance covering the Arab East and Africa, could put a damper not only on the Saudis' aspirations to occupy a leading position in the area but also rob them of their feeling of security and internal stability.[44]

American efforts to silence the Saudis were successful in that the wrath of the Arab regimes was directed at Sadat's Egypt and not at the United States. Oil continued to flow, trade continued to grow, and more Arab money continued to be poured into the United States economy for investment.

While the Saudi position in the Arab world and the world of oil was being undermined by the American policy in the Arab region and by changing conditions in the demand for oil, another force of historical dimension contributed its share to undermine the position of the Saudis in the region. This force was the Iranian Revolution, which succeeded in overthrowing the monarchy in Iran and replacing it with the Islamic Republic in 1979.

Although the Iranian Revolution and the Iran-Iraq War strengthened the market position of Saudi Arabia and other Arab oil-producing countries, such strength proved to be transitory as demand for oil continued to decline and as new non-OPEC supplies continued to reach the market. More important, as Arab oil and Arab oil-producing economies have become so thoroughly integrated in and dependent upon the international economic system through imports, exports, trade, financial investment, and real investment, it has ceased to be conceivable to challenge Western economic interests for some Pan-Arab political considerations. Nothing illustrates this point as well as the myth of Arab oil power more vividly than the posture of resignation and utter helplessness that the Arab governments adopted during the Israeli invasion of Lebanon in 1982. Nor had the Arab governments done anything since 1982 to change this political situation.

NOTES

1. *Middle East Economic Survey* (*MEES*), January 3, 1977, 1–2.
2. *MEES*, July 3, 1978, 2.
3. *MEES*, July 25, 1977, 3.
4. *MEES*, May 22, 1978, ii.
5. See Pierre Terzian, *OPEC: The Inside Story* (London: Zed Books, 1985), vii.
6. *MEES*, January 10, 1977 (Supplement), 8.
7. *MEES*, July 25, 1977, 3–5.
8. *MEES*, August 28, 1978, 2.
9. Ali Tawfik Sadik, "Managing The Petrodollar Bonanza: Avenues and Implications of Recycling Arab Capital," *Arab Studies Quarterly* 6, Nos. 1 & 2 (1984): 28–34.
10. *MEES*, May 15, 1978, 2.

11. *MEES*, June 5, 1978, 1–2.

12. See "Report of OPEC's Ministerial Committee on Long Term Strategy," *International Currency Review*, July 1980, pp. 9–15. See also *MEES*, March 3, 1980, 1–2; May 12, 1980, 1–4; and September 22, 1980, 5–8.

13. *MEES*, May 12, 1980, 3.

14. OPEC, *Annual Report, 1980* (Vienna), 44.

15. See *Petroleum Intelligence Weekly* (*PIW*), June 4, 1979, 44.

16. OPEC, *Annual Report, 1980* (Vienna), 44.

17. Ibid.

18. OPEC, *Annual Report, 1981* (Vienna), 36.

19. See "Prices—Conservation Effects on World Oil Demand," *Petroleum Times Price Report*, July 1, 1983.

20. OPEC, *Annual Report, 1980*, 19.

21. International Energy Agency, *World Energy Outlook* (Paris, 1982), 22.

22. Fadhil al-Chalabi, "Energy Conservation Policies of the Consuming Countries: A Producer's Point of View," *OPEC Review* (December 1977), 25.

23. Ibid, 27.

24. See *PIW*, June 4, 1979, 4.

25. OPEC, *Annual Report, 1981*, 124.

26. *MEES*, April 27, 1981 (Supplement), 1.

27. *MEES*, September 20, 1982 (Supplement), 6.

28. *MEES*, April 5, 1982, 5.

29. See *MEES*, July 27, 1981, pp. 1–2, and September 7, 1981, 2.

30. For the text of the GCC statement see *MEES*, October 18, 1982, 3.

31. For an analysis of the relationship between these factors see J. E. Hartshorn, "Netbacks and the Price Collapse," *MEES*, March 17, 1986, D1–5.

32. See *MEES*, April 21, 1986, A7.

33. For data on OPEC output, export, and income for the period 1967–1987 see *MEES*, November 28, 1988, D1–3. For a good analysis of the factors that led to the collapse of OPEC's market share see Fadhil al-Chalabi, "The Role of OPEC in Market Stabilization (1985)," in Robert Mabro (ed.), *OPEC and the World Oil Market: The Genesis of the 1986 Price Crisis* (Oxford: Oxford University Press, 1986), 131–137.

34. See Ghassan Tueni, "After October: Military Conflict and Political Change in the Middle East," *Journal of Palestine Studies* 3, No. 4 (Summer 1974): 114–130.

35. See Muhammad Hassanein Heykal, "The Saudi Era," *Journal of Palestine Studies* 6, No. 4 (Summer 1977): 159–164.

36. Ibid, 161.

37. Ibid, 164.

38. Ibid, 161. This of course is in addition to the withdrawal of Israel from the territories it occupied in the 1967 war.

39. See Sadiq al-Azm, "The View from Damascus," *Journal of Palestine Studies* 7, No. 3 (Spring 1978): 154–167, especially p. 157.

40. See Sadiq al-Azm, "Illusions about America," *Journal of Palestine Studies* 7, No. 1 (Autumn 1977): 175–178.

41. See *MEES*, January 17, 1977, ii–iii.

42. See an interview with Yamani, "Oil Price Collapse Part of Western Plan to Dominate OPEC," *OPEC Bulletin*, June 1986, 3.

43. For an excellent analysis of such United States threats see Marwan R. Buheiry, *U.S. Threats of Intervention Against Arab Oil 1973–1979* (Beirut: Institute for Palestine Studies, 1980).

44. al-Azm, ''The View from Damascus,'' 158.

8

DIMENSIONS OF ARAB ECONOMIC DEPENDENCY

The last seven chapters analyzed several issues pertaining to the integration of Arab economies in the world economic system. Among these forces were the gradual incorporation of these economies into the European-dominated international economic order in the eighteenth century when most of the Arab region was part of the Ottoman Empire; the imposition of the colonial system on most of the Arab region where the hegemonic control of the Ottoman Empire was successfully challenged; the formal imposition of colonial or imperial control by Britain and France on the remaining parts of the Arab region in the aftermath of the defeat of the Ottoman Empire in World War I; the rise of Arab nationalism; the emergence and rise of dependent oil industry; and the creation of the state of Israel in the midst of the Arab region and the consequent wars that together with oil shaped much of the developments in the twentieth-century Arab world.

This chapter undertakes an analysis of some of the implications of the more significant changes in Arab economies as well as some of the measures of dependency. This in turn will set the stage for the analysis in the following chapter of some of the trends that are likely to shape the future of the Arab economies in the decades to come.

ECONOMICS OF THE ARAB STATE SYSTEM

It has been maintained that the initial formations of what came to be known as Arab states could be traced back to a period before the nineteenth century in the sense that the states were locally rooted, enjoyed legitimacy in the eyes of their people, and had recognizable boundaries or at least a core territory where their authority endured over time.[1] European penetration of the Arab region, which gained momentum during the first half of the nineteenth century, reached its height in the aftermath of World War I when Britain and France controlled either directly or indirectly virtually all of the Arab region.

Regardless of the nature and the modalities of foreign control, both Britain and France exerted their control through some form of centralized administration and increased the region's economic contacts with Europe, thus exposing the economies to the effects of free trade and aided in the creation of groups that tended to be nationalist. An interesting phenomenon in the evolution of the Arab state system was the conflict between colonialism and imperialism and some of the economic and social strata to which European penetration gave rise. As Ilya Harik observed:

Interestingly enough, the forces which tied the Arab countries to the world economy in a colonial and dependent relationship also generated the seeds of the destruction of colonialism, that is, nationalism. . . . Colonialism introduced some contradictory trends in the area. It generated economic forces which tied the Arab economies to the West in a dependency relationship, on the one hand, and made for the domestic integration of state and society, on the other. A new class of businessmen, landlords and professionals emerged and held high the torch of nationalist resistance to imperialism.[2]

In those countries where forces of nationalism succeeded in gaining political independence from a colonial power, the underlying economic structure and its dependency relationship on the former colonial powers remained unchanged. Even in those few Arab countries where forces of nationalism were both genuine and powerful, these countries either could not or chose not to transform their economic dependency relationship to a more equitable and independent pattern of relationships. This failure to repattern relationships with the international economic system may be attributed to the nature of relationships between centers and peripheries in the postcolonial era as well as to factors peculiar to the Arab region.

It can be safely said that the two most important forces that shaped most developments in the Arab region in the postcolonial period—the second half of the twentieth century—are Arab nationalism and oil. The rhetoric and the writings of the Arab nationalists, most of whom came from the relatively advanced core Arab states, Egypt, Iraq, and Syria, have always advocated the paramount importance of Pan-Arabism, which has Arab unity as its ultimate objective. The legitimacy of the ''Arabness'' of a regime or a state was to be judged by the professed adherence of that regime to the ultimate goal of having a single state, the territory of which would be coterminous with the geographical territory of the Arab region. These Pan-Arab positions were challenged, however, more frequently than not by the conservative regimes in the Arab world who were more interested in associating their regimes with the Western system of alliances than in Pan-Arab enterprises. Thus Iraq, for instance, opted in 1955 to join the Baghdad Pact, a United States–backed regional military alliance of Turkey, Iraq, Iran, and Pakistan at a time when the tide of Arab nationalism under the leadership of Nasser of Egypt was on the rise.

Another important challenge to Arab nationalism that came from Arab regimes was to posit Islam as a countervailing force and a movement that would dwarf Arab states in the much larger number of Muslim states. Thus Saudi Arabia led a movement in the 1960s with the slogan that the Arab world was a part of the larger Islamic world and that Islam was a bond that supersedes nationalist loyalties.[3] In their attempt to curb Pan-Arab success the Saudis were willing to align themselves with the Iranians in an effort to create a Pan-Islamic organization, eliciting this comment from Nasser: "The reaction in the Arab world has allied itself with colonialism in order to destroy the Arab nationalist idea."[4] Yet neither the perceived threat of Arab nationalism nor the adherence to Islam pushed the economies of the Arab states system in the direction of the conservative elements of the system. Instead it was the combination of the rising oil revenue and the 1967 defeat of the nationalist states—Egypt and Syria—at the hands of the Israeli army that enabled conservative states to play a crucial role in regional developments.

It was one of those monumental accidents of history that most of the oil resources in the Arab region should be concentrated in a small number of conservative Arab states whose governments' first and foremost allegiance was to protect the sovereignty of the individual state from the encroachment of the ideals of Arab nationalism.

In his "The Rentier State in the Arab World" Hazem Beblawi points to certain conflict between the political objectives of Pan-Arabism and the political agenda and economic objectives of conservative oil producers. Thus by channeling some of their oil income to non-oil-producing states the former hope to enhance and maintain their tranquility and political stability. He goes on to say that:

Pan-Arabism and Arab money were, to a great extent, and in different hands, the stick and the carrot, used to bring about a very subtle equilibrium in sharing oil rent. By conferring and/or withholding superlegitimacy over individual states, the advocates of pan-Arabism used their political clout as a source of financial aid. By distributing and/or promising aid, the carrot in the hands of the oil states helped them buy peace and stability. Arab finance was thus more a counterpart than a complement to pan-Arabism.[5]

FINANCIAL FLOWS AND THE PHENOMENON OF DERIVATIVE DEPENDENCY

The oil price explosion of the early 1970s and its attendant increase in the national income of oil-producing countries influenced inter-Arab patterns of relationships in a significant and perhaps lasting manner in two important areas. First, it changed suddenly and dramatically the distribution of gross national product among Arab countries. Second, it gave rise to considerable flows of human and financial resources among the countries of the region, giving rise to a new phenomenon among developing countries—the phenomenon of derivative or secondary dependency.[6]

As a measure of the magnitude of change in the distribution of income among Arab countries that the oil price rise brought about, it is sufficient to note the combined Arab GNP jumped from $55 billion in 1972, the last year prior to the sharp price change, to $145 billion (or by $90 billion) in 1975, the first full year when oil output returned to normal and when the new price structure was well in place. Of the $90 billion increment 52 percent went to three countries—Saudi Arabia, Kuwait, and the United Arab Emirates—which have less than 7 percent of the total Arab population. Another 23 percent of the rise in GNP went to Algeria, Iraq, and Libya with 21 percent of the Arab population. By contrast the non-oil-producing countries, with 71 percent of the Arab population, accounted for only 17 percent of the increase in Arab GNP during this period. The magnitude of the redistribution of income among Arab countries can be seen in the dramatic rise in the share of the Gulf Cooperation Council (GCC) countries in the combined GNP of the Arab countries. In 1972 the six GCC member countries accounted for 26 percent of the combined Arab GNP. By 1975 their share had jumped to 46 percent, only to rise again to 50 percent in 1980 when their combined population was less than 8 percent of the Arab population of 163 million. Although the decline in the demand for oil and its price affected the level of national income of the GCC countries, they continued to retain a disproportionately high share of Arab GNP. Thus in 1985 the GCC countries accounted for 9.4 percent of the Arab population of 192 million and 45 percent of its $380 billion GNP.[7] Last but not least the changes that were brought about by the rise in the price of oil may be appreciated by comparing the economies of Egypt and Saudi Arabia. Thus in 1972 Saudi Arabia's GNP was $6.8 billion or 86 percent of Egypt's GNP of $7.9 billion. By 1975 the relative importance of the two economies had so dramatically changed that Egypt's GNP of $9.3 billion had become a fraction of that of Saudi Arabia's of $40.4 billion.[8]

It was inevitable that the redistribution of economic fortunes among Arab states would result in a change in the relative political importance in favor of the sparsely populated and more economically underdeveloped and socially backward GCC states. The shift in inter-Arab political power in the aftermath of the October war was a process that can be traced to the defeat of Arab armies in the 1967 June war when Saudi Arabia and Kuwait started to determine Arab political and economic agenda by using their surplus financial resources. The phenomenon of the rising political/economic importance of the Gulf which was accompanied by the relative political/economic decline of the more advanced Arab countries was aptly captured by the title of a chapter in *Rich and Poor States in the Middle East* by Malcolm Kerr, "Egypt in the Shadow of the Gulf."[9]

The sudden and sharp increase in the revenue from oil led some observers to think that a new era of development and social and political change was about to begin among the Arab countries, leading up to some form of economic integration. The main reason for such expectation is the obvious fact that resource endowments among these countries were different enough to provide a rationale for integration.

In the case of the GCC states, for instance, oil was the primary resource endowment, since they possess virtually no other resources that can provide a foundation for a viable state. Their thin population base is reflected by lack of a labor force capable of meeting the rising needs of economies that were poised to attain high rates of economic growth. By contrast, the availability of skilled manpower and other resources in countries such as Egypt, Syria, and Jordan was thought to provide an essential integrative factor among the Arab economies.

By the same token, balance-of-payments surpluses of the GCC countries were thought to provide another integrative force if such funds were to be made available to non-oil-producing Arab countries. In other words, the oil price revolution was thought to have removed the bottleneck of capital shortage, a factor much emphasized by development economists.[10] Contrary to all available evidence the belief that non-oil-producing Arab countries would have access to the wealth of the oil states persisted in some circles long after the oil price increase.[11] Such beliefs proved to be illusory in spite of the fact that large numbers of Arab skilled workers and professionals moved to the GCC states to help, together with non-Arab workers, to operate the economies of those states.

It should be observed that the other side of this labor movement was the considerable flow of remittances to the economies of labor-exporting countries. In addition to the flow of worker remittances, governments of oil-producing states, as was observed in an earlier chapter, transferred considerable sums of money to non-oil-producing states in the form of loans, grants, and other types of economic assistance. Moreover, Arab private capital was invested in these economies for profit.

Yet these major flows of factors of production failed to lead to the emergence of the much hoped for Arab economy. Why? Those who had hoped for some kind of Pan-Arab distribution of oil income could not have taken note of the failed attempts by the League of Arab States to move the Arab states in that direction. The accumulated experience of Arab states over more than four decades in Pan-Arab undertaking amply demonstrates that at no time were the Arab states willing to coordinate or subordinate (not to mention sacrifice) their narrow, localized interests for the sake of Pan-Arab considerations. In other words, the independent sovereign state that is a member of the League of Arab States and its interests as these interests are defined by its elites has the first and the overriding claim on all the resources at the disposal of this political entity.[12]

The desire to accelerate the pace of economic growth and to increase public spending in the oil states, which could not be met by local manpower, forced the oil states to resort to the labor pools of other countries. The availability of Arab workers and their willingness to move to the labor-short oil-producing states prompted many observers to declare that these new flows of labor and capital have contributed to a higher stage of organic relations among Arab countries, leading for the first time to what might be termed an "Arab economy.''[13] Yet neither statistical evidence nor analysis was provided to support such a contention. On the contrary the evidence points in the opposite direction, that oil wealth led to the emergence of two distinct groups of economies in the Arab region with a substantial degree of dependency by the nonoil states on the oil-producing states precisely because of the vast movement of labor and capital.

It was estimated that in 1975 there were 1.8 million migrant workers in the Arab world with 72 percent drawn from within the Arab region and 20 percent from Asian countries. By 1980 the number of migrant workers had reached 3.4 million with Arab workers constituting 67 percent or 2.3 million of the total while Asian countries supplied the other 33 percent or 1.1 million workers.[14] It is important to stress that without these foreign workers the economies of the oil states could not have functioned at levels deemed necessary by their governments. This is particularly the case with the oil-exporting countries of the Arab Gulf states and Libya. In addition to meeting its labor shortage, a labor-importing country derives other important economic benefits. Since foreign labor has already received its training in the country of origin, the labor-receiving country would not have to incur the cost of human capital formation. Another source of saving for the labor-receiving country is that foreign workers tend to accept lower wages and work longer hours. They also tend to have a relatively high rate of turnover, thus enabling employers to exploit them at the peak of their productivity.[15]

It is important to remember that the determining factor in an employer's decision to hire workers is not a sense of nationalism or Arabism. It is rather the motive of profit maximization, which ultimately determines the size and the ethnic composition (Arab and non-Arab) as well as the skill structure of imported workers.

It is relevant to note in this connection that the rise in the number of non-Arab workers in the Gulf region was helped by at least two other factors. Governments in labor-exporting countries such as India, Korea, the Philippines, and Pakistan played an active role in organizing the flow of their workers to oil-producing states in order to augment their foreign exchange earnings. Another factor was the adoption of a contract-awarding system requiring foreign employers to supply and care for their own workers, who were expected to leave the country once a project was completed. A corollary of this innovation in recruiting foreign workers was to absolve the GCC governments from having to respond to pressure to give preference to Arab over non-Arab workers.[16]

Although it is true that labor migration generated foreign exchange earnings to labor-exporting countries, the flow of labor had some important long-term adverse consequences for the economies of those countries. One of the more serious consequences of this phenomenon is that migration does not necessarily draw upon the excess segment of available labor, since demand for migrant workers tends to be biased toward higher skills. This meant that those countries of origin that had suffered from shortages of professional and skilled workers found themselves forced to cope with the effects of shrinking pools of professional and skilled workers. This seems to be true whether the country of origin is Egypt, the Sudan, Yemen, or Jordan.[17]

The distortive effects of professional migration on the future course of economic development in labor-exporting countries are very serious. In the case of Egypt it is really impossible to measure the magnitude of present and future economic losses to the Egyptian economy due to the migration of a major portion of its university teaching staff or the migration of 2 million of the cream of its labor force. The brain drain from Egypt was of such magnitude that it prompted certain ministries such as the ministry of health and the ministry of planning to protest the policy of open-door migration especially as regards physicians and engineers.[18] The problem would be compounded for countries with smaller labor forces with a narrower range of skills.

Another problem associated with the flows of labor and remittances is the impact of these remittances on the patterns of consumption and the implications of this particular linkage to balance of payments and ultimately to external debt. As migrant workers are exposed to higher and diversified levels of consumption in labor-receiving countries, they tend not only to increase their own consumption but also to transfer this new pattern of consumption to their home countries. This demonstration effect will stimulate consumption with a high import component. Thus, according to Saad Eddin Ibrahim, personal consumption in Jordan increased by a little more than three times in the period 1971–1979 while imports of consumer goods increased by seven times during the same period. This high correlation between remittances and imports of durable consumer goods was also found in other labor-exporting countries.[19] While the flows of labor and remittances constituted crucial dependency linkages between nonoil states and the Arab Gulf states, other linkages were forged that broadened and deepened the dependency of the nonoil states on economic and political decisions taken by the oil-exporting states.

The sudden rise in oil income and wealth was viewed by certain Arab states as something that most of the Arabs would share. The reasoning behind this view was that without the losses and sacrifices of Egypt and Syria in the course of the October 1973 war the increase would not have taken place. Accordingly it was claimed that the oil states with balance-of-payments surpluses should see to it that these ''Arab'' financial resources were deployed to serve all Arab countries. Egypt for instance claimed that in its various confrontations with Israel it had suffered between $12 and $15 billion in war losses and it called for an ''Arab Marshall Plan'' to rebuild the country. In 1976 President Sadat sought $10–12 billion in Arab financial support for Egypt's Five-Year Plan. Instead Egypt found itself getting a commitment of $2 billion from the newly formed Gulf Organization for the Development of Egypt.[20]

In contrast to this perception, the oil states had an entirely different view as to how to use their surpluses. For them the surpluses should not be viewed as ''Arab'' funds. Instead the surpluses belonged to the governments of Saudi

Arabia, Kuwait, the United Arab Emirates, Qatar, and other individual countries, which were going to dispose the surpluses and use them according to their own political and economic interests. From this perspective financial transfers were to be determined by factors that these governments thought served their own particular interests and not by the needs of other Arab countries.

In the case of Egypt, for instance, John Waterbury observed, "Saudi Arabia and Kuwait came to the conclusion that what they were providing was essentially balance of payments support to sustain a way of life, based on consumer subsidies, that Egypt could not afford." Furthermore, they adopted the position that further credit would be contingent upon Egypt's compliance with the International Monetary Fund's package of restrictive economic measures commonly known as IMF conditionality.[21] The relatively small amount of official aid and the requirement that Egypt comply with Western forms of conditionality coupled with the wasteful consumption and the flaunting of wealth in which the surplus oil countries indulged prompted an Egyptian observer in 1975 to write of the indifference of those who possessed petrodollars to the plight of those who had shed "petroblood."[22]

One measure of such indifference is reflected in the size of official development assistance that the oil states provided to other Arab countries. Data compiled by Mohammad Imady, former director general of the Arab Fund for Economic and Social Development, show that Arab bilateral development aid to Arab countries during the period 1974–1981 amounted to $24 billion or an average of $3 billion per year.[23]

In addition to this aid, which was provided by governments and national funds for external development, multilateral Arab organizations provided an average of $.6 billion per year in loans to Arab countries. It is important to note that while the Arab region received about $30 billion in various forms of economic assistance and loans, the accumulated surpluses of petrodollars had amounted to $350 billion by the end of 1981. It is also relevant to note that while a few Arab states had hoarded so much wealth in Western financial markets, other Arab states found themselves resorting to the same markets for borrowing at onerous interest rates.[24]

In addition to these channels for the transfer of economic assistance and loans there were two other mechanisms for the flow of financial resources to Arab countries. One was the formation of joint Arab projects where a host country provided a proper environment to attract private Arab capital. The other took the form of joint projects that were funded by Arab and non-Arab capital. It was estimated that by 1981 about $10 billion, mostly in service and construction industries, had been invested in such projects.[25]

One of the significant consequences of the sharp rise in oil income was the expansion and growth of an Arab banking industry with an active international dimension. Yet in their dealings with major prospective borrowers in the Arab world these Arab banks found it easier and more profitable to extend their loans in conjunction with Western banks. As one Arab economist observed, these joint loans provided Arab capital with non-Arab cover in order to accommodate the desire of borrowing countries to deal with Western banks.[26]

In addition to official flows in the form of economic assistance and commercial flows in the form of investment and loans there was the significant flow of workers' remittances. The size of these remittances is determined by several variables including the number of migrant workers, skill structure, length of stay, and wage and salary structure in the employing country. Available data, which tend to underestimate the actual size of these flows, indicate that there had been a sharp upward shift in these transfers. Thus Arab workers in the Gulf region increased their transfers from $353 million in 1973 to $4 billion in 1979 and to nearly $6 billion in 1984. The distribution of these receipts among labor-exporting countries depends, of course, on the number of workers and their skill structure.

Egypt was the sender of by far the largest number of workers whose remittances amounted to $127 million in 1973 and increased to $3.4 billion in 1984. Sudan's receipts, on the other hand, went up from only $4 million in 1973 to $260 million a decade later, while Jordan's receipts increased from $45 million at the start of the period to $510 million by 1979 and to more than $1 billion in 1983. North Yemen's receipts jumped from $135 million in 1973 to nearly $1 billion a decade later. These figures indicate that worker remittances have become an important component of the GNP. In the case of Egypt their share in GNP was negligible in 1973 but amounted to 13 percent in 1979 and 10.4 percent in 1984. In the case of North Yemen it increased from 17 to 46 percent of the GNP between 1973 and 1979. For Jordan the share of remittances in GNP increased from 7 to 27 percent between 1973 and 1984.[27] The importance as well as the danger of the flow of remittances to the receiving countries may be appreciated when it is realized that these flows in the case of Jordan represented between 53 and 160 percent of that country's exports between 1974 and 1984; in the case of the Sudan the ratios were between 1 and 48 percent; in the case of Egypt the ratios were between 21 and 115 percent. These flows also enabled these countries to finance between 17 and 38 percent of imports in the case of Jordan, 13 and 34 percent in the case of Egypt, and 60 and 92 percent in the case of Yemen during the period 1974–1984.[28]

While such flows may seem helpful in meeting balance-of-trade and balance-of-payments deficits, they tend at times either to create or increase such deficits. The primary explanation is that the availability of these funds provided the foundation for a certain pattern of consumption that could not be satisfied by the local economy. In other words, these remittances were used to promote and sustain a consumer demand that had to be satisfied by imports of durable consumers goods—automobiles, television sets, and the like—in addition to nondurable consumer goods. Moreover, the returning workers by displaying their acquisitions of these consumer durables tended to create a consumption demonstration effect that impacted on the rest of the society, hence contributing to general rise in imports, which could not be matched by a similar increase in exports. In the case of Jordan for instance about 27 percent of private consumption in 1973 was met by imports of consumer goods. By 1979 the ratio increased to 41 percent. Parallel with this trend was the rise in the ratio of worker remittances to total private consumption from 8 percent to 35 percent during the same period.[29]

It should be stressed that the consequences of labor migration and workers' remittances transcend consumption patterns and increased imports, since these flows tend to generate inflation, affect the distribution of income, change the structure of the economy, distort savings and investment patterns, compromise the effectiveness of fiscal and monetary policies, and cause labor shortages and bottlenecks in the labor-exporting countries. These conclusions were supported by a careful analysis of the impact of migration and remittance transfer on the economy of Yemen by Nader Furgani, who agreed with J. C. Swanson's conclusion that labor migration had become a transmitting belt of petrodollars from the oil states to the West due to the rise in consumption spending in labor-exporting countries.[30]

OIL AND THE PHENOMENON OF DERIVATIVE DEPENDENCY

It is clear from these indicators how the economies of the nonoil states in addition to oil-producing countries have become dependent on oil and the revenue from it. Dependence, according to Theotonio Dos Santos, means a situation in which one economy is conditioned by the development and expansion of another economy. Interdependence under these conditions becomes dependence when some countries (the dominant ones) can expand and be self-sustaining while other countries (the dependent ones) can do this only as a reflection of that expansion.[31]

The pattern of economic relations between Arab economies and the international economic system is a good illustration of this dependency condition. The oil economies, like many raw-material-exporting countries, rely by and large on the export of a single commodity, the demand for which is determined by economic conditions and policies in industrialized countries over which the oil states have no control. Even the limited control that the oil-producing countries had over prices in the 1970s proved to be of short duration. Developments in the international energy market and economic changes in industrialized countries in the 1970s forced oil-producing countries to reduce their prices and their oil output and exports and to cope with lower levels of national income.

Following Dos Santos' definition the case of the dependence of the economies of Arab oil-producing countries is self-evident. This is so because, as was stated earlier, the oil sector is the most important sector as a source of national income, exports, and foreign exchange earnings. Demand for crude oil is derived demand in that it is determined by the demand for its products, which in turn is a function of the level of economic activity in oil importing countries. It follows, then, that economic conditions in oil-producing countries are going to be determined by economic conditions and policies in industrial countries. In other words, the perceived economic independence and power that many Arab states thought they acquired in the 1970s proved to be of very transitory nature if not illusory.

What is more significant is that the rise in oil wealth and income increased the role of the oil sector in the economy and freed the state from having to impose and/or raise taxes to meet financing needs of its expanded social and development programs. This means that government economic policies are ultimately externally determined by the forces that determine the demand conditions for and the prices of crude oil. This was made painfully clear to all OPEC countries when, between 1980 and 1986, their combined oil revenue declined by 76 percent from $287 billion to $77 billion. This sharp reduction in oil income produced deficits in national budgets and balance-of-trade and payments, and led to economic retrenchments, political instability, unemployment, and unprecedented levels of foreign debt.

What about the nonoil Arab states? Again following Dos Santos' definition, one can easily say that like the oil states, they suffered from similar conditions of dependence in that they have a narrow range of exports, which in turn gave rise to trade and payments imbalances and foreign indebtedness. And like all other developing countries, they have not been able to expand significantly their industrial sectors or modernize their agriculture. These conditions may be described as primary dependency. The primary dependency problem of the nonoil Arab countries is complicated by what might be characterized as derivative or secondary dependency, since these countries suffer also from the particular linkages that they developed with Arab oil-producing states.

As the oil states were forced by the decline in oil income to contract spending in both private and public sectors, the flow of financial resources to other Arab countries had to decline. The decline in Arab official development assistance is a case in point. In 1980 the development aid of the Arab members of OPEC amounted to $9.6 billion, or 3.2 percent of their combined GNP. By 1987 such aid constituted 1.1 percent of their GNP or $3.3 billion, a 65 percent decline from the 1980 level.[32]

Another dimension of the derivative dependency is related to the impact of the decline in oil revenue on the demand for labor from non-oil-producing countries. As was stated earlier, the rise in oil income during the 1970s and the first half of the 1980s removed savings and foreign exchange constraints and propelled the oil-based economies to increase spending. They were forced to resort to other labor markets to meet the rising demand for labor, which their own labor pools could not meet. But as the sharp decline in oil income forced the oil-based economies to lower their spending, the rate of growth of foreign labor started first to slow down and then to falter. This meant that the rate of increase in worker remittances upon which these economies had become dependent as a major source of foreign exchange had to decline accordingly. But since certain patterns of consumptions, both public and private, had evolved on the premise that remittances would continue to flow, the change in the economic conditions of the oil economies forced labor-exporting countries to adopt certain economic austerity measures to counteract the relative decline in remittances, things to which they would not have to resort if they had not become dependent on the earnings of their nationals working abroad.

The decline in the demand for labor had other significant and long-term implications for the economies of labor-exporting countries. In the first place the decline does not seem to be a temporary phenomenon. On the contrary, the number of workers returning to their country of origin in the latter part of the 1980s tended to exceed the number of new migrant workers. The Arab League for instance has estimated that about 1.5 million workers from Egypt, Jordan, Palestine, and the two Yemens working in the Arab Gulf states will be forced to return to their country of origin once their contracts expire. The reentry of large numbers into economies already suffering from unemployment would compound the problems that these economies are facing in absorbing new entrants into the labor force.[33]

ARAB DEPENDENCY: SOME INDICATORS AND MEASUREMENTS

Several Arab economists attempted to provide a definitional framework as well as quantitative measurements of dependency. According to Mohammed Mahmoud al-Imam, for instance, dependency is a phenomenon that entails the acceptance of economic choices and options beneficial to outside forces. From this it follows that measurements of dependency tend to concentrate on the structure of external economic relations such as foreign capital and technology, relative importance of foreign trade to domestic output, and the ability of the economy to satisfy national demand.[34]

More recently Ibrahim al-Aysawi attempted to develop a comprehensive system to measure dependency. In addition to indicators of economic dependency he developed indicators of six other forms of dependency such as food, technology, cultural, information, military, and political.[35] Al-Aysawi delineated forty-five indicators to measure economic dependency. Some of these indicators include the ratios of imports and exports to GDP; the ratio of imports to exports; concentration ratios of imports and exports by commodity, source, and destination; relative importance of consumer and intermediate and capital goods to total imports; external debt and debt service ratios; role of foreign investment in the national economy; and the relative contribution of manufacturing to GDP.[36]

Another attempt to measure Arab economic dependency was made by Mohammad Azhar al-Sammak, who developed eight indices to measure the degree of economic exposure to imports and exports; relative importance of exports to GNP; concentration of exports; export of raw materials; range of exports; geographic concentration of exports; geographic concentration of imports; and the degree of technological dependency. Some of his findings, which are summarized in the following paragraphs, not surprisingly reveal a high degree of dependency.[37]

Al-Sammak showed that the degree of economic exposure, which relates the sum of exports and imports to the value of gross domestic product (GDP), was found to be 50 percent in 1970 but rose to 84 percent in 1982. In certain cases this particular measure shows that the total of exports and imports was much higher than the GDP. In 1982, for instance, it was found that foreign trade amounted to 104 percent of the GDP in Jordan, 148 percent in Bahrain, 109 percent in Oman, 182 percent in Kuwait, and 271 percent in South Yemen. The ratios for Libya, Iraq, and Saudi Arabia were 90 percent, 87 percent, and 82 percent respectively.

Although it was expected that oil would constitute the bulk of exports, it was revealing that most such exports took the form of crude oil rather than petroleum products, thus leaving a good part of the value added to be garnered by countries other than the oil-exporting countries.

The geographic distribution of both exports and imports provides a good insight into the nature of dependency, where most of the foreign trade is conducted with the West. It was found that the top two trading partners bought up to 35 percent of the exports of certain Arab countries. By the same token, it was found that between 20 and 59 percent of the imports of Arab countries came from two trading partners.

Looking at the global distribution of Arab foreign trade, it was found that in 1983 the industrial countries accounted for 75 percent of the Arab world's imports and 66 percent of its exports while the developing countries were responsible for 15 percent of the Arab world's imports and absorbed 25 percent of its exports with the remaining 8 percent of the foreign trade accounted for by the Arab countries themselves.[38]

Dependence on foreign trade, especially imports, is much heavier than the figures reveal. This is so because imports cover a wide range of goods and services including basic food necessities such as wheat, rice, and meat; consumer durable and non-durable goods; industrial inputs; capital goods; and arms. These imports have become an integral part of the Arab economies at a time when these economies have become increasingly dependent on oil income. With the expansion of both military and civilian employment, personal income and living standards became increasingly dependent on imports, which in turn made it politically and socially difficult to reduce imports even at a time when export earnings and national incomes were declining. Thus between 1980 and 1986 Arab countries' export earnings declined by $153 billion, from $238 to $85 billion, or by 64 percent. Imports, by contrast, declined during the same period by $14 billion, from $108 to $94 billion, or by 13 percent.[39]

Although countries with accumulated surpluses could draw down their reserves to finance trade deficits, most Arab countries had no such option. This, in turn, meant that these countries had no choice but to finance their trade deficits through borrowing and therefore adding to their existing external debt burden. The magnitude of the deterioration of external debt conditions of the Arab countries can be seen in the quadrupling of the debt in a period of ten years. In 1975 the foreign debt of the non-oil-producing countries amounted to $18 billion. This debt for the same group of countries rose to $99 billion in 1986 with 61 percent of the debt being carried by Egypt and Morocco. If we were to include also the external debt of the oil-producing states, the debt would rise to $29 billion in 1975 and $147 billion in 1986.[40]

Trade dependency, heavy though it might be, is compounded by technological dependency. The latter form of dependency is reflected in the bulk of Arab imports that are manufactured goods that embody advanced technologies. Arab countries also rely on foreign inputs of technical know-how, patents, and technical management. In short, Arab technological dependency is almost total. As Samir Makdisi observed, "At this stage of their development the Arab countries can only be receivers of technological know-how, though some progress in building national institutions devoted to the development of indigenous technology is being made. In other words, the scope for autonomous action in this field appears much more restricted than in other fields."[41]

An important element in the deepening of Arab dependency in the oil era may be seen in the declining food self-sufficiency in the Arab region. The production of wheat, which is considered by the Arab League and the Arab Fund for Economic and Social Development as *the strategic food commodity in the Arab world*, met in the second half of the 1970s 43 percent of total consumption. By contrast, during the first half of the 1980s it satisfied only 34 percent of domestic consumption. The production of other food items such as rice, sugar, and meats also failed to keep up with domestic consumption, leading to increased dependence on the economies of the industrialized countries, which happen to be also major exporters of these food items.[42]

The failure of agriculture to expand in response to rising domestic consumption was not offset by a rise in the relative importance of the manufacturing industry. Neither food processing nor petrochemical nor textile nor raw material nor construction materials nor capital goods industries were able to meet local demand or function at full capacity. This in turn meant that the contribution of manufacturing to Arab GDP remained modest. This may be seen in the changing relative importance of manufacturing to GDP from 10 percent in 1973 to 11 percent in 1986. The contribution of the industrial sector, which is dominated by the oil sector, declined from 62 percent to 39 percent while that of agriculture declined from 13 percent to 11 percent during the same period. The service sector on the other hand expanded its share of GDP from 38 percent to 50 percent between 1973 and 1986.[43]

CONCLUDING OBSERVATIONS: THE POLITICAL ECONOMY OF ARAB DEPENDENCY

In trying to assess the nature of the political economy of Arab dependency during the modern period, roughly from the middle of the nineteenth century to the present, one has to take into account four crucial forces that shaped the nature and the evolution of Arab economies. These four forces are: (1) the Ottoman legacy, which lasted for four centuries until the outbreak of World War I; (2) European colonial control, which ran at times concurrently with the Ottoman control but lasted to the end of World War II; (3) Arab nationalism, which sought liberation from foreign domination and aspired for Arab unity; and (4) oil, which worked as a force to accelerate the process of integrating the Arab economies on the one hand and thwarting the objective of Arab unity on the other.

It can be said without exaggeration that the Ottoman period had a lasting influence on the evolution of Arab economies and their relationship to the world economic system. The Ottoman influence derives from three primary sources. First, the distortive effects of the colonial pattern of relationships forced the Arab provinces to become a source of revenue for the Ottoman government, hence leaving little savings to be invested in the local economies of the provinces. Second, the weakness of the Ottoman Empire in the face of powerful European capitalism forced the former to open its economy and those of the provinces to the penetrating influences of the latter, introducing another set of distortive effects and new linkages of dependency. Third, the Ottomans created local classes and elites who found their economic and political interests to be compatible with those of the European colonial powers.

The second major force that shaped the political economy of the Arab region was the direct and indirect European control of political institutions and economic wealth in the Arab countries. The disappearance of the Ottoman ''intermediation'' for Arab dependency provided for the direct linking of Arab economies with European capitalism through exports, imports, financial and banking services, and the creation of local elites who derived their power from European colonial powers—mainly Britain and France.

While the Arab countries were under Ottoman and European rule, there were political forces in the Arab world who believed that the Arabs should expel foreign influence and domination and should ultimately have the fragmented Arab states encompassed and unified in one political entity. Although the League of Arab States was created in 1945 to facilitate forms of political and economic integration, if not unity, its experience over the last several decades proved to be an unmitigated failure. One should hasten to add, however, that the failure of the Arab League was a reflection of Arab states' interest in individual and separate rather than joint or collective development. This in turn reflected each state's interest in developing and protecting its linkages and interests with the external world on the one hand and its commitment to the concept of the sovereignty of the state on the other. These two forces were joined in the oil era in such a forceful combination as to render any serious consideration of Arab unity to be no more than an exercise in futility.

The last and most important force that shaped and continues to shape the composition and direction of Arab economies in the twentieth century and beyond is oil. While oil has provided certain income to oil-producing states, oil operations have become the mechanism that has linked the economies of these states ever more closely to the international economy and to the changing economic conditions and policies of industrial countries. But the significance of oil as a mechanism of dependency has gone beyond the traditional patterns that govern relations between raw-material-exporting countries and the West. The importance of oil as a mechanism of dependency has been enhanced due to at least three factors.

First, the sharp rise in oil income to countries with low absorptive capacity resulted in the emergence of balance-of-payments surpluses, which have been recycled back into the financial markets of the industrial countries, thus creating strong linkages in banking and finance between the two groups of countries. The placement of funds in the main financial centers of the world has meant also that the freedom of action on the part of the oil states has to be compromised, since the governments of industrial countries could freeze these financial assets any time they deem appropriate.

Second, the sharp rise in oil prices enabled governments to increase very sharply their spending on social programs, infrastructure, and industrial development. The removal of the foreign exchange constraint made it possible to increase private consumption to levels that would not have been possible if oil income had not increased. The obverse side of the increase in public and private spending was massive increase in imports, which covered agricultural and food products, durable and nondurable consumer goods, capital goods, arms, and technology. This reliance on foreign goods and services to sustain all sectors of the economy has its obvious dangers for the importing countries especially at times when oil income falls, since any drastic change in spending patterns may endanger the social, political, and economic stability of these countries.

Third, the level and the demographic composition of population in the oil states were such that they have had to rely on foreign labor to work in virtually every sector of the economy. The influx of large numbers of Arab and non-Arab workers has entailed the transfer of large sums of money in the form of workers' remittances to labor-lending countries. This flow of funds together with the economic assistance that the oil states have supplied to the nonoil states has created what might be described as derivative or secondary dependency. As oil revenue declines as a result of a decline in demand for oil or a fall in its price or both, the demand for these workers tends to decline. The resultant decline in the flow of workers' remittances together with the decline in economic assistance has had the effect of slowing down the rate of economic growth in many labor-sending countries such as Egypt, Jordan, and Yemen. In short, so long as the Arab states, both oil-exporting and non-oil-exporting, continue to rely on the revenue from oil to finance private and public spending, then the inevitable consequence will be their continued and deepened dependence on changing economic conditions in industrial countries.

NOTES

1. For a more detailed analysis of the evolution of the Arab states system see Ilya Harik, "The Origins of Arab State System," in Ghassan Salame (ed.), *The Foundations of the Arab State* (London: Croom Helm, 1987), 19–46.

2. Ibid, 40–42.

3. Ghassan Salame, "Integration in the Arab World: The Institutional Framework," in Giacomo Luciani and Ghassan Salame (eds.), *The Politics of Arab Integration* (London: Croom Helm, 1988), 268–270.

4. Ibid.

5. See Hazem Beblawi, "The Rentier State in the Arab World," *Arab Studies Quarterly* 9, No. 4 (Fall 1987): 383–398, especially p. 392.

6. In addition to the specific sources cited, this section draws heavily on Abbas Alnasrawi, "The Arab Economies: Twenty Years of Change and Dependency," *Arab Studies Quarterly* 9, No. 4 (1987): 357–382.

7. Ratios were computed from data published by Arab Monetary Fund, *National Accounts of the Arab States, 1972–1983* (Abu-Dhabi, 1984), League of Arab States et al., *Joint Arab Economic Report, 1987*, and World Bank, *World Development Report, 1988* (Washington, D.C.: World Bank, 1988).

8. In 1987 Egypt's GNP of $34 billion represented 44% of Saudi Arabia's GNP of $78 billion in that year. See *World Development Report, 1989*, 164–165.

9. See Malcolm H. Kerr and El Sayed Yassin (eds.), *Rich and Poor States in the Middle East: Egypt and the New Arab Order* (Boulder, Colo.: Westview Press, 1982), 1.

10. For a detailed treatment of these points see Alnasrawi, "The Arab Economies."

11. See for example Hossein Askari and John Thomas Cummings, "The Future of Economic Integration Within the Arab World," *International Journal of Middle East Studies* 8 (1977): 289–315, and Essam Montasser, "The Arab Economy and Its Developing Strategy: A New Arab Economic Order," in Kerr and Yassin, *Rich and Poor*, 99–128.

12. For a good elaboration on this point see Muhammad A. Shuraydi, "Pan-Arabism: A Theory in Practice," in Hani A. Faris (ed.), *Arab Nationalism and the Future of the Arab World* (Belmont, Mass.: Association of Arab-American University Graduates (AAUG) Press, 1986), 95–114.

13. A good example of this unwarranted optimism may be found in Montasser, "The Arab Economy," 99–128.

14. The 1975 ratios were derived from League of Arab States, *Towards a Joint Arab Economic Action* (in Arabic), 1980, vol. 3, p. 93, and the 1980 ratios were derived from Ibrahim Saad Eddin and Mahmoud Abdel-Fadil (eds.), *Movement of Arab Employment: Problems, Effects and Policies* (in Arabic) (Beirut: Centre for Arab Unity Studies, 1983), 70.

It is to be noted that Nader Furgani estimated the number of Arab migrant workers at 3.4 million. One explanation for Furgani's higher figure for Arab workers was the fact that Iraq in the 1980s became an important labor-importing country due to its war conditions. See his *Migrants in Arabs' Land: On Labor Migration in the Arab World* (in Arabic) (Beirut: Centre for Arab Unity Studies, 1987), 62.

15. For a more detailed treatment of these points see Ali Labeeb, "Causes of the

Spread of Asian Employment,'' in Nader Furgani (ed.), *Foreign Employment in the Arabian Gulf Countries* (in Arabic) (Beirut: Centre for Arab Unity Studies, 1983), 123– 128.

According to one estimate, between 1973 and 1983 some 20 million Arab workers have migrated within the Arab world, affecting another 100 million dependents and relatives. See Arab Thought Forum, *The Returnees from the Oil Fields* (in Arabic) (Amman: Arab Thought Forum, 1986), 6.

16. See Labeeb, "Causes of the Spread of Asian Employment," 125–128.

17. See Ibrahim Saad Eddin Abdalla, "Migration as a Factor Conditioning State Economic Control and Financial Policy Options," in Giacomo Luciani and Ghassan Salame (eds.), *The Politics of Arab Integration* (London: Croom Helm, 1988), 141–158.

18. For data on the migration of the teaching staff see Saad Eddin Ibrahim, "Oil, Migration and the New Arab Social Order," in Kerr and Yassin, *Rich and Poor*, 45. On the corrupting influence of oil wealth on Egypt's labor force see Muhammad H. Heykal, "Arab Unity Issues and Arab Society," *Al Mustaqbal Al Arabi*, No. 29 (July 1981): 6– 19. See also Saad Eddin Ibrahim, "Causes and Effects of Labor Exporting in Egypt," *Al Mustaqbal Al Arabi* (in Arabic), No. 35 (January 1982): 57–87.

It is instructive to note that in the case of North Yemen about 54 percent of its 2.6 million labor force in 1981 was employed abroad. This migration played havoc with the agricultural sector, as it forced a reduction in the cereal cultivated land area by one-third, which in turn led to increased imports, higher agricultural wages and inflation, lower agricultural output, and a forced change in the structure of agricultural output. See Ahmad al-Qaseer, "Impact of External Migration on the Social Structure in the Yemen Republic," *Al Mustaqbal Al Arabi* (in Arabic), No. 70 (December 1984): 118–127.

19. Saad Ibrahim, "Causes and Effects," 145.

20. See John Waterbury, *The Egypt of Nasser and Sadat: The Political Economy of Two Regimes* (Princeton, N.J.: Princeton University Press, 1983), 417.

21. Ibid.

22. Ibid.

23. See Mohammed Imady, "Patterns of Arab Economic Aid to Third World Countries," *Arab Studies Quarterly* 6, Nos. 1 & 2 (Winter/Spring 1984): 88.

24. Abdel Hasan Zalzala, "The Economic Role of the League of Arab States," *Al Mustaqbal Al Arabi* (in Arabic), Nos. 42, 43, and 44 (August, September, and October 1982): 157–158.

25. Ibid.

26. Burhan al-Dajani, quoted in Fouad Moursi, "Impact of Arab Oil on the International Relations," *Al Mustaqbal Al Arabi*, No. 14 (April 1980): 53.

27. Data on remittances were derived from Saad Eddin and abdel-Fadil, *Movement of Arab Employment*, 78, and Samir Radwan, "Arab Manpower: Reality and Future Dimensions" (in Arabic), *Al Mustaqbal Al Arabi* (March 1988), pp. 41–65, especially Table 8. Radwan estimates that during the last decade there were some 25 million migrant workers in the world and that about 20 percent of them were in the Arab world.

According to one study Arab worker remittances amounted to $7.3 billion out of total worker remittances of $11.3 billion in 1983. See Tayseer abdel-Jaber, "The Current Situation of Labor Exchange in the Arab World and Future Possibilities," in Arab Thought Forum, *The Returnees from the Oil Fields*, p. 37.

28. See Radwan, "Arab Manpower."

29. Ibid, 88.

30. For a fuller analysis of the economic consequences of migration and remittances see Saad Eddin and abdel-Fadil, *Movement of Arab Employment*, 75–128. See also Saad Eddin Ibrahim, "Causes and Effects," 57–87; Nader Furgani, "Exporting Manpower and Development: The Case of Yemen Arab Republic" (in Arabic), *Al Mustaqbal Al Arabi*, No. 35 (January 1982), 88–106; and Bassam K. al-Saket, "The Transfers of Migrant Workers and Their Uses: The Case of Jordan" (in Arabic), *Al Mustaqbal Al Arabi*, No. 35 (January 1982): 107–120.

31. Theotonio Dos Santos, "The Structure of Dependence," *American Economic Review*, May 1979, 231–236.

32. See World Bank, *World Development Report, 1989*, 201.

33. League of Arab States et al., *Joint Arab Economic Report, 1986*, 85.

34. Mohammad Mahmoud al-Imam, "Role of Joint Arab Action in Achieving Independent Development," in Nader Furgani (ed.), *Independent Development in the Arab World* (in Arabic) (Beirut: Centre for Arab Unity Studies, 1987), 831.

35. Ibrahim al-Aysawi, *Measuring Dependency in the Arab World* (in Arabic) (Beirut: Centre for Arab Unity Studies, 1989), 40.

36. Ibid, 42–53.

37. See Mohammed Azhar al-Sammak, "Measuring Economic Dependency of the Arab Nation and Its Possible Geopolitical Effects," *Al Mustaqbal Al Arabi* (in Arabic), September 1986, 61–81.

38. See Samir Makdisi, "Economic Interdependence and National Sovereignty," in Giacomo Luciani and Ghassan Salame (eds.), *The Politics of Arab Integration* (London: Croom Helm, 1988), 111–140.

39. See International Monetary Fund, *Direction of Trade Statistics Yearbook, 1987* (Washington, D.C., 1987).

40. Data for 1975 may be found in Arab Monetary Fund, *The Arab States: Economic Data and Statistics, 1975–1983* (Abu Dhabi, 1985), 54. The 1986 data were published in *Middle East Economic Survey (MEES)*, March 2, 1987, B7.

41. Ibid., 118.

42. For more data on Arab imports of various items see League of Arab States et al., *Joint Arab Economic Report, 1985*, 49–54.

43. Ibid, 62–71. See also Arab Banking Corporation, *Industrialization in the Arab World* (Bahrain, 1986), 6.

9

THE ARAB ECONOMIES: PRESENT CONDITIONS AND FUTURE OUTLOOK

The analysis in the previous chapters dealt with the impact of the forces that shaped the evolution of modern Arab economies as well as the forces responsible for the integration of these economies into the world economic system. Statistical measures designed to show the nature of dependency of Arab economies on the world economic system were also presented.

In this chapter the analysis will focus on the future likelihood of the evolution of Arab economies and the trends that might affect such evolution. It is postulated that the future of Arab economies will, to a considerable degree, be affected by developments in the demand for crude oil and the price of oil; by the size of the external debt and the relative importance of the debt service; and by the extent of the tendency toward privatization. In order to set the stage for the analysis, a review of some of the more important economic variables will be undertaken first.

THE ARAB ECONOMIES: MAJOR CHARACTERISTICS

In 1987 the combined gross national product (GNP) of the Arab economies amounted to $402 billion for a total population of 202 million. This GNP was divided between the oil-based economies or the first group (Algeria, Iraq, Libya, Kuwait, Saudi Arabia, Qatar, United Arab Emirates, and Oman), which had 31 percent of the population but accounted for 67 percent of the GNP or $268 billion; and the nonoil states or the second group (Egypt, Syria, Jordan, Lebanon, North Yemen, South Yemen, Morocco, Tunisia, Sudan, Djibouti, Somalia, and Mauritania), which had 69 percent of the population but received the remaining 33 percent of the GNP, or $134 billion. The disparity in the distribution of income within the Arab world becomes sharper and wider if we note that four of the first-group countries (Saudi Arabia, Qatar, Kuwait, and United Arab Emirates) are classifed by the World Bank as high-income countries. These four countries, which account for merely 8.6 percent of the population, received $128 billion (32 percent of total GNP) giving them $14,419 per capita—slightly above that of West Germany. At the other end of the scale per capita GNP for the countries of the second group ranged from $290 for Somalia to $1,640 for Syria.[1]

Another feature of Arab economies is their integration into world trade. In the early 1980s the ratio of trade—exports plus imports—to GDP reached 91 percent. Although the ratio fell to 61 percent, primarily due to the decline in oil exports, this was not matched by a corresponding decline in the ratio of imports to GDP, indicating the high degree of Arab economic dependency on the world economy. In absolute terms exports fell from their 1980 peak of $234.3 billion to $98.5 billion in 1988, a decline of $135.8 billion. By contrast the decline in imports amounted to $31.9 billion, since imports fell from their peak of $138.3 billion in 1982 to $106.4 billion in 1988.

The high degree of the dependency of Arab economies on the oil sector may be seen in the change in the relative importance of that sector to GDP. Thus during the period of high oil prices the oil sector contributed nearly 49 percent of the GDP in 1980. The decline in oil exports led to a sharp decline in the contribution of the oil sector to 19 percent in 1987. The contribution of the oil sector to the GDP of the economies of the first group declined from 60 percent to 26 percent during the same period. It is to be noted that the share of oil in the GDP is determined by the external forces of world demand for oil and consequently the contribution of the oil sector to GDP. Therefore, if oil prices are to rise in the future, so will the contribution of oil to GDP.

What about the nonoil sectors? Economic activity outside the oil sector may be grouped into four sectors: services, agriculture, construction, and manufacturing. In the decade of the 1980s these sectors exhibited varying rates of performance.

The service sector was by far the most important nonoil sector, contributing 56 percent of the nonoil GDP in 1980 and 58 percent in 1987. Agriculture was another sector that raised its contribution to nonoil GDP; it rose from 12 to 15 percent between 1980 and 1987 with most of the increase taking place in Algeria, Saudi Arabia, Iraq, Egypt, and Syria.

The other two sectors lost grounds in their relative importance to nonoil GDP. The construction sector's share declined from 17 to 11 percent between 1980 and 1987, while that of manufacturing declined from 13 to 12 percent during the same period. While the decline in construction was due primarily to the completion of the infrastructural projects in the countries of the first group, the decline in the role of industry reflected the inherent weakness of this sector, at least at this stage of Arab economic development.

One of the more significant aspects of Arab economies is the relatively high levels of consumption relative to GNP. Thus, in 1980 both public and private consumption absorbed 52 percent of the GDP but 99 percent of the nonoil GDP.

By 1987 the ratios changed to 72 and 88 percent respectively. The obverse side of high consumption is low savings ratios. A combination of declining oil revenue in the 1980s together with the completion of major infrastructure projects led to a serious decline in capital formation from $116 billion in 1981 to $93 billion in 1987. Investment spending in the countries of the first group declined from $93 billion to $68 billion in the same period.

FOREIGN INDEBTEDNESS: RISE AND FUTURE PROSPECTS

One of the more striking economic developments in the 1980s was the emergence of the Arab economies as a major indebted group of countries in the Third World. The external debt of the Arab economies, which amounted to $15 billion in 1975, rose to $49 billion in 1980 and reached $181 billion in 1988. As a share of Third World debt Arab external debt increased from 8 percent in 1975 to 15 percent in 1988. Measured against Arab GNP, the ratio of the external debt increased from 10 percent in 1975 to 13 percent in 1980 and 46 percent in 1988. But if we remove the $33 billion external debt of the four Gulf countries (Saudi Arabia, Kuwait, United Arab Emirates, and Qatar) from the calculation on the grounds that their considerable holdings of foreign assets more than offset their debt, we find that the $148 billion remaining debt represents 55 percent of the combined GNP of the other indebted Arab countries.[2]

Within the indebted countries the debt burden as measured by its relative importance to GNP varied considerably. Thus in 1987 the ratio of external debt to GNP was 15 percent in Syria, 31 percent in Algeria, 70 percent in Tunisia, 102 percent in Sudan, 109 percent in Egypt and 118 percent in Morocco. Similarly the ratio of debt service to exports ranged from 16.5 percent in Syria to 49 percent in Algeria. It is worth noting that the debt service amounted to $7.8 billion in 1980 and rose steadily to reach $10.8 billion in 1988. It is also worth noting that between 1983 and 1988 Arab countries increased their external debt by $22.3 billion, but they paid $38.7 billion in debt service, indicating net capital outflow of $16.4 billion in a four-year period.

Given these indicators, the question that needs to be answered is what caused the external debt to rise by 269 percent in the Arab countries between 1980 and 1988 while the corresponding increase in Third World debt amounted to 92 percent during the same period? In attempting to explain the rise in Arab external debt, one must deal with factors common to all developing countries as well as factors that are more or less unique to conditions in the Arab region.

Factors responsible for the rise in Third World external debt include the deterioration of developing country terms of trade in the 1980s; the widening gap between exports and imports, which resulted in larger current account deficit; the sharp increases in the price of crude oil in the early 1980s; increases in food imports; military imports; failure of internal economies to meet local demand; impact of both international inflation and recession on the purchasing power of Third World foreign exchange earnings; the sharp rise in nominal and real interest rates in the industrial countries, a rise which was translated into higher levels of debt; United States monetary and fiscal policy; United States budget and trade deficits; and exchange rate instability, which resulted in devaluations and consequently higher debt burdens.[3]

Another factor responsible for the rise in external debt, which began to attract more attention recently, has been the large volume of capital that was moved by its owners from the Third World, including Arab countries, to the economies of the industrial countries. In a recent study of the phenomenon of capital flight from Arab countries, Ramzi Zaki shows that between 1972 and 1982 capital flight from Egypt amounted to close to $4 billion or 34 percent of the increase in Egypt's foreign indebtedness in the same period. The corresponding ratios for Jordan, Syria, and Tunisia were 33 percent, 96 percent, and 14 percent, respectively.[4]

In addition to these factors there were other forces that tended to affect the indebtedness of Arab countries in a special manner. One such factor is the financial flows from the oil states to the nonoil states. As was indicated in the last chapter, the oil price revolution of the 1970s prompted the oil-producing states to engage in a policy of accelerated development, which entailed the flow of a large number of workers from the nonoil states. The obverse side of this flow of labor migration was the flow of remittances from the oil states to the nonoil states. With all their beneficial dimensions, these financial flows were externally determined as far as the recipient countries were concerned. In other words although these flows helped to pay for imports and meet budgetary needs, their levels and their continuance were contingent upon policy considerations in the labor-importing countries. Moreover, these flows provided easy access to higher consumption—both public and private—which entailed higher imports that could not have been supported by individual country GDP. But this state of triangular economic interrelationship between oil states, nonoil states, and the world economy, as was to be seen in the 1980s, was too fragile to stand any downward change in the price of oil or in the need for the migrant workers.

The decline in the world demand for Arab oil and the decline in the price of oil led to a sharp decline in revenue of the oil states, which led to a reduction in spending in the private and public sectors in absolute or relative terms or both. Taking Saudi Arabia as a case in point, it was estimated that its oil revenue amounted to $34 billion in 1976, $116 billion in 1981, and only $17 billion in 1986. Correspondingly public and private consumption increased from $15 billion in 1976 to $83 billion in 1983 only to slump to $61 billion in 1986. By the same token gross domestic investment rose from $10 billion in 1976 to peak at $37 billion in 1983 only to fall to $17 billion in 1986.

These sharp declines in oil revenue and spending had the effect of reducing demand for labor and consequently worker remittances. But since the governments of the nonoil states have in the meantime grown dependent on this source of revenue and foreign exchange to finance imports, budget, and development spending, these governments found themselves resorting to external borrowing to bridge the resource gap caused by changes in the oil-based economies.

Not unlike the effect in the decline in demand for labor is the decline in the flow of aid from the oil states to the nonoil states. Suffice it to note that Arab oil states' development aid increased from $4.9 billion in 1976 to $9.5 billion in 1980 but by 1987 such aid declined to $3.3 billion. And since 53 percent of this aid went to other Arab countries, it is not difficult to see how such a decline would have an effect similar to that of the decline in worker remittances.

Another reason for the rise in Arab external debt is also oil-related in that the rise in oil revenue, worker remittances, and aid provided the resource base to expand investment, consumption, and imports to levels that could not have been supported by the local economies of the nonoil states. This anomalous state can be appreciated by looking at the composition of expenditures in relation to GDP. In the case of Sudan, Syria, Egypt, and Morocco the ratio of their consumption to GDP for the years 1976–1986 ranged between 80 percent and 96 percent. And in the case of North Yemen, South Yemen, and Jordan the corresponding ratios ranged between 105 percent and 158 percent. The magnitude of the resource gap naturally becomes larger when gross investment, which ranged between 13 percent and 53 percent depending on the year and the country, is added to consumption. This in turn means that these countries really had little choice but to lower spending and resort to borrowing once the inter-Arab financial flows began to decline.

It is worth noting that investment tended to absorb a disproportionately larger share of the decline in spending than in consumption. One explanation for this outcome is that most of the capital formation is undertaken by the state and consequently was much easier to adjust than lowering consumption, an act that could give rise to unacceptable social and political costs. Moreover, a significant portion of the remittances was invested in housing and similar forms of investment, which had to be suspended once the flow of funds began to decline.

The rise in Arab external debt may be explained also by the rise of Arab dependency on food imports, which constitutes 75 percent of all agricultural commodity imports, and made the Arab world one of the highest food-importing regions in the world. With only 4 percent of the world population the Arab world imports about one-fifth of the world imports of cereals. And on a per capita basis it was calculated that net agricultural imports in the Arab world as a whole amounted to $84 in 1986 compared to $58 in Europe, $11 in Asia, or $4.4 in Africa.[5] In the absence of agricultural development policies that would raise output, increase self-sufficiency, and lower the food imports bill current account deficits will continue to force many Arab countries to increase the size of foreign debt.

Another factor that contributed to the rise of external indebtedness was the heavy defense burden that most Arab governments have undertaken. In the period 1977–1987 the countries of the Middle East, including Iran and Israel, devoted between 11 percent and 16 percent of GNP and between 29 percent and 32 percent of their government budgets to military expenditures. These ratios, it must be added, were the highest in the world.[6] A corollary of this heavy spending is the unavoidable reliance on foreign suppliers for military equipment, technology, and services, since these countries—with exception of Israel—have to import the bulk of their military supplies from abroad. Thus during the same period the ratio of military imports to total imports was computed to range between 3 percent and 75 percent depending on the country and the year.[7] And since governments are reluctant to cut defense spending, it follows that they would be prepared to incur more external debt rather than reduce military spending.

ECONOMICS OF PRIVATIZATION IN THE ARAB CONTEXT

The sharp rise in oil revenue increased the power of the state immensely by placing at its disposal vast amounts of financial resources. Consequently, the public sector expanded dramatically in all oil states, which by now had the bulk of Arab GNP. Similarly there was a major increase in the social services and welfare functions of the state. What distinguished the oil states from the nonoil states as far as the public sector was concerned was their approach to the goods-production function of the public sector. Thus while countries like Iraq, Syria, Egypt, and Algeria continued to look at the public sector as the centerpiece of economic policy and the primary agent of change, the market-oriented economies of the oil states tended to accentuate their commitment to the private sector as the latter was encouraged and given opportunities to expand its role in the growing oil-based economies.

What enabled the private sector to expand its role was the sharp increase in government spending on imports, foreign contracts, factories, industrial complexes, and other needs, which entailed the services of classes of people who performed functions of intermediation between foreign contractors and suppliers on the one hand and governments and local enterprises in exchange for commissions and other financial rewards.[8] It goes without saying that the emergence of such classes had the effect of expanding the private sector on the one hand and strengthening its linkages to the international economic system and its multinational corporations on the other.

It is worth noting in this context that although the internal cycling of oil revenue in the GCC countries resulted in a high degree of inequality in the distribution of income, it nevertheless succeeded in broadening the base of private property to include the largest portion of population. Moreover, the same phenomenon was extended to labor-sending countries as the migrant workers were able to accumulate sizable financial assets relative to their incomes in their country of origin.[9]

In addition to strengthening private property and the private sector during this period, the oil era witnessed the integration of Arab capital and finance in the international financial system as owners of such assets preferred to place their resources in foreign rather than in Arab financial institutions or Arab instruments of debt. A related aspect of this change was the emergence of an Arab banking industry located outside the Arab World that was helped by the rise of oil income and the emergence of balance-of-payments surpluses and the globalization of financial markets, which integrated further Arab funds in the international system.[10] The rise of a new class of Arab bankers and financiers in the oil era and its integration in the global financial system had several effects. These include the broadening and extension of the private sector, its integration in the international financial system, and its influence in conjunction with international lending agencies on the economic orientation in the Arab World. This influence was strengthened by the fact that this class had become part of an international elite whose interest in profit maximization transcends the national interests of the Arab people.

While the role and the size of the public sector in most Arab economies tend to a large extent to be influenced by what happens to oil revenues, the decade of the 1980s seems to have witnessed some important structural and qualitative changes that cannot be attributed to the changing fortunes of the oil sector alone. As far as the impact of oil was concerned, quantitative changes in the role of the state and therefore the public sector can be expected. A decline in oil income is bound to cause declines in the size of the budgets, social services, imports, capital spending, and development. It also gave rise to balance-of-trade and payments deficits and increased foreign debt especially in the case of countries such as Egypt, Jordan, and the two Yemens, which allowed their consumption patterns to be influenced by consumption standards in oil-producing countries. Although both Iraq and Algeria are major producing countries, their foreign indebtedness increased due primarily to the collapse of the price of oil. In the case of Iraq one must add, of course, the economic effects of the eight-year war-related costs and debt. Egypt had long before the oil collapse embarked on the road of an open economy, which had as its centerpiece the encouragement of the private sector and foreign investment.

The move in favor of the private sector was helped by the decline in oil revenue, which forced governments to shrink their role in the economy by reducing the scope of public sector services and subsidies. By shifting the responsibility of performing certain functions to the private sector, governments can divert attention from themselves to the private sector should the latter fail to live up to the task. Moreover, by encouraging the private sector, governments can claim neutrality in matters of social justice and income and wealth distribution by falling back on the old cliché of supply and demand and market forces. It was at this very juncture that many people began to advocate privatization—the subject of the balance of this section.

It is a well-known fact, of course, that advocacy for the sale of public sector enterprises to the private sector has become a significant voice in shaping the debate regarding the future direction of Arab economies. Seminars were held and books and articles were published to discuss the merits or the shortcomings of this approach to economic problems.[11]

The entire structure of the analysis in favor of privatization is based on the *belief* that the private sector is more efficient than public sector enterprises. It follows from this that society will be able to maximize output or minimize cost of production given the inevitable constraint of limited resources. A central problem with the argument of the advocates of privatization is that it is based on the belief rather than analysis. In other words they base the whole argument on premise that the private enterprise in virtually all economies regardless of their stage or the process of their historical development is more efficient than public sector enterprises. This position was summed up very neatly by an Arab economist as follows:

Public Sector ownership is not necessarily the solution to market failures. . . . It became clear that public sector's shortcomings could be more serious and damaging to economic development than the market's failure. . . . Rather than dismembering the state, privatization is intended to revitalize it as well as to rehabilitate the price mechanism. . . . Privatization is part of a wider concept, that is, the rehabilitation of proper economic indicators. Without promoting competition in the meantime, the private sector could be as inefficient as the public sector.[12]

Other Arab economists expressed the same belief in the superiority of the efficiency of the private sector over that of the public sector when they said, "It is generally supposed that the private sector is more efficient economically than the public sector, especially in certain activities. Hence, the call for privatization stems from the need for higher productivity and efficiency."[13]

It should be noted that these economists, and the many other economists who share their position, have yet to tell us why and how the private sector is more efficient. As a matter of fact one can provide data to show why the private sector is not efficient and that public sector enterprises are more efficient and more profitable than private sector enterprises. Thus, it was noted that there were 600 private sector firms in Egypt on the verge of bankruptcy, and it was found in Kuwait that out of 300 private sector firms that were audited only seven, or 2.3 percent of the total, were found to be profitable.[14] On the other hand, it was found that public sector enterprises were as profitable or more profitable than private enterprises in Tunisia, Algeria, Iraq, Uganda, South Korea, Turkey, Brazil, Tanzania, and Ethiopia.[15]

Before prescribing the need for a market economy to the developing countries of the Arab region, it is necessary to see whether some of the economic arguments support the position taken by the advocates of privatization. As was indicated earlier, advocates of privatization share the belief that the private sector tends to be more efficient and therefore more productive. Given this belief, it follows that the scarce resources should be allocated by the private sector if we were to maximize output. But this position is too simplistic to be taken seriously.

To begin with, the very concept of efficiency needs to be clarified and defined. There are at least two types of efficiency. The first relates to the market in which the firm operates. This is allocative efficiency, which depends upon the output levels of firms with given cost structure. The second type is the internal efficiency of the firm and depends upon the total cost to the firm of producing a given output. This means that a firm may be internally efficient but its allocative efficiency is not, or vice versa. The policy implication of this two-tier efficiency is that privatization may improve internal efficiency but will worsen allocative efficiency if the enterprise has large market power. To avoid this unintended waste of resources, two conditions must be present. First, the industry in which the privatized firm is operating must exhibit rigorous competition, something that we may not want to have or cannot have in developing economies such as the Arab economies, since such competition may become the source of another form of waste. The second condition is that regulatory mechanisms and constraints must be present to insure that monopolistic conditions do not emerge. It is clear from this analysis that in the economics of privatization, ownership is only one of three factors that affect economic performance, the other two factors being the competitiveness of the industry and government regulating mechanisms.[16]

When discussing the merits of the private versus public sector, one should be careful not to accept the terms of the debate as set by the advocates of free enterprise because once you accept their premise of efficiency as the sole determinant of resource allocation, you will lose the debate. Societies, as we noted in the course of discussing the rise of the public sector in the Arab World, must have objectives other than profit maximization when they choose their economic systems or economic organizations for the purpose of allocating their scarce resources. Therefore, if we were to say that the objective of an economic system is *welfare maximization* and not *profit maximization*, then there would be no reason to conclude that resources would not be allocated efficiently. Indeed, welfare maximization would not lead to efficiency in resource allocation, but public ownership would be superior to the private alternative, since it provides government with additional policy instruments to correct deviations between social and private returns that arise from failures in goods and market factors.[17] Moreover, public ownership will do away with the economic distortions associated with taxation policies, which proponents of privatization advocate to compensate for the transfer of payments from taxpayers to shareholders.

In short, government ownership has several advantages over the private alternative for the society as a whole. These advantages include welfare maximization and income and wealth distributional benefits, giving policymakers additional policy instruments and conserving resources that are wasted in stock market trading, takeovers, and mergers, which lead to the distortion of investment patterns and needs.

To say that public ownership and welfare maximization are superior alternatives to private ownership and profit maximization does not mean that all activities are to be monopolized by the public sector. Competition from public and private sectors can be introduced perhaps to the point of becoming an incentive mechanism. Goods that the public sector has little or no incentive to produce can also go to the private sector. The guiding principle, however, remains the same and that is welfare maximization. And this in turn will determine the composition of national output, which can be accomplished only through public ownership.

The last point in this analysis is the importance of marginal social cost. While the private sector is guided in its pricing policies by the private marginal cost, which tends to underestimate the true cost of production, public sector enterprises could be persuaded to base their pricing decisions on the marginal social cost. If this is going to be the case in the public sector, as it should be, then profitability comparisons between public and private enterprises become not only misleading but irrelevant.[18] In other words, the much talked-about allocative efficiency becomes not only irrelevant but a false dilemma as well.

INTERNATIONAL CONTEXT OF PRIVATIZATION

As with the evolution of Arab economies within a certain international economic context, the present debate in the Arab world regarding the merits of the two systems cannot be separated from its international context. Many observers seem to date the emergence of an advocacy body in favor of the private sector to the policies of the Margaret Thatcher government in the United Kingdom and of the Reagan administration, with their emphasis on the role of the private sector in the economy. Given the role that United States aid plays in many countries and given the special influence that the United States government has in the councils of the World Bank and the International Monetary Fund and given the economic orientation of policymakers in these two Western-dominated bodies, it was only logical that the policies of these three sources of funds would be directed to promote private sector role and influence. The heavy burden of debt of many Third World countries only made it easier to force the debtor countries to agree to implement policies of privatization.

It is worth noting that for almost two decades—the 1960s and 1970s—the World Bank was disposed in favor of lending to state enterprises, thus shifting its pro-market-forces stance that had governed its lending policies between 1946 and 1960. But as the decade of the 1970s was coming to a close and politics in many countries were shifting to the right, the World Bank changed its position toward state-owned enterprises. The change in thinking was revealed in the early 1980s in a bank document entitled *Accelerated Development in Sub-Saharan Africa: An Agenda for Action*, which remains the bank's guide in its "policy dialogue" with developing countries. The central message of that document was that African governments should stop blaming their countries' plight on the capriciousness of nature, on poor terms of trade, or on stagnant flow of aid. Instead, African governments were told to blame their own excessive and misguided interventionist economic policies. The document went on to deliver a sweeping indictment of state-owned enterprises.[19]

The irony in this posturing is that, like most other developing countries, the African countries in most cases have followed international and other Western agencies' policy prescriptions for development. It was the thing to do to rely on the state as the primary mover of development. And multinational corporations were eager to enter into joint ventures with state-owned enterprises. With the failure of Keynesian economic policies in the 1970s, which failed to correct the twin problems of inflation and stagnation in Western economies, and the general shift toward the political right, the public sector and state-owned enterprises came under attack. They were not to be reformed or improved but were to be replaced by private enterprises.

Walter Vernon's comments on this subject are worth quoting. Although he warned United States policymakers not to base their policies on any general assumptions about the inherent superiority of the private sector, he nevertheless went on to pin much of the blame for the difficulties of developing countries on state-owned enterprises and urged an active and interventionist policy by United States aid-giving agencies in these words:

To be sure, U.S. policy cannot remain aloof from all issues that involve the domestic policies of an aid-receiving country. As long as the U.S. government pursues a policy of supporting the development process in poor countries, it cannot fail to take cognizance of institutions and policies that greatly inhibit development and that reduce the value of international aid to such countries. In numerous instances, the operations of state-owned enterprises have appeared to be inhibiting that process, and the search for alternatives has seemed altogether justified. In such cases, U.S. officials cannot conscientiously flinch from exploring the implications of privatization or of other measures that might deal with the problem.[20]

In addition to the role of the World Bank and United States aid agencies in promoting privatization the IMF made its own contribution in this direction. Although its stabilization policies and conditionality requirements do not typically demand outright privatization, conditionality requirements are such that privatization policies become the logical means of satisfying the IMF's constraints.[21] Another factor that is contributing to the process of privatization is the much talked-about policy of reducing foreign debt of developing countries in exchange for equity interests in their enterprises, both public and private.

To sum up, it can be said that there has been a congruence in the 1980s of several forces that created the conducive environment to push for policies to reduce the scope of the public sector and expand the role of the private sector. While the initial target of such policies was the state-owned enterprises in industrialized countries, the push for privatization was made into a policy prescription for developing countries as well.

It is important to note, as *The Economist* observed, that privatization in many Third World countries is made difficult by the notable lack of private investors.

This may open the door wide for foreign investors to buy important sectors of the national economy.[22]

To summarize, the rise of the public sector in the Arab countries was dictated by the nature of the functions of the state in postcolonial economies. Infrastructure projects and utilities were the main scope of the public sector. The rise of nationalism and the desire for a more equitable society pushed the state in the direction of expanding the public sector to serve as the primary instrument for achieving welfare maximization.

The rise of the oil sector increased the economic power of the state, expanded the public sector but in private-sector-based economies expanded the role of the private sector as well by providing more income to larger numbers of people. In the nonoil economies the availability of funds either from workers' remittances or in the form of outright subsidies from the GCC tended to promote the scope of the private sector.

In concluding this part, it must be pointed out that there exists a fundamental difference between industrialized countries and the developing countries, especially oil-producing countries, as they attempt to sell state-owned enterprises to the private sector. It can be said that state-owned enterprises were financed in the industrialized countries through taxation, that is, through the transfer of funds from the private sector to the public sector. And so the sale of these enterprises to the private sector at a discount, whatever forms that discount may take, will mean in a sense the return of assets that were originally financed by the taxpayers notwithstanding the distributional effects of the transfer.

In oil-producing countries where subsoil minerals belong to the state or the public at large, public enterprises were built by diverting a part of the national income that belongs to the society at large. This in turn means that the sale of these assets to the private sector will amount to the transfer of part of the national wealth, however small it may be, to a group of privileged individuals.

THE FUTURE OF ARAB OIL AND WORLD ENERGY REQUIREMENTS

In 1980 Arab oil-producing countries produced 19.2 million barrels of oil (MBD) or 71 percent of OPEC's total output in that year. By 1989 their output amounted to 12.7 MBD or 64 percent of OPEC's total. Between these two years OPEC output declined from 26.9 MBD in 1980 or 42.8 percent of the world total of 62.8 MBD in 1980 to 23.2 MBD or 36.5 percent of the world total of 63.6 MBD in 1989.[23] In order to understand the prospects for Arab and/or OPEC oil, it is necessary to deal with some of the more important forces that shaped the behavior of oil demand and supply in the recent past.

Historically, the international oil industry was dominated by seven major integrated multinational oil corporations—Exxon, Mobil, Standard Oil of California, Gulf, Texaco, British Petroleum, and Shell. These majors controlled more than 90 percent of the oil production outside the United States and the

Soviet Union in addition to their control over most of the transportation, refining, and marketing facilities. In order to protect their investment and to avoid the disruptive consequences of unregulated development of oil resources, the majors resorted to four strategies. First, the majors resorted to the formation of jointly owned subsidiary oil companies to develop oil resources under their control. This strategy enabled the parent companies, the majors, to coordinate their production plans to avoid excessive output. Second, the majors among themselves entered into long-term contracts, which spelled out where the contracted oil may be sold and the terms at which it could be marketed. The third strategy was to see to it that oil produced in the United States was regulated in such a manner as to meet estimated domestic demand at current prices. Fourth, the oil companies agreed among themselves to use the price quotations of United States–produced crude as the price at which oil was transacted at other oil-exporting points.[24]

This system of single-point pricing was undermined in the post–World War II period as the Middle East became an important oil-producing region and as the number of oil companies operating in the region increased. Given the fact that the cost of production of Middle East oil was much lower than that of American crude, it was only natural for the oil companies to expand the market for Middle East oil by lowering its price. But these price reductions, which were decided upon by the oil companies unilaterally, had the effect of lowering the revenue of oil-producing states, since such revenue was one-half of the difference between the price and the cost of production. The latest price cuts in 1959 and 1960, which lowered government per barrel revenue from 82 cents to 75 cents or by 9 percent, prompted the oil-producing countries to form OPEC in September 1960. OPEC's attempts to raise prices, in order to raise revenue for member countries, proved unsuccessful during the 1960s. OPEC had to wait until 1971 for price increases when such increases were granted by the oil companies under the terms of the Tehran Price Agreement of February 1971, which raised government revenue as a result of price and nonprice changes by 30 cents to 50 cents per barrel.[25]

The 1971 Tehran Agreement was a major turning point in the pattern of relationships between companies and governments in that it acknowledged for the first time the role of governments in price determination. Although the agreement was supposed to last for five years, there were forces at work both within the oil industry and in the international economic system, which caused the agreement to be discarded in October 1973.

The international monetary crisis, which culminated in the suspension on August 15, 1971, of the convertibility of the dollar into gold and the December 1971 devaluation of the dollar, prompted producing governments to demand and receive some compensation for the decline in the value of the dollar vis-à-vis other currencies.

The nationalization by Iraq of most of the assets of foreign oil companies prompted the oil companies in neighboring countries to allow governments to buy equity participation shares in the oil concessions. Neither nationalization nor participation would have succeeded if an imbalance between supply and demand had not emerged in the meantime as will be seen in the following paragraphs.

One of the more important developments in the post–World War II period was the phenomenal increase in oil consumption. Thus oil consumption in the economies of the industrial countries, where most of OPEC oil flows, increased from 8.3 MBD in 1950 to 15.5 MBD in 1960 and to 33.2 MBD in 1970 compared with a level of consumption of 36.6 MBD in 1989. In order to meet this increase in demand, the output from oil fields in OPEC countries had to be increased. In addition output from United States oil fields had to be increased as evidenced by the rise in capacity utilization in Texas from 28 percent in 1964 to 100 percent in 1972. The continued rise in demand, which was strengthened by the economic expansionary policies of the early 1970s in the industrial economies, accentuated by the shift from natural gas to oil and the removal of import controls in the United States, was not matched by an expansion in OPEC oil-producing capacity. In short, the international oil industry was not prepared for the sharp increase in American demand for oil, which rose by 81 percent between 1970 and 1973 compared with 18 percent in Western Europe and 35 percent in Japan during the same period. The sharp rise in demand had the effect of pushing prices and company profits upward while leaving government per barrel revenue unchanged because of the provisions of the Tehran Agreement.[26] The rise in market prices of oil, the stagnation of per barrel government revenue, and the erosion of oil revenue purchasing power moved OPEC to demand that official or posted prices—the price on which government oil revenue is computed—should be adjusted upward to reflect changing market conditions. When negotiation to raise prices started, the October 1973 Arab-Israeli war was already in progress. The refusal of the oil companies to grant the price increase demanded by OPEC together with American military and financial support for Israel prompted OPEC to suspend negotiations and raise the price of oil unilaterally. In addition to the OPEC-sponsored unilateral price increase, from $3 per barrel to $5.11 per barrel, the Arab members of OPEC, except Iraq, decided to lower output and impose an embargo on oil export to the United States. This artificially created oil shortage together with associated panic buying led the spot or open market price to rise sharply above the OPEC official price. This development in turn led OPEC to raise its official price to $11.65 per barrel (more than double the old price) as of January 1, 1974, or nearly four times the price that prevailed only three months earlier.[27] This price remained rather stable until 1978 when the events that preceded the 1979 Iranian Revolution caused oil prices to rise again. This rise was accentuated in 1980 in the context of the Iran-Iraq War, pushing the price to the unprecedented height of $34 per barrel by 1981. Unlike the 1973 price rise, which expressed a serious imbalance between supply and demand, the 1981 price did not reflect such an imbalance and had to be revised downward. Indeed, by 1986 OPEC was in such disarray that for a while prices collapsed to $7 per barrel. The questions that need to be addressed are Why did the price collapse? and What power, if any, does OPEC have to effect price changes in the future?

It is generally agreed that the 1973 price revolution was an important turning point in the history of international oil, not only because the prices were quadrupled, which led to significant redistribution of income from consumers to producers, but also because the decisions to set prices and output were shifted to OPEC member countries. The significance and implications of the latter change to the future of OPEC and the Arab economies cannot be underestimated.

Arab and non-Arab oil-producing countries were, until the early 1970s, the mere recipients of a certain amount of revenue per barrel of oil exported by the oil companies. For nearly twenty years this revenue, which was around 80 cents per barrel, represented the difference between the cost of production and the posted or the tax reference price, the setting of which was the prerogative of the oil companies. Not until 1971 were prices set in negotiations. In 1973 the price-setting function was shifted to governments that were not prepared for the new task, since they were not part of any decision-making processes that affected output and prices.

It will be recalled that the major oil companies that controlled the bulk of OPEC oil were engaged in joint operations and long-term contracts that helped to regulate the rate of growth of production of Middle East oil in such a manner as not to threaten price stability. From oil corporate perspective the system worked well in that it enabled them to introduce the low-cost Middle East oil to the world market without threatening their investments in other parts of the world. In other words oil companies succeeded in maximizing the returns on their worldwide investments by refraining from ruinous competition. In contrast to this corporate ability to stabilize output and maximize returns governments were not similarly positioned to regulate output and set prices.

First and foremost, governments were guided by the principle of the sovereignty of the state, which calls for minimum intervention in the economic policy of the states whether by other states or by international agencies. The history of the failed experiments of the Arab League in matters of economic cooperation and/or integration among the Arab countries, as we have seen in earlier chapters, provides ample evidence as to how jealously those states tended to guard their freedom to make their own decisions. Given the paramount importance of the oil sector in the economies of OPEC countries, it was only natural that these countries try to make most of their decisions with the interest of their national economies uppermost in mind. This in turn meant that decisions with respect to output, investment, and capacity expansion are to be taken without the benefit of the coordination that characterized OPEC oil when it was under corporate control. Indeed, for many years some OPEC member countries refused even to consider the possibility of coordinating production policies. While unable or unwilling to agree on oil production policies, OPEC was able to refrain from price competition for almost a decade after the 1973 price revolution.

OPEC's ability to agree on prices was helped by several factors. These include the continued high demand for oil, since the elasticity of demand for oil is low, and the unavailability of oil outside OPEC. In addition the willingness of Saudi Arabia to play the role of swing producer by lowering its output in times of declining demand and raising its output in time of pending shortages had the effect of stabilizing output and prices. But such stability cannot last for too long. The rise in oil prices encouraged investment in oil fields outside OPEC member countries, where the cost of production was too high relative to pre–1973 prices. In time oil began to flow from Alaska, the North Sea, Mexico, and a number of other non-OPEC countries. Conservation measures that were implemented in the aftermath of the oil revolution began to show results in the form of lower oil consumption per given amount of GNP. Consumption of nonoil sources of energy was allowed to increase in order to lower dependence on oil. These measures and policies were coordinated among industrial economies through their International Energy Agency, which led to severe decline in the demand for OPEC oil, causing OPEC output to decline from a peak of 31.3 MBD in 1977 to a low of 15.4 MBD in 1985. This decline in output was not reflected by a similar decline in revenue because of the sharp rise in prices due to the Iranian Revolution and the Iran-Iraq War. Thus OPEC revenue reached its peak in 1980 at $263 billion but declined to $127 billion in 1985.

The projected decline in both revenue and output in 1986 prompted OPEC to adopt a new policy, which entailed the abandoning of price stability in favor of market share. But such a policy meant the unrestrained output by member countries, which by definition meant further decline in prices. The outcome of the policy meant an increase in output from 15.4 MBD in 1985 to 18.3 MBD, an increase of nearly 19 percent that was accompanied by a decline in oil revenue from $127 billion to $77 billion in 1986, a decline of 39 percent.[28] It is very obvious that a drastic decline in revenue could not be sustained and OPEC found itself resorting to output ceilings again, which had been introduced as an informal arrangement in 1982, and its system of stable prices.

Like all other intergovernmental organizations, OPEC lacks the power to enforce its decisions. This meant that the adherence to output ceilings rests with each member country. Should an individual country find it in its own self-interest to exceed its assigned quota and sell oil at less than the agreed upon price, there is nothing OPEC can do to prevent that from happening. And so between 1982, when output ceilings or quotas were introduced, and 1990 a number of countries at different times either refused to accept their quotas or exceeded their quotas to the detriment of the entire group.

What about the future of Arab oil? The long-term decline in the demand for OPEC oil, which characterized the 1980s and which brought OPEC output from 31.3 MBD in 1977 to 15.4 MBD in 1985, seems to be over. And all studies seem to indicate that a reversal of that trend is taking shape for the 1990s. There are several explanations to this phenomenon. In the first place the decline in the price of oil both in nominal and real terms especially after the price crash of

1986 seems to have stimulated demand for oil. The general economic growth conditions in the industrialized world for much of the 1980s contributed to an increase in the demand for oil. The sharp fall in the dollar after 1985 further lowered real prices for non–United States oil consumers in Western Europe and Japan. Another explanation for the rise in the demand for OPEC oil is the fact that the decline in the price of oil in the 1980s as well as the decline in the productivity of the oil fields outside OPEC had the effect of lowering the supply from non-OPEC sources. The fall in the price of oil provided a general stimulus for the demand for oil to increase.[29] These forces of demand stimulation found their expression in the movement in the demand for oil by the member countries of the Organization for Economic Cooperation and Development (OECD). These countries' demand for oil reached 40.7 MBD in 1979 but declined to 33.2 MBD in 1983 but climbed to 36.6 MBD in 1989. During the same decade oil supply from non-OPEC sources increased from 34.3 MBD in 1979 to 40.4 MBD in 1985 but remained at that level in 1989.

The effects of the reversal in the demand conditions for oil and the stability of supply conditions outside the OPEC region encouraged OPEC to decide for the first time in a decade to raise prices. This was achieved at its July 1990 meeting when it was decided that the minimum reference price for OPEC basket of seven types of crude be raised from $18 to $21 per barrel.[30] Should these trends of rising demand for oil and relative decline in non-OPEC supply continue in the 1990s as seems to be the case, then there is no reason not to expect OPEC and Arab oil to be relied upon to meet an ever-increasing share of the world's demand for oil.

OPEC's own thinking tends to see member countries who hold 76 percent of the world oil reserves to be the only group of countries that can meet the expected rising demand for oil. OPEC's own projections show that world demand for oil—excluding centrally planned economies—will be 55 MBD in 1995 and 58 MBD in the year 2000. On the supply side non-OPEC supplies are estimated to be 28 MBD and 26 MBD in 1995 and 2000 respectively. This means that OPEC will be called upon to provide between 27 MBD in 1995 and 32 MBD in the year 2000. But since OPEC has a current sustainable production capacity of 25 MBD, OPEC must expand its capacity by more than 6 MBD if it is to meet world demand for its oil by the year 2000. To install this additional capacity will cost OPEC $60 billion. With an outstanding external debt of $215 billion, which absorbs a significant part of its revenue to service it, OPEC will be hard pressed to find the necessary capital to expand its production capacity. In other words OPEC would like to see foreign capital being invested to develop its oil fields.[31]

The need for foreign investment to develop oil reserves in OPEC countries had already been voiced by both Iraq and Iran. In the case of Iraq, a country with a significant external debt burden, the government decided to invite foreign companies to participate in the development of oil fields and provide the requisite financing for such development. In order not to add to its debt burdens, the repayment for the development investment will be effected in crude oil produced from those fields where the development took place.[32]

ARAB NATIONALISM, OIL, AND THE FUTURE OF ARAB ECONOMIES

It was postulated that the course of Arab economic development in this century was influenced by three realities: Arab nationalism, foreign dependence, and oil. Arab nationalism sought to reestablish the identity and political aspirations of the Arab populations who lived under the domination of the Ottoman Empire. Arab nationalism sought, in other words, to enable the Arab component of the Ottoman subjects to seek to loosen the grip of Ottoman domination and establish independent Arab states. In their zeal to reach their goals, the leaders of this Arab movement sought to enlist the assistance of other foreign powers—Britain and France. The quid pro quo for this help was for the Arabs to rebel against the Ottomans in World War I on the side of Britain and France. But Britain and France had already agreed among themselves to carve up the Arab region into separate political entities under their control. The new political order that these two European powers imposed on the Arab region strengthened the privileged economic position that they were able to attain during the nineteenth century when the Arab region was already under Ottoman control. And to strengthen their privileged position, they installed political regimes accountable to them but managed by local leadership.

The civilian and military bureaucracies that were necessary for the management of the newly established states were drawn from the early Arab nationalists who sought to break away from Ottoman domination. One of the primary functions of the new states was to help integrate their economies into the international economic system. This stage in Arab nationalist development faced its most severe test in 1948 when Israel was established in Palestine. This historical development exposed the weakness of the Arab regimes that were organized by colonial powers. In a relatively short period of time the regimes in Egypt, Syria, and Iraq were displaced by new regimes that relied on the armed forces for their rule. The new nationalist regimes sought the expulsion of foreign control and declared that Arab unity was one of their major objectives. But the attainment of these objectives was to be undermined by the emergence of oil as the most important sector in most Arab economies.

The position of dominance that Britain and France attained after World War I was further enhanced as they helped their oil companies obtain concession agreements to develop Arab oil. As Arab oil was discovered and developed, the process of integrating the Arab economies into the world economy was accelerated. But oil did more than that. The emergence of Saudi Arabia and other Gulf states as major oil-producing centers and the defeat of the army-based regimes by Israel in the 1967 war shifted the centers of economic, political, and diplomatic power from the core countries of Egypt, Syria, and Iraq to the peripheral oil-producing states. The oil price explosion of the 1970s and the desire of the oil states to develop their economies placed the latter in a much stronger position vis-à-vis other Arab states. This change was helped by the ability of the oil states to provide economic aid to the nonoil states and to provide employment opportunities to vast numbers of Arab workers whose earnings constituted another source of income to the nonoil labor-exporting countries. In short the linkages of integration with and dependency on the world economic system were strengthened as the economies of both groups of countries became increasingly dependent on the industrial countries' demand for oil. The sharp decline in demand, oil exports, and revenue in the 1980s forced adjustments in budgets and development plans and led to a significant increase in external debt in most Arab countries.

But the role of oil in shaping Arab economies is far deeper than just influencing patterns of spending and payments. The availability of oil revenue made it possible in both oil and nonoil states to enjoy levels of consumption that could not have been supported by the nonoil sectors of domestic output. And while the oil states may be forced in a period of recession to draw down on their accumulated savings to support consumption—both public and private—the nonoil states found themselves forced to lower consumption and incur external debt.

What about the future of Arab economies? Looking at the different resource endowments of the Arab region, one is struck by the fact that the countries with the potential for development—Egypt, Iraq, Algeria, Syria, Jordan, Morocco, Tunisia, and Sudan—are capital deficient. These countries may have the natural and human resources, but due to mismanagement, external wars, or civil wars, they find themselves as they enter the twenty-first century overburdened with foreign debt, high population growth rates, high defense burdens, and high levels of unemployment. Moreover, during the era of high oil income these countries neglected to invest in their goods-producing sectors, especially agriculture, giving rise to serious dependency on food imports.

The other countries' economic fortunes are directly related to the demand conditions for oil and the price such demand will set for their oil exports. All oil-exporting countries live by trading in oil as they import most of the things they need. From the perspective of lessening economic and political dependence through economic diversification the oil price revolution was a missed opportunity in the sense that the oil-based economies are no less dependent on this particular sector in the 1990s than they were in the 1970s.

The sudden expansion in oil wealth and revenue could theoretically have ushered in a different era in economic relations among Arab states, which could conceivably have reordered Arab economies in the direction of diversification and self-sufficiency. The ideals of Arab nationalism and Arab unity should have led to a different pattern of income flow among Arab economies. The oil wealth should have persuaded decision makers of the long-term benefits of the economies of scale, market size, specialization, rationalization of decision making, long-term investment, and diversification. In other words, economic policy should have been formulated to benefit from differences in resource endowments and cooperative advantages. But to derive such benefits would have required economic, investment, and planning policies to go beyond established political boundaries. In other words, Arab governments had to engage in coordinating the whole range of economic policies. To do this, however, would have meant that these governments give up at least some of the prerogatives that come with the sovereignty of the state—something those governments were not prepared to do.

Instead of the necessary regional multicountry economic development economic policies tended to have a single-country focus. Arab nationalism may have served as a rallying political movement against foreign domination and intervention but failed to convince policymakers in Arab countries to coordinate and unify. And as the revenue from oil declined, the reaction of the oil states was to reduce spending. But such a reduction had the unavoidable effect of reducing financial flows to nonoil states as economic assistance and worker remittances declined, giving rise to all sorts of economic difficulties including higher budget and balance-of-payments deficits, higher unemployment rates, and larger external debt.

Future rise in the demand for oil will, of course, raise the income of oil-producing states. The rise will not be similar to that of the 1970s and the early 1980s due to the structural changes in supply and demand conditions that have taken place in the decade of the 1980s. This means that the accelerated increase in financial transfers to the nonoil states that characterized the period of oil price revolution will not be repeated. Nonoil states will have to reach their own accommodation with the international economic system in terms of the size of the debt, availability of new loans, rescheduling, terms, economic restructuring, and other arrangements. Regardless of the policies and their instruments countries will be forced to accept lower standards of living than the ones they had hoped to achieve. Social and political tensions are bound to surface in response to the forced absolute or relative decline in income and their consequent expressions by affected social groups.

The prospects of the economies of the oil states may be divided in two groups. The Gulf states and Libya, which are deficient in human and nonhuman resources, are expected to remain dependent on oil and therefore on what will happen to oil demand and supply conditions. Their fortunes will be determined for a long time to come by the economic and energy conditions and policies of the member countries of the International Energy Agency.

While Algeria and Iraq possess significant resource endowments and have relatively advanced economies by Third World standards, their major problems stem from other sources. First they developed, like all other countries, serious dependency on food imports as they neglected to invest in their agricultural sectors. Second, both countries have become for different reasons major indebted countries. Algeria's ambitious industrial development program was built on the premise that oil revenue would continue to rise in the 1980s. The failure of oil revenue to increase coupled with relatively inelastic imports forced Algeria into heavy foreign borrowing. The case of Iraq is different from Algeria in that Iraq started the decade of the 1980s with considerable foreign reserves. Not only did these reserves disappear in the course of the Iran-Iraq War (1980–1988) but the war turned Iraq into a major debtor country. Neither one of these countries will be able to get out of the debt trap without significant increase in their oil earnings, an increase that would generate enough balance-of-payments surplus to pay the debt and in time be diverted to investment purposes. Not unlike the first group of countries, the economic fortunes of Algeria and Iraq will be tied also to oil demand and supply conditions in the IEA group of countries.

In conclusion, it seems that the Arab state system failed to mobilize Arab nationalism or oil wealth as forces to liberate the Arab economies from dependency and underdevelopment.

NOTES

1. It is worth noting that Egypt's GNP, with a population of 50 million or 2.5 times the combined population of the four richest oil states, was $65.8 billion or 53 percent of their GNP. Unless otherwise indicated, economic indicators in this section were derived from League of Arab States et al., *Joint Arab Economic Report* (annual); Arab Monetary Fund (AMF), *Arab Countries: Economic Indicators, 1976–1986* (Abu Dhabi, AMF, 1988), AMF, *National Accounts of Arab Countries, 1972–1983* (Abu Dhabi, AMF, 1984), AMF, *Foreign Trade of Arab Countries, 1976–1986* (Abu Dhabi, AMF, 1988); World Bank, *World Development Report* (annual); International Monetary Fund, *Direction of Trade Statistics Yearbook*; International Monetary Fund, *International Financial Statistics Yearbook*; OPEC, *Annual Statistical Bulletin*.

2. Unless otherwise indicated, external debt data are derived from International Monetary Fund, *World Economic Outlook* (annual), League of Arab States et al., *Joint Arab Economic Report* (annual), Arab Banking Corporation, *Economic and Financial Quarterly*, June 1989, World Bank, *World Development Report* (annual).

3. For a good discussion of the various factors responsible for the rise in Third World indebtedness see, for example, Susan George, *A Fate Worse Than Debt: The World Financial Crisis and the Poor* (New York: Grove Weidenfeld, 1988); Arthur MacEwan, *Debt and Disorder: International Economic Instability and U.S. Imperial Decline* (New York: Monthly Review Press, 1990); Robert Polin and Eduardo Zepeda, "Latin American Debt: The Choices Ahead," *Monthly Review*, February 1987, 1–16; Walter Russel Mead, "The United States and the World Economy," *World Policy Journal* 6, No. 1 (Winter, 1988–1989): 1–45; Jeff Faux, "The Alternative Trap and the Growth Alternative," *World Policy Journal* 5, No. 3 (Summer 1988): 367–413; and Gerald Epstein, "The Triple Debt Crisis," *World Policy Journal* 2, No. 4 (Fall 1988): 625–657. See also Latin American Perspectives, *Debt and the World Economic System* (Special Issue), Issue No. 60, Winter 1989.

4. See Ramzi Zaki, "The Exit from Foreign Indebtedness between Romantic Thoughts and Objective Conception," in Arab Thought Forum, *Balances and Arab External Indebtedness: Alternative Policies for the Protection of Balances and Facing*

Indebtedness (in Arabic) (Amman: Arab Thought Forum, 1987), 87–129, especially p. 114.

5. *Joint Arab Economic Report, 1988*, pp. 62 and 225.

6. See U.S. Arms Control and Disarmament Agency, *World Military Expenditures and Arms Transfers, 1988* (Washington, D.C., 1989), 27–30.

7. Ibid, Table II.

8. For a vivid description of the working of this system see Saad Eddin Ibrahim, *The New Arab Social Order: A Study of the Social Consequences of the Oil Wealth* (in Arabic) (Beirut: Centre for Arab Unity Studies, 1985), 27–34.

9. See Ibrahim Saad El Din Abdallah, "Role of the State in Economic Activity in the Arab World: General Issues and a Future View" (in Arabic), *Al Mustaqbal Al Arabi*, September 1989, 4–36, especially p. 23.

10. For a good analysis of this phenomenon see Hikmat Sharif al-Nashashibi, "Arab Banking Investment in International Financial Markets" (in Arabic), *Al Mustaqbal Al Arabi*, October 1989, 96–106.

11. See for example Said el-Naggar (ed.), *Privatization and Structural Adjustment in the Arab Countries* (Washington, D.C.: International Monetary Fund, 1989); Arab Planning Institute in Kuwait, *Seminar: Role of the State in the Economic Activity in the Arab World* (in Arabic) (Kuwait, May 27–29, 1989); Centre for Arab Unity Studies, "On the Call for the Transfer from the Public Sector to the Private Sector in the Arab World," *Al Mustaqbal Al Arabi*, August 1989, 133–160.

12. Hazem el-Biblawi, "Comment," in el-Naggar, *Privatization*, 137–38.

13. See Ibrahim Helmy abdel-Rahman and Mohammed Sultan Abu Ali, "The Role of the Public and Private Sectors with Special Reference to Privatization: The Case of Egypt," in el-Naggar, Ibid., 143.

14. For the data on the Egyptian firms see *Al Mustaqbal Al Arabi*, August 1989, 142. For the data on the Kuwaiti firms see Majid Hadi Masoud, "Some Economic Structural Imbalances in the Countries of the Arab World and the Role of the Needed Role of the Nationalist Democratic State in their Correction," *Kuwait Seminar*, 36.

15. For the performance of enterprises in Algeria and Tunisia see Sad Hafedh Mahmoud, "An Essay on the Public Sector and Role in Development," *Kuwait Seminar*, 33, and for their performance in all other countries see Yacob Haile-Mariam and Berhanu Mengistu, "Public Enterprises and Privatization in the Third World," *Third World Quarterly* 10, No. 4 (October 1988): 1573–1574.

16. For a good discussion of these issues see John Vickers and George Yarrow, *Privatization: An Economic Analysis* (Cambridge: MIT Press, 1988), chapter 2.

17. Ibid., 27–29.

18. Ibid., 145.

19. See Don Babai, "The World Bank and the IMF: Rolling Back the State or Backing its Role?" in Raymond Vernon (ed.), *The Promise of Privatization: A Challenge for American Policy* (New York: Council on Foreign Relations, 1988), 254–285 especially 260–261.

20. See ibid., 20.

21. See Stuart M. Butler (ed.), *The Privatization Option: A Strategy to Shrink the Size of Government* (Washington, D.C.: The Heritage Foundation, 1985), 4–5. According to Ethan B. Kapstein external forces helped catalyze privatization policy formulation and implementation when the IMF provided support for the Brazilian government's policies of destatization, which were aided by infusion of foreign capital by American Express.

See his "Brazil: Continued State Dominance," in Vernon, *Promise of Privatization*, 142–45.

22. See Haile-Mariam and Mengistu, "Public Enterprises," 1581.

23. Unless otherwise indicated oil and other energy data in this section are derived from BP, *BP Statistical Review of World Energy* (London, Annual); *Annual Statistical Bulletin* (Annual). The term "Arab oil" here refers to the oil produced by OPEC Arab member countries—Algeria, Iraq, Kuwait, Libya, Qatar, Saudi Arabia, and the United Arab Emirates. These seven countries produce over 90 percent of the oil produced in the Arab region. Most of the analysis in this section will focus on OPEC oil rather than on Arab oil per se. This should not affect the conclusions, since Arab oil constitutes nearly two-thirds of OPEC oil.

24. For a fuller analysis of the evolution of the international oil industry see Abbas Alnasrawi, "The Petrodollar Energy Crisis: An Overview and Interpretation," *Syracuse Journal of International Law and Commerce* 3, No. 2 (1975): 369–412; and Abbas Alnasrawi, *OPEC in a Changing World Economy* (Baltimore, Md.: Johns Hopkins University Press, 1985), chapters 2 and 3.

25. For a fuller discussion of these price reductions and the formation of OPEC see Ian Seymour, *OPEC: Instrument of Change* (London: Macmillan, 1980), chapters 2 and 4.

26. For details of price movements in 1973 see *Petroleum Intelligence Weekly* (*PIW*), August 6 and 20, 1973, and *MEES*, September 21, 1973.

27. For a detailed treatment of the circumstances that led to these changes see Seymour, *OPEC: Instrument of Change*, chapter 5.

28. For a fuller treatment of OPEC policies in this particular period see Fadhil J. al-Chalabi, *OPEC at the Crossroads* (Oxford: Pergamon Press, 1989), 77–91.

29. Ibid, 57.

30. *MEES*, July 30, 1990.

31. See Subroto, "How OPEC sees the Crucial Energy Issues of the 1990s," *OPEC Bulletin*, April 1990, 5–10; Subroto, "Energy into the 21st Century: An OPEC View," *OPEC Bulletin*, May 1990, 5–9. See also Saadalla A. al-Fathi, "Security of Oil Supply and Demand: Two Sides of the Same Coin," *OPEC Bulletin*, February 1989, 15–18.

32. See *MEES*, February 12, 1990, and *MEES*, March 26, 1990.

10

EPILOGUE: ARAB NATIONALISM, OIL, DEPENDENCY, AND THE GULF CRISIS

In the first few weeks of August 1990 a number of major developments occurred in the Arab region that tend to support the thrust of the main arguments presented in this study. On August 2, 1990, Iraq invaded Kuwait, which prompted the United Nations Security Council to vote to condemn Iraq's action and to demand the immediate withdrawal of its forces from Kuwait. It also called upon Iraq and Kuwait to enter into intensive negotiations for the resolution of their differences. On August 4, the European Economic Community voted to impose an embargo on oil imports from Iraq and Kuwait. On August 6, the United Nations Security Council adopted another resolution calling for the imposition of a sweeping trade and financial boycott on Iraq. Ten additional resolutions were adopted by the Security Council culminating in the November 29 resolution that empowered member states "to use all necessary means to uphold previous Security Council resolutions demanding Iraq's withdrawal from Kuwait" if Iraq had not done so by January 15, 1991.[1]

For its part, the United States government announced the freezing of all Iraqi and Kuwaiti assets, a step that was followed by other major industrial countries. Moreover, the United States government decided to land military forces in Saudi Arabia and to use its naval forces to blockade all trade with Iraq.[2]

In explaining his decision to send troops to Saudi Arabia, President George Bush stated that his policy was guided by these principles: (1) the requirement of unconditional withdrawal of Iraqi forces from Kuwait; (2) the required restoration of the government that ruled Kuwait prior to the invasion; and (3) the commitment of the United States government, starting with President Roosevelt, to the security and stability of the Gulf. Bush went so far as to equate the importance of the Middle East with that of Europe when he said: "The stakes are high. . . . Our country now imports nearly half the oil it consumes and could face a major threat to its economic independence. . . . We succeeded in the struggle for freedom in Europe because we and our allies remain stalwart. Keeping the peace in the Middle East will require no less.''[3] Following the deployment of American troops, Egypt, Morocco, and Syria sent troops to Saudi Arabia, thus aligning themselves with the United States against Iraq.

The eruption of the crisis, the blockade against oil exports from Iraq and Kuwait (which was annexed by Iraq after the invasion), and the speculative fervor in the oil markets forced oil prices to rise sharply. In order to stabilize prices and increase supply, OPEC, under the strong prodding of Saudi Arabia, authorized its member countries to raise their output to offset the 4-MBD output of Iraq and Kuwait oil that was not reaching the world oil market as a result of the United Nations sanctions and blockade. The events of August 1990 and subsequent developments tend to support the thrust of the main arguments in this study, as will be seen in the following paragraphs.

While the tenets of Arab nationalism with its twin goals of independence from foreign influence and unity among the fragmented Arab states were adhered to in theory, in practice these states tended to follow their own country-centered interests. The Arab state system, as developed in this century, had the prerogatives of the single state as its core. Numerous attempts by the Arab League to develop some form of economic integration among these states failed to receive the necessary political backing of member countries precisely because of some perceived conflict with the economic interest of this or that member country. By the same token, OPEC member countries have on many occasions agreed to certain price and output levels only to find that their own national interest did not adhere to what they had already agreed. Nor did Arab countries choose to coordinate their economic planning so as to avoid the wasteful duplication associated with narrowly based planning. Politically these countries followed their own paths despite the periodic lip service that they paid to Arab nationalism and Arab unity when the leaders of these countries met periodically at the summit level. The commitment, in the Arab world, to the preservation of the individual state structure as the core of the political system and ideology was expressed with remarkable clarity by the Iraqi president, Saddam Hussein, in 1982 when he said: ''The question of linking unity to the removal of boundaries is no longer acceptable to present Arab mentality. . . . We must see the world as it is. Any Arab would have wished to see the Arab nation as one state. . . . But these are sheer dreams. The Arab reality is that the Arabs are now 22 states, and we have to behave accordingly.''[4]

The takeover of Kuwait and the consequent division and debate among the Arab states have failed once again to unify the Arab countries. Moreover, the division among the Arab states in their reaction to the takeover was strong evidence attesting to the failure of the Arab state system as it has functioned since its inception in 1945. In that year the League of Arab States was created in order to settle disputes among member states, among other things. Not only did the Arab state system fail to facilitate political and economic integration, but it also failed to protect the takeover of one state by another in spite of all the non-aggression pacts and mutual defense treaties among these states.

The collapse of the Arab state system revealed that for certain states such as Kuwait and Saudi Arabia their very political existence was dependent on the military power of the West under the leadership of the United States. In the case of Kuwait it was the United States that pledged to secure the withdrawal of Iraq from Kuwait and the return of the ruling family to its position of power, a pledge that was backed by the combined weight of its diplomacy and military force. The United States government also committed itself to the preservation of the territorial and political status quo in Saudi Arabia, where the American troops were deployed.

The takeover of Kuwait exposed the inherent contradiction between Arab nationalism with its twin emphasis on unity and independence from foreign influence and the requirement of the sovereign state. The deployment of American troops to protect the political system of Saudi Arabia and to demand the withdrawal of Iraq from Kuwait was testimony to the fact that existing political arrangements and borders cannot survive without a Western protective shield and that the interests of a number of Arab states lay with the West.

The decision by several Arab states to endorse the presence of Western troops in Saudi Arabia and the decision by Egypt, Morocco, and Syria to associate themselves militarily with the West must be taken as supporting evidence of the importance that ruling governments in the Arab world attach to the individual state system and the inherent limitations of Arab nationalism. On the basis of interviews in the Gulf region, one observer concluded that rich, conservative Gulf nationals foresee a long American presence in a number of Gulf states, that the opinions of the rest of the Arab world will simply not matter with such a protective umbrella, and that Arab nationalism and the Arab League are finished.[5]

OIL AND THE CRISIS

A considerable part of this study was devoted to an examination of the impact of the development of oil resources on the oil-based Arab economies, the role that oil played in integrating these economies into the international economic system, the dependency of the oil states on this resource as a source of finance and foreign exchange, and the emergence of the phenomenon of derivative dependency in the nonoil states. In the 1990 crisis the role of oil was highlighted at several important junctures.

In one sense the genesis of Iraq's decision to move into Kuwait may be found in the 1980–1988 Iran-Iraq war. In the course of the war, Iraq looked upon itself and was looked upon by Saudi Arabia, Kuwait, and the smaller Gulf states as the defender of the Arab political order against the winds of change emanating from the 1979 Iranian Revolution and the newly established Islamic republic in Iran.[6]

This perception provided the rationale for the infusion of financial resources from Kuwait and Saudi Arabia into Iraq's treasury—funds that were essential for carrying on the war. The newly found community of interests between Iraq and these family regimes explains also Kuwait's decision to allow Iraq to use its facilities for Iraq's imports. It also explains Saudi Arabia's decision to allow Iraq to construct oil pipelines across its territories. The Saudi decision was important for Iraq, since its exporting facilities through the Gulf were destroyed and its pipeline across Syria was closed down by the Syrian government.

The war between Iraq and Iran that erupted in September 1980 created uncertainties in the world oil markets, giving rise to panic buying and in turn causing oil prices to rise sharply from $14 per barrel in January 1979 to $34 per barrel in December 1980. Since Iraq and Iran could not produce at capacity, however, the other countries of OPEC, especially Saudi Arabia, benefited from this price windfall. Moreover, Saudi Arabia increased its output sharply to capture market shares traditionally supplied by Iraq and Iran. Suffice it to say that Saudi Arabia's revenue from oil jumped 188 percent—from $40 billion in 1978 to $116 billion in 1981. During the same period OPEC oil revenue increased 95 percent—from $135 billion to $263 billion. But the increase in output came at a time when the market was suffering from an oil glut.[7]

The Saudi-caused oil glut, together with the success of energy- and oil-saving measures in lowering oil consumption, had the effect of reducing the dependence of industrialized countries on OPEC oil. In addition, the buildup of oil stockpiles and strategic reserves in the industrialized countries, as well as the rise in oil supply from non-OPEC sources, caused OPEC to lose a major part of its share of the world oil market. Suffice it to say that OPEC oil production fell from 27 MBD in 1980 to 15.4 MBD in 1985, with its oil-exports earnings falling from $285 billion to $127 billion during the same period. In order to protect its share of the market from further erosion, OPEC decided to expand its output and sell its oil at lower prices, causing the price of its oil to crash from $27–$28 per barrel in 1985 to less than $10 per barrel in the summer of 1986. This price collapse reduced OPEC oil exports earnings to $77 billion in 1986—the lowest level in the post–1973 period.[8] In an attempt to stabilize prices, output, and revenues, OPEC decided to set a target price of $18 per barrel and to observe a system of output quotas in order to attain that price.

OPEC, however, is an intergovernmental organization with no power to enforce its decisions. Narrow interests of a member country can take precedence over the interests of the group. Several countries at different times produced above their assigned shares of production, causing prices to fall. Several agreements between 1986 and 1990 were made by OPEC to get member countries to observe their assigned quotas but without success, as Kuwait produced above its quota and the United Arab Emirates chose not to accept any quota. While these two underpopulated countries with considerable holdings of foreign reserves were pushing for higher production, Iraq and other countries were interested in stable prices.

When the Iran-Iraq war came to an end in 1988, Iraq, with a population of

17 million—or more than the combined population of Saudi Arabia, Kuwait, the United Arab Emirates, and all other Gulf states—was faced with an economic crisis of major proportions. In the course of the war Iraq had exhausted its foreign reserves and had become a major debtor country. In addition, it faced the expensive task of the postwar reconstruction and the rebuilding of its military forces. Iraq's only hope for coping with these problems was for its revenue from oil to be not just stable but to rise. In order to accomplish this, however, it and Iran had to have the cooperation of other OPEC member countries, especially Kuwait and the United Arab Emirates, to observe production shares within an OPEC-wide system of allocations.

While Iraq's policy stressed output regulation to allow prices to stabilize and then rise, Kuwait's policy stressed the importance of abandoning the quota system altogether because, for Kuwait, quotas were already irrelevant. Member countries, according to Kuwait, should be encouraged to produce as much as they can to see to it that the price of the OPEC basket of crudes does not go above the $18-per-barrel target.[9] This policy, which amounted to a unilateral decision by Kuwait to freeze the price of oil, was unacceptable not only to Iraq but to a number of other countries in OPEC.

Although OPEC oil prices averaged $14.28 and $17.31 in 1988 and 1989 respectively, Kuwait and the United Arab Emirates continued to fail to observe their quotas. And when the price reached close to $20 for a few days in early January 1990, these two countries persisted in their violation of OPEC output quotas to such an extent that the price declined by 32 percent, to $13.67 in June 1990.[10]

In the face of this decline in prices, Iraq started a vigorous campaign of protest against policies of overproduction, which resulted in its loss of revenue. Thus, in early May 1990, Iraq's foreign minister warned the overproducers against continuing with this irresponsible game and suggested that the matter would be taken up at the next Arab summit conference to be convened in Baghdad at the end of the month.[11]

At the Arab summit the Iraqi president criticized the overproducers and highlighted the fact that Iraq was losing $1 billion per year for every $1 per barrel decline in the price of oil. He expressed the belief that the damage that was being inflicted on the Iraqi economy was the equivalent of war: "Wars are sometimes carried out by soldiers . . . and, sometimes, as a result of economic measures." He went on to say that "we cannot tolerate this type of economic warfare which is being waged against Iraq. . . . I say we have reached a state of affairs where we cannot take the pressure. I believe that we will all benefit . . . from the principle of adherence to OPEC resolutions on production and prices."[12]

As the prices continued to be low, the Iraqi government complained on July 15 to the Arab League about the damaging consequence to the Iraqi economy of Kuwait's policy of overproduction. Iraq also accused Kuwait of stealing Iraq's national wealth by extracting, from the Rumaila oilfield that straddles the border between the two countries, oil that belonged to Iraq. It also asked that loans extended by Kuwait to Iraq in the course of the Iran-Iraq war be forgiven on the grounds that, during that war, Iraq has shouldered the responsibility of Arab national defense and Arab sovereignty and the wealth of the Gulf states. These points were reiterated in a public speech given by the Iraqi president on July 17.[13] The failure of negotiations to resolve the Iraqi-Kuwaiti differences prompted Iraq to invade and annex Kuwait.

Iraq's move into Kuwait failed to give it any immediate fiscal relief. On the contrary, the blockade denied Iraq access to the world oil market in order to sell not only Kuwait's oil but its own as well. This meant that the world was deprived of the combined oil exports of Kuwait and Iraq. Expectedly, oil prices increased, and OPEC was called upon to raise output to dampen higher prices. It is worth noting that OPEC had decided only a few days prior to the eruption of the crisis in August to set the price target at $21 per barrel and to set the combined quotas at 22.491 MBD without allowing any member country to exceed its allocated quota for any reason whatsoever.[14] Yet, as soon as the crisis broke out Saudi Arabia made it clear that it would raise its output with or without the consent of OPEC. And before the end of August OPEC decided to suspend the quota system it had approved in July and increase output in accordance with the need of the world market.[15] It goes without saying that oil countries with spare capacity to increase output, especially Saudi Arabia and the United Arab Emirates, are in a position to enjoy considerable increase in their income due to the rise in oil prices as well as the increase in their output.

Soon after the war ended OPEC decided to reintroduce the quota system with a total output of 22.3 MBD—slightly lower than the July 1990 quota of 23.5 MBD. Since neither Iraq nor Kuwait is exporting any oil due to the postwar conditions, Saudi Arabia has been able to appropriate to itself most of these two countries' output, thus raising its share of OPEC's quota from 23.9 percent in July to 36 percent under the new quota arrangement.[16]

DEPENDENCY AND DERIVATIVE DEPENDENCY

The Gulf crisis illustrates the dependence of the oil states and the nonoil states on what happens to the oil sector and on external factors. As soon as the crisis erupted, Iraq found itself blockaded with no access for its traditional export and import markets. Although technically Iraq doubled its oil reserves and increased its export capacity by more than one-half once its takeover of Kuwait was complete, the naval blockade imposed by the United States and its allies made the acquisition of new oil resources meaningless. By imposing an embargo on imports into Iraq, which is dependent on imports for up to 70–80 percent of its food consumption, the United States and its allies gave themselves considerable power over the nature and course of internal developments in Iraq. Only four months after the imposition of the blockade and embargo, their impact on the Iraqi economy was assessed, in a testimony before the House Armed Services Committee, to have had the following effects: (1) more than 90 percent of imports and 97 percent of exports have been shut off; (2) industry appears to be the hardest hit sector as firms found it difficult to cope with the departure of foreign workers and with the cutoff of imported industrial inputs; (3) the embargo has deprived Iraq of roughly $1.5 billion of foreign exchange earnings monthly; and (4) Iraqi's economic problems will multiply as it will be forced to gradually shut down growing numbers of facilities.[17]

The landing of allied troops in Saudi Arabia created a different form of dependency on the United States, which gave the latter considerable leverage over political and economic developments, especially in oil matters, in that country as well as in other Gulf states. As Sam Nakagama observed: "OPEC will never be the same. . . . It will become a kind of regulated public utility in which the United States will have a large voice. Having saved the Saudi royal family as well as the emirates of Kuwait, Dubai, Abu Dhabi and Qatar, the U.S. will emerge with considerable influence over their political and economic policies."[18] Indeed, OPEC's decision to raise output was influenced considerably by United States pressure, which was described as having amounted to a direct order.[19]

Nor were the nonoil states spared from the consequences of the crisis. According to a study by the United Nations, it was estimated, for example, that oil at $40 a barrel would cost poor oil importing countries $64 billion on their trade balances and developed market economies $177 billion.[20] In addition to these oil-related losses, there are other factors that contributed to the economic losses of nonoil countries, especially in the case of those countries that were affected directly by the crisis.

The economic consequences of the takeover and the blockade forced large numbers of foreign workers to leave Kuwait, Iraq, and Saudi Arabia and to return to their respective countries of origin—be they Egypt, Jordan, Yemen, the West Bank, Pakistan, Bangladesh, India, Sri Lanka, or the Philippines. In all these cases the act of return deprived these countries of an important source of foreign exchange as worker remittances were flowing while the workers were employed outside their economies.

In the case of Egypt, for example, it was estimated that if the two million Egyptian workers were to return home, it would cost Egypt $2.5 billion in remittances or the equivalent of 60 percent of Egypt's commodity exports.[21] In addition to remittances there are other sources of loss of foreign revenue such as tourism, trade with Iraq and Kuwait, royalties and service fees. According to a World Bank study, non-oil losses were estimated to be the equivalent of 2.9 percent of Egypt's GDP in 1990, 4.3 percent in 1991, and 3.4 percent in 1992. In the case of Jordan, the ratios were estimated to be 21.6 percent, 26.8 percent, and 26.8 percent respectively.[22] While Egyptian, Jordanian, and Palestinian workers found themselves forced to leave Iraq and Kuwait in the aftermath of the invasion, Yemeni nationals working in Saudi Arabia found themselves forced to leave the kingdom because the Saudi government introduced new measures restricting work and residency of Yemeni workers. The Saudi government that introduced these measures in retaliation to the Yemeni government's position on the dispute forced more than one half million Yemeni workers to leave Saudi Arabia, in addition to the 200,000 workers who had to leave Kuwait.[23]

In addition to the economic losses of these dislocations, the burden of the returnees to their home economies will be large, as most of these workers will not be able to find jobs and will thus increase the rate of unemployment.

ARAB NATIONALISM, OIL, THE UNITED STATES, AND THE NEW WORLD ORDER

When Iraq invaded Kuwait the initial reaction of the United States government was to resort to diplomatic means and economic pressure and sanctions to force Iraq out of Kuwait. Yet a few days later the character, dimensions, and consequences of the invasion were transformed when President George Bush decided to send troops to Saudi Arabia. According to Bush, "the mission of our troops is wholly defensive. . . . They will not initiate hostilities, but they will defend themselves, the Kingdom of Saudi Arabia, and other friends in the Persian Gulf."[24] As time went on, however, the numbers of the troops increased, their mission changed from a defensive to an offensive one, and the objectives of the policy expanded. Thus, in addition to the defense of Saudi Arabia, the Bush administration added to its objectives the removal of Iraqi forces from Kuwait by means of a counter invasion; the destruction of the Iraqi regime; the destruction of Iraq's military and industrial capacity, so it would not be able to make war in the future; the elimination of its nuclear potential; and the inclusion of a defeated and disarmed Iraq in "a new security structure," of which the vital component would be a permanent United States garrison or garrisons in the Gulf area.[25] In addition to these objectives, President Bush outlined yet another objective, which he called a New World Order.

The notion of a New World Order was articulated by President Bush in his September 11, 1990, address before a joint session of Congress. In that address he reiterated that the United States's objectives in the Persian Gulf were: (1) Iraq must withdraw from Kuwait completely, immediately, and without condition; (2) Kuwait's legitimate government must be restored; (3) the security and stability of the Persian Gulf must be assured; and (4) American citizens abroad must be protected. The president went on to say:

We stand today at a unique and extraordinary moment. The crisis in the Persian Gulf, as grave as it is, also offers a rare opportunity to move toward a historic period of cooperation. Out of these troubled times, our fifth objective—a New World Order—can emerge; . . . This is the vision that I shared with President Gorbachev in Helsinki. He and other leaders from Europe, the Gulf, and around the world understand that how we manage the crisis today could shape the future for generations to come. . . . Recent events have surely shown that there is no substitute for American leadership.[26]

On January 16, 1991, the United States Air Force and Navy launched missile and bombing attacks against Baghdad and other cities in Iraq. The bombing, which continued for several weeks, led to the destruction of Iraq's military capabilities, civilian infrastructure, industrial capacity, water supply and power systems, and transport and communications networks. Before the end of February Iraq was forced to withdraw from Kuwait and accept all United Nations resolutions, by which time it had suffered enormous human and economic destruction. The extent of the destruction was described by a special United Nations mission to Iraq: ''Nothing that we had seen or read had quite prepared us for the particular form of devastation which has now befallen the country. The recent conflict has wrought near-apocalyptic results upon the infrastructure of what had been, until January 1991, a rather highly urbanized and mechanized society. Now, most of means of modern life support have been destroyed or rendered tenuous. Iraq has, for some time to come, been relegated to a pre-industrial age, but with all the disabilities of post-industrial dependency on an intensive use of energy and technology.''[27]

Given the destruction of Iraq at the hands of the United States and its Western and Arab allies, the question remains, What place will there be for Arab nationalism and Arab oil in the Middle East in the post–Gulf War period.

It is safe to say that the Iraqi defeat will remove the last pretense that Arab nationalism is a force in Arab political discourse—a force for political independence and unity. The centrality of the individual state will be strengthened and reinforced. This trend will be reinforced should Saudi Arabia and the other Arab Gulf states enter into a formal United States–led new security system. Given Egypt's and Syria's economic difficulties, it is difficult to imagine these two countries not associating themselves, at least indirectly, with the new security system. As for Jordan and Yemen, the two Arab countries in the Middle East that condemned both the Iraqi invasion of Kuwait and the introduction of foreign troops into the region, they are too small, too poor, and too dependent to provide any countervailing force to the new system. It should be stressed that historically only Iraq, Syria, and Egypt had the prerequisites of leadership in the Arab world. And for the Arab countries of North Africa, there is no reason to believe that any one of them has the capacity or the inclination to provide such leadership. On the contrary, an argument can be made that these countries will, for economic considerations, tend to gravitate toward Western Europe rather than toward the Arab East.

As for oil, it is only logical to expect the United States to play a more active role in determining oil policies of the Gulf states and thus of OPEC as a whole. Oil will continue to play its role as a mechanism for further economic and financial integration and dependency. At the regional level oil-producing states will feel less pressure to share some of their income with other Arab countries in the name of Pan-Arabism. Nor will they feel pressured to give preference to Arab over non-Arab workers in their economies. This in turn will widen the gap between the ''haves'' and the ''have nots'' in the Arab world.

The projected inability of most Arab governments to meet the aspirations of the majority of their population for improved economic and political conditions will constitute the major source of instability to Arab regimes. Should the Palestinian question remain unresolved, Arab regimes will have to contend with another source of instability in addition to their other grievances. In short, regardless of the outcome of the current crisis, the Arab world is poised to enter a new period of prolonged instability.

CONCLUDING OBSERVATIONS

The crisis in the Gulf illustrates once again that the interests of the individual state both in the Arab state system and in the OPEC system take precedence over the common interests of the group. This observation leads one to the conclusion that Arab nationalism as a political force will be dormant for a long time to come, as the ruling elites of each sovereign state will seek to maximize (or minimize) their own economic and political gains (or losses) by forging or reforging alliances with the West, especially with the United States.

Given the nature of the structures of various Arab economies, oil will continue to play a crucial role in determining economic, political, and social outcomes in virtually all states. Oil in a sense has become the primary determining force of both intra- and interstate patterns of relations, superseding all other forces including Arab nationalism.

Moreover, dependence on oil means dependence on changing demand conditions for oil in the international economic system. Since the bulk of Arab oil is sold to industrialized countries, it follows that economic development and change in the Arab region will continue to be governed by economic policies and change in the industrialized countries. The very nature of the integration of Arab economies into the world economic system will preclude a different outcome. The introduction of American and other Western armed forces into the region will only reinforce this phenomenon.

Finally, and at the risk of drawing historical comparisons, it can be argued that the landing of Western armed forces in Saudi Arabia and the Gulf region, and the invasion of Iraq, is reminiscent of the conquering of the Middle East by the British and French armies in the course of World War I. In other words, is the Arab world entering a new era of Western colonialism?

NOTES

1. For a summary of United Nations Security Council resolutions see *Middle East International*, December 7, 1990, p. 8.

2. Given the fact that the crisis was still in progress as this book went to press, it is to be expected that most of the information in this Epilogue came from news reports. Unless otherwise indicated, four dailies have been relied upon for the factual information: *New York Times, Christian Science Monitor, Wall Street Journal*, and *Washington Post*.

3. For the text of President Bush's address of August 8, 1990, see U.S. Department of State, Bureau of Public Affairs, *The Arabian Peninsula: US Principles* (Washington, D.C.: Government Printing Office, August 1990).

4. Quoted in Christine Moss Helms, *Iraq: The Eastern Flank of the Arab World* (Washington, D.C.: The Brookings Institution, 1984), 114.

5. See Kathy Evans, "The Gulf States," *Middle East International*, August 31, 1990, 20.

6. For a brief summary of viewpoints regarding the Iran-Iraq war, see Abbas Alnasrawi, "Iraq's Perspective," in *Consistency of U.S. Foreign Policy: The Gulf War and the Iran-Contra Affair*, ed. Abbas Alnasrawi and Cheryl Rubenberg (Belmont, Mass.: Association of Arab-American University Graduates (AAUG) Press, 1989), 133–55.

7. It is significant to note that as early as 1981 the Iraqi president was voicing his criticism of the Saudi policy of overproduction, saying that it was intended to weaken Iraq and prolong the Iran-Iraq War. For these criticisms and for a more detailed analysis of Saudi oil policy during the Iran-Iraq War, see Abbas Alnasrawi, "Economic Consequences of the Iraq-Iran War," *Third World Quarterly*, 8, No. 3 (1986): 869–95, especially 886–92.

8. Data on output, revenue, and prices are derived from OPEC, *Annual Bulletin of Statistics*, and *Middle East Economic Survey* (MEES), various issues.

9. For a fuller exposition of Kuwait's oil policy, see *MEES*, February 12, 1990.

10. For oil price movements in this period see *MEES*, April 16, 1990 and June 11, 1990, and *OPEC Bulletin*, August 1990.

11. *MEES*, May 7, 1990.

12. *MEES*, July 23, 1990.

13. For the text of Iraq's memorandum to the Arab League, Kuwait's response, and the Iraqi president's speech, see *MEES*, July 23, 1990.

14. *MEES*, July 30, 1990.

15. It is worth noting that OPEC oil output declined from 23.5 MBD in July to 19.6 MBD in August. By September it rose to 22.7 MBD and by November it rose again to 23.6 MBD. See *MEES*, December 17, 1990, A9 for OPEC oil production data for the year 1990. For OPEC's decisions in July and August, see *OPEC Bulletin*, September 1990, 6–8.

16. See the *New York Times*, March 13, 1991, D1.

17. See *New York Times*, December 6, 1990, A16.

18. Quoted by David R. Francis, "Will Priorities At Home Suffer?", *Christian Science Monitor*, August 28, 1990, 1.

19. See Youssef M. Ibrahim, "OPEC Members Close to Raising Output Ceiling," *New York Times*, August 28, 1990, D6.

20. See "The Costs of War," *The Nation*, December 24, 1990, 793.

21. *MEES*, August 27, 1990.

22. See *MEES*, October 1, 1990, B3.

23. Arab Organization for Human Rights, *News Bulletin*, December 1990, 1.

24. United States Department of State, Bureau of Public Affairs, *The Arabian Peninsula: US Principles* (Washington, D.C., August 1990), 2.

25. For a more detailed analysis of these objectives, see G. H. Jansen, "Iraq and the US: The Appearance and the Reality," *Middle East International* (October 26, 1990), 19–20.

26. See United States Department of State, Bureau of Public Affairs, *Toward a New World Order* (Washington, D.C.: Government Printing Office, September 1990), 1–2.

27. See the *New York Times*, March 23, 1991, A5.

BIBLIOGRAPHY

Abdalla, Ibrahim Saad Eddin. "Migration as a Factor Conditioning State Economic Control and Financial Policy Options." In Luciani, Giacomo and Ghassan Salame (eds.), *The Politics of Arab Integration*. London: Croom Helm, 1988.

Abdalla, Ibrahim Saad Eddin. "The Role of the State in Economic Activity in the Arab World" (in Arabic), *Al Mustaqbal Al Arabi*, September 1989.

Abdalla, Ismail Sabri. "Observations on the Strategy for Joint Arab Action" (in Arabic), *Studies in Arab Development and Economic Integration*, 1982, 39–76.

Abdulghani, J. M. *Iraq and Iran: The Years of Crisis*. Baltimore, Md.: Johns Hopkins University Press, 1984.

Aflaq, Michel. "Arab Unity Above Socialism." In Anouar abdel-Malek (ed.), *Contemporary Arab Political Thought*. London: Zed Books, 1983.

Akins, James E. "Politics and Saudi Oil Policy," *MEES*, October 12, 1981.

Alnasrawi, Abbas. "The Arab Economies: Twenty Years of Change and Dependency," *Arab Studies Quarterly* 9, No. 4 (Fall 1987).

Alnasrawi, Abbas. "Dependency Status and Economic Development of Arab States," *Journal of Asian and African Studies* 21, Nos. 1–2 (1986).

Alnasrawi, Abbas. "Economic Consequences of the Iran-Iraq War," *Third World Quarterly* 8, No. 3 (1987).

Alnasrawi, Abbas. *OPEC in a Changing World Economy*. Baltimore, Md.: Johns Hopkins University Press, 1985.

Alnasrawi, Abbas. "The Petrodollar Energy Crisis: An Overview and Interpretation," *Syracuse Journal of International Law and Commerce* 3, No. 2 (1975).

Alnasrawi, Abbas, and Cheryl Rubenberg (eds.). *Consistency of U.S. Foreign Policy: The Gulf War and the Iran-Contra Affair*. Belmont, Mass.: Association of Arab-American University Graduates (AAUG) Press, 1989.

Amin, Samir. *The Arab Nation: Nationalism and Class Struggles*. London: Zed Press, 1978.

Amuzegar, Jahangir. *Oil Exporters' Economic Development in an Interdependent World.* Washington, D.C.: International Monetary Fund, 1983.

Arab Banking Corporation. *Industrialization in the Arab World.* Bahrain, 1986.

Arab Monetary Fund. *National Account of the Arab States, 1972–1983.* Abu-Dhabi, 1984.

Arab Monetary Fund. *The Arab States: Economic Data and Statistics, 1975–1983.* Abu-Dhabi, 1985.

Arab Thought Forum. *Arab Food Security* (in Arabic). Amman: Arab Thought Forum, 1986.

al-Aysawi, Ibrahim. *Measuring Dependency in the Arab World* (in Arabic). Beirut: Centre for Arab Unity Studies, 1989.

al-Azm, Sadiq. "Illusions about America," *Journal of Palestine Studies* 7, No. 1 (Autumn 1977).

al-Azm, Sadiq. "The View from Damascus," *Journal of Palestine Studies* 7, No. 3 (Spring 1978).

Batatu, Hanna. *The Old Social Classes and the Revolutionary Movements of Iraq: A Study of Iraq's Old Landed and Commercial Classes and of Its Communists, Ba'thists, and Free Officers.* Princeton, N.J.: Princeton University Press, 1982.

Beaud, Michel. *A History of Capitalism 1500–1980.* New York: Monthly Review Press, 1983.

Beblawi, Hazem. "The Rentier State in the Arab World," *Arab Studies Quarterly* 9, No. 4 (Fall 1987).

Bina, Cyrus. "Competition, Control and Price Formation in the International Energy Industry," *Energy Economics* 11, No. 3 (July 1989).

Bina, Cyrus. "Limits of OPEC Profits and the Nature of Global Oil Accumulation," *OPEC Review* 14, No. 1 (Spring 1990).

Bishara, Ghassan. "The Middle East Arms Package: A Survey of the Congressional Debate," *Journal of Palestine Studies* 7, No. 4 (Summer 1978).

Blair, John M. *The Control of Oil.* New York: Pantheon Books, 1976.

Buheiry, Marwan R. *U.S. Threats of Intervention Against Arab Oil 1973–1979.* Beirut: Institute for Palestine Studies, 1980.

Butler, Stuart M. (ed.). *The Privatization Option: A Strategy to Shrink the Size of Government.* Washington, D.C.: The Heritage Foundation, 1985.

Cardoso, Fernando H., and Enzo Falleto. *Dependency and Development in Latin America.* Berkeley: University of California Press, 1979.

al-Chalabi, Fadhil. "Energy Conservation Policies of the Consuming Countries: A Producer's Point of View," *OPEC Review*, December 1977.

al-Chalabi, Fadhil J. *OPEC at the Crossroads.* Oxford: Pergamon Press, 1989.

al-Chalabi, Fadhil. "The Role of OPEC in Market Stabilization." In Robert Mabro (ed.), *OPEC and the World Oil Market: The Genesis of the 1986 Price Crisis.* Oxford: University Press, 1986.

Chilcote, Ronald H. *Theories of Development and Underdevelopment.* Boulder, Colo.: Westview Press, 1984.

Cummings, John T., Hossein G. Askari, and Michael Akinner. "Military Expenditures and Manpower Requirements in the Arabian Peninsula," *Arab Studies Quarterly* 2, No. 1 (Winter 1980).

al-Dajani, Burhan. "The Economic Dimensions of the Eleventh Arab Summit Conference'' (in Arabic). In Centre for Arab Unity Studies, *Studies in Arab Economic Development and Integration*. Beirut: Centre for Arab Unity Studies, 1982.

al-Dajani, Burhan. ''The Woes of Arab Economic Development in Time of Oil States' Financial Surplus'' (in Arabic), *Al Mustaqbal Al Arabi*, July 1979.

Deeb, Marius. ''The Socioeconomic Role of the Local Foreign Minorities in Modern Egypt, 1805–1961,'' *International Journal of Middle East Studies* 9, No. 1 (1978).

Dos Santos, Theotonio. ''The Structure of Dependence,'' *American Economic Review* 60, No. 2 (May 1970).

Engler, Robert. *The Politics of Oil: A Study of the Private Power and Democratic Directions*. Chicago: University of Chicago Press, 1961.

Epstein, Gerald. ''The Triple Debt Crisis,'' *World Policy Journal* 2, No. 4 (Fall 1988).

Evans, Kathy. ''The Gulf States.'' *Middle East International* (August 31, 1990).

abdel-Fadil, Mahmoud. *Arab Economic Thought and Issues of Liberation, Development and Unity* (in Arabic). Beirut: Centre for Arab Unity Studies, 1982.

al-Fathi, Saadalla, A. ''Security of Oil Supply and Demand: Two Sides of the Same Coin,'' *OPEC Bulletin*, February 1989.

Faux, Jeff. ''The Alternative Trap and the Growth Alternative,'' *World Policy Journal* 5, No. 3 (Summer 1988).

Francis, David R. ''Will Priorities at Home Suffer?'' *Christian Science Monitor* (August 28, 1990).

Frank, André G. ''The Development of Underdevelopment.'' In James D. Cockcroft, André Gunder Frank, and Dale I. Johnson, *Dependence and Underdevelopment: Latin America's Political Economy*. Garden City, N.Y.: Anchor Books, 1972.

Frank, André Gunder. *World Accumulation, 1492–1789*. New York: Monthly Review Press, 1978.

Furgani, Nader. ''Exporting Manpower and Development: The Case of Yemen Arab Republic'' (in Arabic), *Al Mustaqbal Al Arabi*, January 1982.

Furgani, Nader. *Migrants in Arabs' Land: On Labor Migration in the Arab World* (in Arabic). Beirut: Centre for Arab Unity Studies, 1987.

Furgani, Nader (ed.). *Independent Development in the Arab World* (in Arabic). Beirut: Centre for Arab Unity Studies, 1987.

Furtado, Celso. ''Economic Development of Latin America.'' In Peter F. Klaren and Thomas J. Bossert (eds.), *Promise of Development: Theories of Change in Latin America*. Boulder, Colo.: Westview Press, 1986.

Gauhar, Altaf. ''The Hidden Cost of the Arms Race,'' *South*, July 1982.

George, Susan. *A Fate Worse than Debt: The World Financial Crisis and the Poor*. New York: Grove Weidenfeld, 1988.

Hammad, Mujdi. *The Arab Military and the Unity Question* (in Arabic). Beirut: Centre for Arab Unity Studies, 1987.

Hammadi, Sadoon. ''Arab Nationalism and Contemporary Challenges'' (in Arabic). In Centre for Arab Unity Studies, *The Evolution of Arab Nationalist Thought*. Beirut, 1986.

Harik, Ilya. ''The Origins of Arab State System.'' In Ghassan Salame (ed.), *The Foundations of the Arab State*. London: Croom Helm, 1987.

Hartshorn, J. E. ''Netbacks and the Price Collapse,'' *MEES*, March 17, 1986.

Hasan, Salman. *Studies in the Iraqi Economy* (in Arabic). Beirut: Dar Al Taliaa, 1966.

Haseeb, Khair El Din (ed.). *The Future of the Arab Nation: The Challenges and the Options* (in Arabic). Beirut: Centre for Arab Unity Studies, 1988.

Helms, Christine Moss. *Iraq: The Eastern Flank of the Arab World*. Washington, D.C.: The Brookings Institution, 1984.

Heykal, Muhammad Hassanein. "The Saudi Era," *Journal of Palestine Studies* 6, No. 4 (Summer 1977).

Heykel, Mohammad H. "Arab Unity Issues and Arab Society," *Al Mustaqbal Al Arabi*, July 1981.

Hirst, David. *The Gun and the Olive Branch: The Roots of Violence in the Middle East*. London: Futura Publications, 1978.

Hourani, Albert. *Arabic Thought in the Liberal Age, 1798–1939*. London: Oxford University Press, 1962.

al-Husri, Sati. "The Primacy of Arabism." In Anouar abdel-Malek (ed.), *Contemporary Arab Political Thought*. London: Zed Books, 1983.

Ibrahim, Saad Eddin. "Causes and Effects of Labor Exporting in Egypt" (in Arabic), *Al Mustaqbal Al Arabi*, January 1982.

Ibrahim, Saad Eddin. "Oil, Migration and the New Arab Social Order." In Malcolm H. Kerr and El Sayed Yassin (eds.). *Rich and Poor States in the Middle East: Egypt and the New Arab Order*. Boulder, Colo.: Westview Press, 1982.

Ibrahim, Saad Eddin. *The New Arab Social Order: A Study of the Social Consequences of the Oil Wealth* (in Arabic). Beirut: Centre for Arab Unity Studies, 1985.

Ibrahim, Saad Eddin. *Society and State in the Arab World* (in Arabic). Beirut: Centre for Arab Unity Studies, 1988.

Ibrahim, Youssef M. "OPEC Members Close to Raising Output Ceiling." *New York Times* (August 28, 1990).

Imady, Mohammed. "Patterns of Arab Economic Aid to Third World Countries," *Arab Studies Quarterly* 6, Nos. 1 & 2 (Winter/Spring 1984).

al-Imam, Mohammad Mahmoud. "Role of Joint Arab Action in Achieving Independent Development" (in Arabic). In Nader Furgani (ed.), *Independent Development in the Arab World*. Beirut: Centre for Arab Unity Studies, 1989.

International Energy Agency. *World Energy Outlook*. Paris, 1982.

International Monetary Fund. *International Financial Statistics Yearbook*. Washington, D.C., annual.

International Monetary Fund. *World Economic Outlook, 1983*. Washington, D.C., 1983.

Ismael, Tareq Y. *The Arab Left*. Syracuse, N.Y.: Syracuse University Press, 1976.

Issawi, Charles. *An Economic History of the Middle East and North Africa*. New York: Columbia University Press, 1982.

Issawi, Charles, and Mohammed Yeganeh. *The Economics of Middle Eastern Oil*. New York: Frederick A. Praeger, 1962.

Itayim, F. "Arab Oil—The Political Dimension," *Journal of Palestine Studies* 3, No. 2 (Winter 1974).

abdel-Jaber, Tayseer. "The Current Situation of Labor Exchange in the Arab World and Future Possibilities (in Arabic). In Arab Thought Forum, *The Returnees from the Oilfields*. Amman: Arab Thought Forum, 1986.

Jansen, G. H. "Iraq and the US: The Appearance and the Reality." *Middle East International* (October 26, 1990).

al-Kawwari, Ali Khalifa. *Toward an Alternative Strategy for Comprehensive Development* (in Arabic). Beirut: Centre for Arab Unity Studies, 1985.

Kazeeha, Walid. "Arab Nationalism in the Stage Between the Two World Wars" (in Arabic), *Al Mustaqbal Al Arabi*, January 1979.

Kazeeha, Walid. "The Concept of Arab Unity in the Early Twentieth Century" (in Arabic), *Al Mustaqbal Al Arabi*, November 1978.

Kazeeha, Walid. "The Social-Political Foundations of the Growth of the Contemporary Nationalist Movement in the Arab East" (in Arabic), *Al Mustaqbal Al Arabi*, No. 6, March 1979.

Kerr, Malcolm H., and El Sayed Yassin (eds.). *Rich and Poor States in the Middle East: Egypt and the New Arab Order*. Boulder, Colo.: Westview Press, 1982.

Khadduri, Walid. "Arab Oil Decisions for the Years 1973–1974: A Study of Arab Decision Making" (in Arabic). In *How Decisions Are Made in the Arab Nation*. Beirut: Centre for Arab Unity Studies, 1985.

Kissinger, Henry. *Years of Upheaval*. Boston: Little, Brown, 1982.

Kubba, Ibrahim. *This is the Road of July 14: Defense Before the Revolution's Court* (in Arabic). Beirut: Dar al Taliaa, 1969.

Labeeb, Ali. "Causes of the Spread of Asian Employment" (in Arabic). In Nader Furgani (ed.), *Foreign Employment in the Arabian Gulf Countries*. Beirut: Centre for Arab Unity Studies, 1983.

Latin American Perspectives. *Debt and the World Economic System* (Special issue), No. 60 (Winter 1989).

League of Arab States et al. *Joint Arab Economic Report*. Abu Dhabi. Annual.

League of Arab States, *Specialized Arab Organizations: Basic Information and Founding Document* (in Arabic). Tunis, 1984.

League of Arab States, *Toward Joint Arab Economic Action (Main Paper): Document Presented to the Eleventh Arab Summit Conference, Amman, Hashemite Kingdom of Jordan, 1980*. Tunis, 1980.

Leeman, Wayne A. *The Price of Middle East Oil: An Essay in Political Economy*. Ithaca, N.Y.: Cornell University Press, 1962.

MacEwan, Arthur. *Debt and Disorder: International Economic Instability and U.S. Imperial Decline*. New York: Monthly Review Press, 1990.

Matr, Jamil, and Hilal, Ali El Din. *The Arab State System: A Study in Arab Political Relations*, 5th edition (in Arabic). Beirut: Centre for Arab Unity Studies, 1985.

Mead, Walter Russel. "The United States and the World Economy," *World Policy Journal* 6, No. 1 (Winter 1988–1989).

Montasser, Essam. "The Arab Economy and Its Developing Strategy: A New Arab Economic Order." In Malcolm H. Kerr and El Sayed Yassin (eds.). *Rich and Poor States in the Middle East: Egypt and the New Arab Order*. Boulder, Colo.: Westview Press, 1982.

Moursi, Fouad. "Impact of Arab Oil on International Relations" (in Arabic), *Al Mustaqbal Al Arabi*, April 1980.

Moursi, Fouad. *A Second Look at Arab Nationalism*. Cairo: Al-Ahali Books, 1989.

Nadhmi, Wamidh Jamal Omar. "The Nationalist Thought of Sati al Husri" (in Arabic). In Centre for Arab Unity Studies, *The Evolution of Arab Nationalist Thought*. Beirut: Centre for Arab Unity Studies, 1986.

el-Naggar, Said (ed.). *Privatization and Structural Adjustment in the Arab Countries*. Washington, D.C.: International Monetary Fund, 1989.

al-Nashashibi, Hikmat Sharif. "Arab Banking Investment in the International Financial Markets" (in Arabic), *Al Mustaqbal Al Arabi*, October 1989.

OPEC. *Annual Bulletin of Statistics*. Vienna.

Owen, Roger. *The Middle East in the World Economy, 1800–1914*. London: Methuen, 1981.

al-Pachachi, N. "The Development of Concession Arrangements in the Middle East," *Middle East Economic Survey*, March 29, 1968.

Polin, Robert, and Eduardo Zepeda. "Latin American Debt: The Choices Ahead," *Monthly Review*, February 1987.

al-Qasser, Ahmad. "Impact of External Migration on the Social Structure in the Yemen Republic" (in Arabic), *Al Mustaqbal Al Arabi*, December 1984.

Radwan, Samir. "Arab Manpower: Reality and Future Dimensions" (in Arabic), *Al Mustaqbal Al Arabi*, March 1988.

abdel-Rahman, Osama. *The Single Revenue and the Prevailing Spending Orientation* (in Arabic). Beirut: Centre for Arab Unity Studies, 1988.

Ramsis, Nadya. "Western Theory and Arab Development" (in Arabic), *Al Mustaqbal Al Arabi*, June 1984.

"Report of OPEC's Ministerial Committee on Long Term Strategy," *International Currency Review*, July 1980.

Rodinson, Maxime. *The Arabs*. Chicago: University of Chicago Press, 1981.

Rodinson, Maxime. *Marxism and the Muslim World*. New York: Monthly Review Press, 1981.

Rouhani, Fuad. *A History of O.P.E.C.* New York: Praeger Publishers, 1971.

Saad Eddin, Ibrahim, and Mahmoud Abdel-Fadil, (eds.). *Movement of Arab Employment: Problems, Effect and Policies* (in Arabic). Beirut: Centre for Arab Unity Studies, 1983.

Sadik, Tawfik Ali. "Managing the Petrodollar Bonanza: Avenues and Implications of Recycling Arab Capital," *Arab Studies Quarterly* 6, Nos. 1 & 2 (1984).

Sadowski, Yahya. "Patronage and the Ba'th: Corruption and Control in Contemporary Syria," *Arab Studies Quarterly* 9, No. 4 (Fall 1987).

Salame, Ghassan. "Integration in the Arab World: The Institutional Framework." In Luciani, Giacomo and Ghassan Salame (eds.), *The Politics of Arab Integration*. London: Croom Helm, 1988.

al-Sammak, Mohammed Azhar. "Measuring Economic Dependency of the Arab Nation and Its Possible Geopolitical Effects" (in Arabic), *Al Mustaqbal Al Arabi*, September 1986.

Saudi, Abdulla. "Arab Banking and the Eurocurrency Market," *OAPEC Bulletin*, August/September 1982.

Sayigh, Yusif A. "Arab Economic Integration and the Pretext of National Sovereignty" (in Arabic), *Al Mustaqbal Al Arabi*, March 1979.

Seymour, Ian. *OPEC: An Instrument of Change*. London: Macmillan Press, 1980.

Shaheen, Edward. "Step-By-Step in the Middle East," *Journal of Palestine Studies* 5, Nos. 3 & 4 (Spring/Summer 1976).

Shuqair, Muhammad L. *Arab Economic Unity: Its Experiences and Expectations*, 2 vols. Beirut: Centre for Arab Unity Studies, 1986.

Shuqair, Mohammad Labib. "The Economic Dimension in Arab Unity Thought: The First Stage, from the Beginning of Arab National Thought to the Mid-Fifties" (in Arabic), *Al Mustaqbal Al Arabi*, September 1978.

Shuraydi, Muhammad S. "Pan Arabism: A Theory in Practice." In Hani A. Faris (ed.), *Arab Nationalism and the Future of the Arab World*. Belmont, Mass.: AAUG Press, 1987.

Stavrianos, L. S. *Global Rift: The Third World Comes of Age*. New York: Morrow, 1981.

Stivers, William. *Supremacy and Oil: Iraq, Turkey, and the Anglo-American World Order, 1918–1930*. Ithaca, N.Y.: Cornell University Press, 1982.

Stocking, George W. *Middle East Oil: A Study in Political and Economic Controversy*. Nashville, Tenn.: Vanderbilt University Press, 1970.

Stork, Joe, and Jim Paul. "Arms Sales and the Militarization of the Middle East," *MERIP Reports*, February 1983.

Subroto. "Energy into the 21st Century: An OPEC View," *OPEC Bulletin*, May 1990.

Subroto. "How OPEC Sees the Crucial Energy Issues of the 1990s," *OPEC Bulletin*, April 1990.

Terzian, Pierre. *OPEC: The Inside Story*. London Zed Books, Ltd., 1985.

Tibi, Bassam. *Arab Nationalism: A Critical Enquiry*. New York: St. Martin's Press, 1981.

Tueni, Ghassan. "After October: Military Conflict and Political Change in the Middle East," *Journal of Palestine Studies* 3, No. 4 (Summer 1974).

United States Arms Control and Disarmament Agency. *World Military Expenditures and Arms Transfers*. Washington, D.C., annual.

U.S. Senate Committee on Foreign Relations, Subcommittee on Multinational Corporations, *The International Petroleum Cartel, The Iranian Consortium and U.S. National Security*. Washington, D.C.: Government Printing Office, 1974.

U.S. Senate, Committee on Foreign Relations, Subcommittee on Multinational Corporations. *Multinational Oil Corporations and U.S. Foreign Policy*. Washington, D.C.: Government Printing Office, 1975.

U.S. Senate, Select Committee on Small Business. *The International Petroleum Cartel*. Washington, D.C.: Government Printing Office, 1952.

U.S. Department of State. *U.S. International Energy Policy, October 1973–November 1975*. Washington, D.C.: Government Printing Office, 1975.

U.S. Department of State. *U.S. Policy in the Middle East: December 1973–November 1974*. Washington, D.C.: Government Printing Office, 1975.

U.S. Department of State, Bureau of Public Affairs. *The Arabian Peninsula: US Principles*. Washington, D.C.: Government Printing Office, August 1990.

United States Department of State, Bureau of Public Affairs. *Toward a New World Order*. Washington, D.C.: Government Printing Office, September 1990.

Vernon, Raymond (ed.). *The Promise of Privatization: A Challenge for American Policy*. New York: Council on Foreign Relations, 1988.

Vickers, John, and George Yarrow. *Privatization: An Economic Analysis*. Cambridge: MIT Press, 1988.

Warriner, Doreen. *Land Reform and Development in the Middle East: A Study of Egypt, Syria, and Iraq*. London: Royal Institute of International Affairs, 1957.

Waterbury, John. *The Egypt of Nasser and Sadat: The Political Economy of Two Regimes*. Princeton, N.J.: Princeton University Press, 1983.

Willrich, Mason, and Melvin A. Conant. "The International Energy Agency: An Interpretation and Assessment," *Journal of American Society of International Law*, April 1977.

Woodward, Bob. *Veil: The Secret Wars of the CIA, 1981–1987*. New York: Simon and Schuster, 1987.

World Bank, *World Development Report*, Washington, D.C., annual.

Zaki, Ramzi. *The Arab Economy Under Siege* (in Arabic). Beirut: Centre for Arab Unity Studies, 1989.

Zaki, Ramzi. "The Exit from Foreign Indebtedness between Romantic Thoughts and Objective Conception" (in Arabic). In Arab Thought Forum, *Balances and Arab External Indebtedness: Alternative Policies for the Protection of Balances and Facing Indebtedness*. Amman: Arab Thought Forum, 1987.

Zalzala, Abdel Hasan. "The Economic Role of the League of Arab States" (in Arabic), *Al Mustaqbal Al Arabi*, August–October 1982.

Zalzala, Abdel Hasan. "The Challenges Facing Arab Economic Integration" (in Arabic), *Al Mustaqbal Al Arabi*, November 1980.

INDEX

About the Author

ABBAS ALNASRAWI is Professor of Economics at the University of Vermont. His previous publications include *Financing Economic Development in Iraq: The Role of Oil in the Middle Eastern Economy; Arab Oil and United States Energy Requirements* (1982); *OPEC in a Changing World Economy*, and, as co-editor, *Consistency of U.S. Foreign Policy: The Gulf War and the Iran-Contra Affair's Foreign Policy* (1989). Since 1971 he has published numerous articles, monographs, and chapters on Arab and mid-Eastern economies.